T0244118

DECLINE

FROM THE TOP

DECLINE
FROM THE TOP

Snapshots From America's Crisis and Glimmers of Hope

Matt Purple

Since 1947
REGNERY
An Imprint of Skyhorse Publishing, Inc.

Regnery books may be purchased in bulk at special discounts for sales promotion, corporate gifts, fund-raising, or educational purposes. Special editions can also be created to specifications. For details, contact the Special Sales Department, Regnery, 307 West 36th Street, 11th Floor, New York, NY 10018 or info@skyhorsepublishing.com.

Regnery® is an imprint of Skyhorse Publishing, Inc.®, a Delaware corporation.

Visit our website at www.regnery.com.

Please follow our publisher Tony Lyons on Instagram @tonylyonsisuncertain.

10 9 8 7 6 5 4 3 2 1

Library of Congress Cataloging-in-Publication Data is available on file.

Cover design by David Ter-Avanesyan

Print ISBN: 978-1-68451-462-5
eBook ISBN: 978-1-5107-8255-6

Printed in the United States of America

For Claire. The country may be going downhill but you've made my life so much better.

Contents

Prologue: Crashing Down   ix

CHAPTER 1
The Apple Jacks Generation   1

CHAPTER 2
Spaceship Earth's Melted Plastic   17

CHAPTER 3
The Smartphone Surveillance State   37

CHAPTER 4
The Sound of Silence   51

CHAPTER 5
The Return of *X-Files* Politics   63

CHAPTER 6
The Final Frontier Is Now Closed   75

CHAPTER 7
To Live and Die in the USA   89

CHAPTER 8
Drinking Alone   103

CHAPTER 9
Of Congregationalists and Commitophobes   121

CHAPTER 10
Dystopian Chic Comes to the Swamp   135

CHAPTER 11
Wokeness Is the Religion of Decline   147

CHAPTER 12
The Battle of the Sexes Bogs Down   173

CHAPTER 13
The American Dream, Now Available for Monthly
Installments of $12,999.99   187

CHAPTER 14
Capitalists Without Chests, Politicians Without
Brains   201

CHAPTER 15
Our Godzilla Versus Mothra Politics   217

CHAPTER 16
Advise and Descent   231

CHAPTER 17
From the Halls of Okinawa to the Shores of
Benghazi   247

CHAPTER 18
American Gladiators   263

Afterword: It Begins with Us   275

Index   283

Prologue: Crashing Down

By the dawn of the twenty-first century, the United States had become more powerful than any other nation in human history. The Cold War was over; the Berlin Wall had come tumbling down and with it the Soviet Union. Without the commies getting in our way, we were free at last to do what we do best: carpet the globe with our aircraft carriers, Doritos Locos Tacos, and DVDs of the twenty-sixth *American Pie* movie.

America's reach and influence had no parallel throughout history. Ancient Athens? A glorified port city. Rome? Marcus Aurelius had nothing on Oprah's ratings. Even our most obvious imperial forebear, Great Britain, had merely ruled the seas. "The sun never sets on the British Empire"? We could broadcast sunsets to TVs worldwide, then superimpose CGI Transformer battles in front of them, then export T-shirts with said Transformers on them to every bazaar in sub-Saharan Africa. Which we did, by the way.

For some Americans (and non-Americans too), the aroma of this dominance was intoxicating. From our Cold War victory came a sense that our country was all but invincible, that we could flex our muscles wherever and however we saw fit—even that we could remake the world. The only limit was our imagination. In 1990, columnist Charles Krauthammer declared a "unipolar moment" in which global power was now vested in a single entity, the United States.

Krauthammer believed this unipolar moment would be brief. He predicted Germany would soon rise as the leader of Europe and Japan as a hegemon in East Asia. (He was half right.) Yet he also advised against returning to the boring old days of "realpolitik" and "balance-of-power politics." By that he meant the cold-eyed exercise of power, the mere movement and exchange of pawns on the global chessboard. Krauthammer wanted to think big. Queen to d8 and check![1]

Even more audacious was the thinker Francis Fukuyama, who in 1992 published *The End of History and the Last Man.* The book has since become a poster child for civilizational hubris, but it's a far more serious work than it gets credit for. Fukuyama posits that because liberal democracy satisfies man's need for recognition—his *thymos*—by giving him rights and allowing him a say in his nation's affairs, it is the best form of government. But Fukuyama goes further, arguing that liberal democracy is also the *final* form of government. Like Hegel, Fukuyama sees politics as a process of historical evolution, and liberal democracy is its logical zenith, an ideal system that can never be improved upon.[2]

---

1   Charles Krauthammer, "The Unipolar Moment," *Foreign Affairs* 70, no. 1, January 1, 1990, https://www.foreignaffairs.com/articles/1990-01-01/unipolar-moment.

2   Francis Fukuyama, *The End of History and the Last Man* (New York: Free Press, 1992).

In other words, not only had America triumphed over authoritarian socialism, that triumph was on a grand and philosophical scale. The enlightened side had won; the last great ideological conflict was over.

Intellectuals are like weathervanes: they capture the moods and trends of their times. And there was reason to think in Fukuyama's time that we really had entered some kind of glorious endgame. The early 1990s had seen the former Soviet republics and even Russia herself (or so it seemed) flip from Marxist dictatorships into liberal democracies. Moscow was no longer run by communists but drunks, a vast improvement. Fascism was the province of two or three yellow-toothed European third-party ranters. Even Maoist China seemed to be liberalizing. The great pull of politics seemed toward individual liberty, open markets, property rights—American values.

Adding to this sense of destiny was that life in the United States was pretty good and getting better. The domestic ills of the 1960s and 1970s, which had taken a heavy toll on the national psyche, seemed to be resolving in our favor. The economy was galloping ahead, with years of labor strikes and stagflation a distant memory. Crime had plummeted; the nation's capital was no longer an island of marble in a sea of gun violence; the endless building fires in the burning Bronx had at last been doused.

And a bright future was beaconing courtesy of a nifty new invention called the World Wide Web. Yes, as the Rest of the World annoyingly pointed out, the internet was *technically* invented in Europe. But it was packaged and popularized right here in the good old US of A, and by the late 1990s, it was as American as cheeseburger pie. Microsoft and Netscape were both American companies. So too, less subtly, was America Online. And while the internet today is chiefly useful for calling those who even mildly disagree with you "c**ts," back then it was sheathed in a real sense of fruited-plain techno-optimism.

America was growing, rising, flexing, plugging in—all while the Rest of the World seemed to be shrinking to within reach. Globalization, the free flow of people and capital across borders, and of ones and zeroes across networks, had turned the entire planet into a market for American corporations. Even the former Iron Curtain was now open for business.

In 1996, *New York Times* columnist Thomas Friedman came up with yet another pop explainer of post–Cold War hubris, the Golden Arches Theory of Conflict Prevention. It held that "No two countries that both have a McDonald's have ever fought a war against each other."[3] This was true not only because it's extremely difficult to crawl through a trench after eating a Double Quarter Pounder with Cheese, but because a McDonald's franchise had become an emblem of a nation's openness to trade and globalization. And McDonald's nations were thriving. Why would a country want to endanger all that investment, all that prosperity, by sending in the tanks?

You may be aware that both Russia and Ukraine had a McDonald's as of February 2022. Picture Grimace loading up a Kalashnikov . . . but not yet. Because, again, the national mood at the time Friedman was writing really did make it seem like the Happy Meal might be an overlooked tool of soft power. We had won the Cold War because our economy had outlasted the Soviets', hadn't we? Why shouldn't that same economy now export peace to other dark crevasses of the globe? Why shouldn't it open lines of dialogue and close arteries worldwide?

The Rest of the World, unsurprisingly, wasn't always thrilled with this dominance. But what were they supposed to do? America haters, especially in Western Europe, had long viewed the United States through

---

3   Thomas L. Friedman, "Foreign Affairs Big Mac I," *New York Times*, December 8, 1996, https://www.nytimes.com/1996/12/08/opinion/foreign -affairs-big-mac-i.html.

the prism of various self-flattering stereotypes and snobberies. Yet by the turn of the millennium, even the most observed of anti-American tropes had become hopelessly passé.

Consider this anti-Americanism (which still circulates in the UK): Americans don't understand irony. Could anything have been further from the truth? By the year 2000, Americans were positively drowning in irony, unable to so much as order a pizza without affecting a Daria-like voice inflection insinuating that the very institutions of cheese, sauce, and mushrooms were some grand cosmic joke. We were so ironic that some began to worry we were *too* ironic. This prompted Jon Stewart of *The Daily Show* to give a non-ironic defense of the ironic against this school of the non-ironic anti-ironic.[4]

"Americans don't understand irony"? We had dragged irony into an infinity mirror. Or how about this anti-American trope: American beer tastes like piss. By the early twenty-first century, the legalization of home brewing by that party animal Jimmy Carter had touched off a craft beer revolution. The average beer consumer was no longer a portly fella in a Dallas Cowboys T-shirt sitting on the couch. He was a pencil-thin mustachioed hipster murmuring "mmm, hints of pinecones and formaldehyde" as he sniffed his octuple-imperial Gulf Coast IPA from out of a tulip glass.

There seemed to be no stereotype we couldn't innovate away. And who were these Old World snobs to judge us anyhow? Hadn't we taken in their poor, their marginalized, their potato-famished, their *Untermenschen*—and hadn't we then fashioned a new nation out of the talents their fatherlands had spurned? We had turned Europe's creaking class systems into a mortal weakness, exploiting all that untapped

---

4   "Irony is Dead," *The Daily Show With Jon Stewart*, Created by Madeleine Smithberg and Lizz Winstead, performed by Jon Stewart, season 6, Mad Cow Productions, 2001.

ingenuity. Sure, we had our own class-related issues, starting with our history of racism against African Americans. But even that seemed to be in the rearview come the start of the Roaring Twenty-First.

The journalist Tom Wolfe in the year 2000 wrote an essay called "Hooking Up," on which this prologue is loosely based. In it, he marveled at just how completely America had transcended the old bogey of class. The word "proletariat," he noted, had become "so obsolete it was known only to a few bitter old Marxist academics with wire hair sprouting out of their ears." America's working class had become a comfortable middle class—electricians wearing gold chains, air-conditioning repairmen out on pleasure yachts with their third wives.

This high standard of living had led to other pathologies, namely sexual decadence (hence the title of Wolfe's essay). Still, it was truly amazing just how thoroughly the Marxist forecast of class conflict, clung to by so many twentieth-century intellectuals, hadn't come to pass. American workers had no time to revolt against the bourgeois; they were too busy closing on a second house in the Keys.[5]

So completely checkmated were the old-line Marxists that a new political creed had grown up around global capitalism. This school is often called "neoliberalism," and while that word may be accurate (it is both relatively new and grounded in certain liberal ideas), it implies a stronger degree of conformity than ever existed. It's best thought of as a disposition, a mood. It looks across oceans with a smile and a friendly wave. It favors openness in both markets and borders. There are no strangers here; only industrious innovators waiting to arrive on our shores. And while there are plenty of neoliberals in other countries,

---

5   Tom Wolfe, "Hooking Up: What Life Was Like at the Turn of the Second
     Millennium: an American's World," *Hooking Up* (New York: Farrar,
     Straus and Giroux, 2000).

neoliberalism's optimism and forward thinking make it an easy fit for the United States.

Little surprise, then, that free-market neoliberalism took root in the patriotic and pro-business Republican Party. Yet it was the rise of Bill Clinton that signaled game over for the Marxists. Clinton declared himself a New Democrat, opposed to runaway government spending and impromptu riots outside the Pentagon. The most famous line from his presidency was . . . actually it was "I did not have sexual relations with that woman," but the *second* most famous line was "the era of big government is over."

For Clinton, this was a neoliberal rallying cry, separating him from his party's old-line leftists. And unlike with the sexual relations stuff, on this, Clinton was (sometimes) good to his word. He worked with the GOP to reduce the number of people on welfare. He hammered out the North American Free Trade Agreement and other trade deals. He deregulated Wall Street. Old-school progressives, skeptical of commerce and smelling slightly of grass, were now politically homeless. Clinton and his New Democrats had harnessed the nation's optimism and they would ride it gleefully, decadently, into the sunlit uplands of the new millennium.

***

Nobody thinks this way anymore.

Once, Americans looked confidently to the future. Today, we're gloomy, unsettled, haunted by visions of a country coming apart. Once we were a "hyperpower," as the unnecessarily Anglo-named journalist Peregrine Worsthorne called us,[6] and the "indispensible nation," as

---

6   Peregrine Worsthorne, "The Bush Doctrine," *Sunday Telegraph*, March 3, 1991.

former secretary of state Madeleine Albright put it.[7] Today, no comparison seems too dire. The United States is late-stage Rome; the United States is the Weimar Republic; the United States is the United States circa 1860. Analogies to fictional dystopias roll off the tongue: George Orwell's *Nineteen Eighty-Four*, with all of its state-surveilled bleakness, or Gilead in Margaret Atwood's *The Handmaid's Tale*, which many journalists seem to think is the only book that has ever been written.

The average young American in 2024 doesn't exude optimism. He hears about the American dream and wonders where it's gotten off to.

A young American today probably went to a four-year liberal arts college where he learned that his country is the most oppressive in the world (as well as that the quadratic equation is racist, iambic pentameter is violence against women, and so on). He'll graduate with a load of student debt, which will take him decades to pay off. And he'll enter a job market where inflation takes constant bites out of his paycheck.

Our young American might turn on the news where he's likely to hear about yet another mass shooting. Back in the halcyon 1990s, school shootings were still a relatively new phenomenon, and it wasn't until 1999 that the horrific massacre at Columbine High School shook the nation by its collar. Yet since then, they've come to seem like just another segment of the news, sandwiched between the weather and the lotto numbers. While our young American knows his odds of dying in a mass shooting are infinitesimally small, it's still enough to make him wince every time he hears a car backfire.

That isn't all that gives him pause. It seems like the world around him pulsates with political hostility. Gone are the days of neoliberal consensus. Every political debate is now a firefight, with

---

7   "Interview With Secretary of State Madeleine K. Albright," *The Today Show*, hosted by Matt Lauer, February 19, 1998, https://1997-2001.state.gov/statements/1998/980219a.html.

Democrats accusing Republicans of being fascists and Republicans accusing Democrats of being Marxists. On Capitol Hill, the only thing Republicans and Democrats can seem to agree on is shoveling more taxpayer money into a gas stove. And then he just read that Democrats supposedly want to ban gas stoves so who even knows how that's going to work.

If our young American turns on cable news, he'll find neither much in the way of "news," as his parents and grandparents understood it, nor much in the way of "debate," as when William F. Buckley Jr. helmed the TV show *Firing Line*. Today, almost all cable "news" is commentary. And even if our young American agrees with some of that commentary, it's not like he feels connected to the hosts. They seem to be selling him a narrative he doesn't like while the commercials seem to be selling him a catheter he doesn't need.

So it's onto the internet, where our young American is active on TikTok . . . Snapchat . . . *sigh*. He wades through a Pacific of belfies, *Mean Girl* GIFs, vitriol from the partisans, but it just leaves him feeling *desolate*. It's all empty calories, swigs of stale Sierra Mist, and now he's even less happy than he was before. Once it was believed the internet would bring us together, let us read Plato's *Republic* by day and video-chat about Glaucon's errors by night. Instead, he finds only vitriol on Twitter and the same glamor shots from the same unattainable "influencers" on Instagram.

Our young American now clicks over to a Quora forum where someone has asked a question: "Can America be saved?" The answers are overwhelmingly in the negative. Cynical Americans sigh with exhaustion. Smug Canadians and Brits sneer about how *the United States is the poorest rich country in the world*. This rankles our young American's innate patriotism, but he also can't help but think they have a point. He studied abroad in college, where he got the storybook version of Europe, all chocolate romances and whistling trains. It looks

like a dream against the congested superhighway honking just outside
his apartment.

Our young American closes his laptop. He knows he needs to find
something to do, but he's not sure what. He isn't aware of any local
associations he could join. He isn't religious, and while he keeps an
open mind—he tells girls he's "spiritual"—it's not like he's about to step
inside a church. He has friends, but they see less of each other since the
COVID-19 lockdowns, and he tends to think calling them up would
be an imposition. Oh well, he thinks, as he fires up his computer and
sticks his hand down his pants. There's always that.

I've just set up a contrast, two caricatures, and admittedly both are
touched up for effect. The 1990s weren't always *that* glorious, as we'll
discuss in the first chapter, while 2024 isn't one long cringe scene from
Euphoria. But even allowing for some polemic license, these depictions
should resonate with anyone familiar with either time period.

Is it any wonder this is affecting how Americans perceive their
country? According to Gallup, 77 percent of us say we're dissatisfied
with the way things are going, compared to a mere 28 percent when
Gallup asked in early 2000.[8] Gallup also finds that only 39 percent
are "extremely proud to be an American," compared to 70 percent in
2003.[9] A YouGov poll says close to half of all Americans believe the
United States may soon "cease to be a democracy."[10] An ABC News/
Ipsos survey from January 2024 found 69 percent think the American

---

8   "Satisfaction With the United States," Gallup, December 20, 2023,
     https://news.gallup.com/poll/1669/general-mood-country.aspx.

9   "Extreme Pride in Being American Remains Near Record Low," Gallup,
     June 29, 2023, https://news.gallup.com/poll/507980/extreme-pride
     -american-remains-near-record-low.aspx.

10   "Yahoo! News Survey—January 6," Yahoo! News/YouGov, June
     13, 2022, https://www.scribd.com/document/578506037/Yahoo
     -News-Survey-January-6th.

dream is an empty promise, up twenty-two points over a similar poll taken in 2010.

This lack of faith in the American project is gravely worrying. There are many theories as to why civilizations fall, and surely just as many reasons, but one of the most convincing comes from the historian Kenneth Clark. Civilization, Clark says, "requires confidence—confidence in the society in which one lives, belief in its philosophy, belief in its laws, and confidence in one's own mental powers." He adds, "So if one asks why the civilization of Greece and Rome collapsed, the real answer is that it was exhausted."[11]

Can there be any doubt that Americans today are exhausted? Clark's comments call to mind the work of another Brit, a BBC reporter, who amid the chaos of the final days of the 2020 election campaign, went to Philadelphia and asked a voter whether he feared what might come next.

The man thought about it, then shrugged. "Rome fell," he said.[12]

***

This is a book about decline. It's a book about the decline we see when we turn on the news and then turn it off five seconds later in abject despair. But it's also about the decline we see in our day-to-day lives, the decline we've grown accustomed to and perhaps don't think that much about.

Being a cranky conservative, I much prefer to dwell on the negative rather than the positive. So let's discuss what this book is not.

This book is not, first of all, a comprehensive account of our decline, my *Decline and Fall of the American Empire* (the title notwithstanding).

---

11   Kenneth Clark, *Civilisation* (London: John Murray, 2015).

12   "Divided America: the battle for the White House in a fractured nation—BBC News," YouTube, uploaded by BBC News, November 6, 2020.

There may yet come a time for such a work, but it won't be until long after the Visigoths have stormed the Outer Banks. In the meantime, we're still living in the midst of the events and trends this book aims to chronicle. There is thus no singular, settled narrative of how all this came to pass. The bogeys so often blamed for our civilizational decline—capitalism, decadence, neoliberalism, Kris Jenner—can't on their own explain how we got here. What this book does instead is to take an amused and observed look at the individual factors behind decline with the understanding that the composite picture is complicated and not yet finished.

Another thing this book is not is a data dump. Click around the internet for numbers on our decline and you'll find plenty—and plenty are cited in these pages. But observation, not calculation, is this book's tool of choice. As George Orwell put it, "To see what is in front of one's nose needs a constant struggle." As he put it less charitably, "We have now sunk to a depth at which restatement of the obvious is the first duty of intelligent men."

This book is also not a work of partisanship. That may come as a surprise, given that I've written for no fewer than ten right-leaning publications, campaigned for several GOP candidates, and once had a bumper sticker on my dorm room wall that read, "Vote Democrat: It's Easier than Thinking" (*ha ha!* I cackled when I was alone on a Friday night).

But then the fastest way to grow exhausted with partisanship is to experience it from the inside. That's especially true if you're a conservative, for whom a key goal should be to make life *less* political. And while my own political leanings will inevitably surface, I don't think decline is entirely the fault of either the left or the right. The destructive effects of internet culture can't be pinned solely on Democrats or Republicans. Neither can our failure to return to the Moon, the hollowing-out of flyover towns, or the abject uselessness of Congress.

Likewise does this book not spend a lot of time on the presidential race. Both Joe Biden and Donald Trump will shout and shamble their way across these pages but I don't dwell too much on either one. This is because I view them as downstream from larger problems, which are more the focus of my writing here. But it's also because I finished this book in early 2024, when everyone in my profession was screaming about the election. I've spent much of my career screaming about elections, and I'm starting to sound like Marge's sisters from *The Simpsons*. I'm hoarse. I need a break.

Finally, this is not a work of gloom and doom. Anyone who wants pessimism about America can switch on social media and find it by the dollop. But then, as we've seen, that pessimism itself is a driver of our downfall, stuck in a feedback loop with all the other problems we're experiencing. And when it comes to scoping out the future, all the old rules still apply. Determinism is still bunk. There is no dark tide of history sweeping us toward our demise. We got here through decisions we made freely, and we may yet get out of here through decisions made more wisely.

Who knows? It was only twenty-five years ago that we thought we were on top of the world. To decline, you have to come down from somewhere, and so it is that we turn the DeLorean back to what now seems like a golden age. Please keep your Moon Shoes inside the vehicle and don't pet the Pokémon.

CHAPTER 1

The Apple Jacks Generation

There's an old TV commercial that I think captures the 1990s better than any other cultural artifact. Four young boys are sitting around a garage, eating Apple Jacks cereal in the middle of the afternoon (as one does) when in struts their hopeless, pathetic, harebrained, possibly mentally unwell father.

"I don't get it," the fumbling, bumbling dad says as he searches for his stupid Allen wrench or whatever. "Why do they call them Apple Jacks if they don't taste like apple?"

The little shits all look at each other knowingly. One of them mocks the father, *"They don't taste like apple,"* and the rest crack up. The towering monument to paternal folly stands there for a moment, hoping to hold his ground against this monsoon of humiliation. Then he turns around and slinks away, likely ruing the day he was ever born.

Or at least that's how I remembered the commercial. Rewatching it on YouTube made me realize it went a little easier on the dad than I'd recalled from my childhood.[1] Yet the ad is still classic 1990s. Within its thirty seconds is contained an entire generation.

The kids sitting in the garage were my age, the millennials, the most studied and parsed and orally swabbed demographic in the history of the world. Endless research has been done into the millennial cohort by battalions of social scientists, yet all this time the answer was hiding in plain sight. What explains the millennials? We know why Apple Jacks don't taste like apple.

To grow up in the 1990s was to have your youth constantly glamorized and repackaged back to you. It was to be told by endless voices from off the TV, "You're young! You're hip! You're *savvy*! We want to know all about *you*!" It was to understand that *you* were the prime demo for the TGIF showrunners and the Tamagotchi salesmen, *you* were what all the earworm jingles and bright colors were blaring at. Only *you* knew what *you* wanted, and what *you* wanted was regarded by advertisers as some of the most coveted information on the planet. *You* were thus privy to knowledge your parents didn't have. *You* knew why Apple Jacks don't taste like apple.

Here was an inversion of the traditional understanding of wisdom. Most civilizations have maintained that knowledge comes to the old and battle-tested, not the young and inexperienced. You have to mature in the world before you can understand its most mysterious cereal-related secrets. It isn't until old age that, as Cephalus puts it in Plato's *Republic*, "the passions relax their hold" and "we are freed from the grasp not of one mad master only, but of many," allowing wisdom to thrive.[2]

The mentality millennials were raised under was more in the vein of the radical philosopher Jean-Jacques Rousseau: there was something

1   "Apple Jacks Commercial (1996)," YouTube, uploaded by mycommercials, November 20, 2009.

2   Allan Bloom, *The Republic of Plato* (New York: Basic Books, 2016), ch. 1, book 1.

pure and uncorrupted about our youth. We were attuned to the zeitgeist, knowledgeable of its ways, uncorrupted by the breakfast-based ignorance of our elders. We knew why Apple Jacks didn't taste like apple.

In retrospect, it can seem a bit cheap that the reason we were taught to think this way was to move product, to make Apple Jacks and zillions of other wares seem exclusive to the young and therefore desirable. Yet there was an underlying ethos here too. This ethos was, ironically enough, propagated by that least commercial of generations, the baby boomers. Once upon a time, the boomers had rejected capitalism, yet in addition to flirting with Marx, they'd also bragged about "never trusting anyone over thirty" and staying "forever young." It was this latter impulse that won out. As abstract dreams of working-class revolution dispelled into neoliberal reality (at least for the time being), the boomers became the bourgeois their college selves had despised. They went to work in advertising, and brought with them the fanciful if alluring idea of youth as glamor.

The boomers, of course, did not remain "forever young": they succumbed to gravity until they were beyond the help even of the readily available Botox they'd pioneered. But if they couldn't quite gulp from the Fountain of Youth, they could at least sluice its waters toward their children. "Forever young" was a boomer motto but it became a millennial curriculum. And it made the experience of childhood feel precious, maybe even native to us, a trait rather than a temporal state, like having blue eyes, one that maybe, just maybe, might last forever.

Why would we want to grow up? Then we might forget why Apple Jacks don't taste like apple.

***

If millennials were conditioned to prize our youth, then we were also—and this is key to understanding us—forced to grow up suddenly.

The terrorist attacks of September 11, 2001, marked the spiritual end of the 1990s, the moment we were all ejected from our Nerf foam cocoons at maximal velocity onto the cold floor of the real world. Our home was no longer indestructible; our youth was no longer our refuge; a mushroom of evil smoke hovered over our idyll. Millennials have a reputation for being spoiled, and at least some of that is deserved, but give us credit: in the aftermath of those attacks, we enlisted in the military at an impressive clip.

I'll revisit 9/11 in future chapters, but suffice it to say it wasn't the destruction of the Twin Towers that came to define the millennial generation. It was everything that came afterward.

First up was the debacle of the Iraq war, which sent a message: *you and your country aren't as powerful as you think and not everyone wants to be you.* Then came the economic crash in 2008 and the end of the thriving economy we'd come to take for granted. Then the slowest economic recovery since the Great Depression, the failure of Obamacare, the sense that no matter what the government tried to do it ended up just deferring or compounding our problems. Then the pyrotechnics of the Trump presidency, COVID-19 lockdowns and mask and vaccine mandates, the George Floyd riots, the January 6 riot, the humiliation in Afghanistan, inflation, rising crime.

The calm of our childhoods had given way to a cascade of crises. At least some of us nineties kids had grown up with a vague, inchoate patriotism, not so much an impulse to wave the flag as a kind of innate gratitude, a sense that we were stupidly lucky to be living in the most peaceful and prosperous country at the most peaceful and prosperous time in the history of the world. Now we were being confronted with the disproof of this birthright. Blow after blow had been landed on the national psyche, leaving us to wonder not just whether our country reigned supreme but whether it could function at the most basic level.

For the golden children of history, the keepers of the Apple Jacks riddle, this was a hard awakening. After being conditioned to think such a thing wasn't possible, millennials had become spectators to decline.

***

I am, as it happens, so millennial it hurts. I was born in 1987, which means the 1990s spanned my first conscious memory through my graduation from middle school. I was the quintessential nineties kid: Nickelodeon on the TV, wood-paneled minivan in the driveway (why did anyone ever think timber looked stylish on a sliding door?).

I wouldn't describe my childhood as idyllic, but I would describe it as still. Very, very still. Still and twofold. Two cars in the garage. Two thirds of an acre under the house. Two parents at the dinner table. Two hours between us and the nearest big city.

I mention all this not because I want to indulge nineties nostalgia (though I do and will constantly throughout this chapter), but because I want to caution against my own biases. My childhood might have been still, but there are plenty for whom the 1990s were anything but still, starting with most Rwandans and Albanians and continuing through plenty of Americans living in inner cities and deindustrialized towns.

So was my experience representative of a better time? Or did I grow up in privilege and am now stretching that privilege across an entire decade? Or am I just responding to my forever-young conditioning, pining for an age when Nintendo 64 mattered more than oil changes?

The question of personal bias versus social reality is a difficult one, which is why we say things like "history is written by the winners." Yet consider as a point in my favor that much of the millennial generation feels the way I do. Boomers tend to miss their young adulthoods, their 1960s protest days when they smashed monogamy and burned bras and thought "surely this will in no way have any adverse effects on our children." Millennials can miss their young adulthoods too, but they also miss their eighth birthday parties at Chuck E. Cheese. That isn't normal. How many Silents pine for the days of keeping their elbows off an empty table during the Great Depression? The sheer universality of our longing makes it seem like more than just some generational whimper for the infantile.

It also isn't just millennials who feel this way. A wide-ranging poll by Kelton Global and *National Geographic* found the 1990s run roughly even with the 1980s as Americans' choice for the last great decade. According to Kelton, nearly three quarters said they would vote for Bill Clinton if he ran for president again and a majority said TV was better in the 1990s. (Movies alone were said to be better in the present day, though I think that's the hill I'd die on. *Goodfellas? Apollo 13?* The first *Jurassic Park?*)

Now consider that the Kelton poll was taken in 2014, before COVID-19 and other assorted chaos.[3] I think we can safely assume a poll taken in 2024 would find the 1990s beckon even more seductively.

In fact, we don't have to assume too much, because the headlines betray the mood. Google "90s better time," and here's a sample of what you'll find: "The best decade ever? The 1990s, obviously," "6 reasons the 90s were really the best generation to live," "20 reasons why the 90s were the best decade to grow up," "Why the 90s is the best decade ever," "1990s: the good decade," "1990s things people miss," "I would murder a man in cold blood to bring back the 1990s" (okay I made up that last one).

Punch in "90s worst time" and you'll get a few bites too: "26 reasons why growing up in the 90s was the fucking worst." But then that seems less like serious analysis than cynical contrarianism—which

---

3   "Were the nineties the Last Great Decade?" National Geographic and Kelton Global, June 25, 2014, https://www.prnewswire.com/news-releases/were-the-90s-the-last-great-decade-264613751.html#:~:text=It%20would%20seem%20that%20the,the%20'90s%20with%2022%25.

was a hallmark of the 1990s! You see how it is? You can't hope to resist. (I imagine the author of that article waking up at three in the morning, padding over to a glass display case, and checking to make sure his Beanie Baby raccoon and flamingo are still arranged *just so*.)

Nostalgia for the 1990s gets a bad rap, and certainly it can be crass and mass-marketed (just like the decade it so fondly remembers). But the point is it's not an invention of corporate America or the millennial mind playing tricks on itself. It's a very real and widely felt phenomenon. And it's borne out of the unfortunate events that have come since, the generation caught in the middle, and the inescapable impression that the country has slipped into decline.

***

One of the upsides of living in a big liberal society is you can always find someone to oppose a motion. Think granite is a rock? No doubt there is someone at large right now who thinks granite is very much not a rock and who is willing to die arguing this point on a Twitter account called @TheCountertopConspiracy.

So it is that across the river from the cottage industry that is nineties nostalgia has grown up another cottage industry of nineties skepticism. These people aren't mere contrarians. They don't trash the 1990s per se, so much as try to expose it as more nuanced than it seems.

The realists have their own documentary series called *The Dark Side of the nineties*. Produced by Vice and narrated by Mark McGrath, the lead singer of the band Sugar Ray, its episodes look at everything from exploitative trash TV like *The Jerry Springer Show* to the mad rush to buy Beanie Babies that eventually culminated in a homicide to doomsday cults like the Branch Davidians to the East Coast versus West Coast hip-hop war that saw the slayings of both Tupac Shakur and Biggie Smalls.

Watching *The Dark Side of the nineties,* your first impression is that one reason we remember that decade so fondly is because social media didn't exist back then. The abuse and trauma suffered by the supermodels of that era, for example, which is documented in one of the episodes, likely would have been an online sensation had it been a problem in the 2020s. And it's hard to think of anything that would have discredited trash TV faster than a moralizing Twitter mob on a mission.

But *really*, I mean *really* . . . doesn't that sound kind of cool? Doesn't a world where Twitter doesn't exist, where societal vices are sometimes kept in the shadows without us needing to performatively upbraid them, smack of an Atlantis? This is never more the case than in the series' second episode, about the Viper Room, a private club in Hollywood opened by Johnny Depp as a refuge for celebrities who needed to unwind. The Viper Room is supposed to be a part of nineties Mordor because River Phoenix, brother of actor Joaquin, died of a drug overdose just outside. And certainly we don't want to detract from the tragedy of his death.

Yet as the documentary flips through photos of Johnny Depp and girlfriend Kate Moss smoking cigarettes, Jennifer Aniston lounging about with Counting Crows frontman Adam Duritz, Cameron Diaz smiling coolly as a longneck dangles from her fingers, you can't help but think *this is awesome.*[4] And *what a shame this couldn't exist today.* Because it couldn't exist today. There is no such thing anymore as a totally dark club, a little haven where you can drink and smoke in peace knowing you're invisible to the gawkers. If the Viper Room was still open, someone would eventually post a photo

---

4   "Dark Side of the nineties," directed by Richard Rotter, featuring Mark McGrath, aired July 2021–August 2022 on Vice TV, produced by Railsplitter Pictures and Insight Productions.

to Instagram showing Celebrity A making out with Bartender B even though he was linked to Pelvis Model C. Or Movie Star A telling jokes about Ethnic Group B whose Political Lobby C would demand he be banished to Deserted Island D.

Our eyes and our indignation would barge into the Viper Room like a vice squad, stomping about until it had been reduced to some boring vegan phantom of its former self. And then we would congratulate ourselves because we'd had the foresight to *care*.

This is the overwhelming impression of the 1990s that's left by the Vice doc, as a time when problems could be kept gloriously under wraps. *The Dark Side of the nineties* demands sunlight—it's right there in the title. Yet by purporting to expose the decade's flaws, it reminds you that in living through that decade you might have been fortunate enough to miss those flaws entirely.

***

This lack of social consciousness, in the best sense, was very much a feature and not a bug. It's difficult to imagine today, but the one imperative imposed by the nineties was that you be the opposite of an activist. Chuck Klosterman, in his excellent pop-history *The Nineties*, sums it up this way: "It was perhaps the last period in American history when personal and political engagement was still viewed as optional."

And perhaps even less than optional. Today's culture is often criticized for its "slacktivism," its effort-free hash tags typed from reclined chairs. Yet the cool thing in the nineties wasn't to be a slacktivist but a slacker. As Klosterman puts it, what "informed the experience of nineties life" more than anything else was "an adversarial relationship with trying too hard."[5] You didn't just have the choice to ignore

---

5   Chuck Klosterman, *The Nineties: A Book* (New York: Penguin Press, 2022).

politics; it was what every young person in good standing was expected to do. Elections, causes, political candidates—these things simply weren't cool.

This apathy was so pronounced as to have once been considered a warning light for the country's future. The 1996 election, between Bill Clinton, Bob Dole, and Ross Perot, saw voter turnout plunge to its lowest rate in a presidential contest since 1924, when the gloriously boring Calvin Coolidge was elected. There was a sense in the nineties that we had entered a lazy post-political age. You weren't supposed to be an "ally" because there was nothing to ally with. To fight for a cause was lame.

Few writers have chronicled this slacker inclination better than Klosterman. Klosterman is one of those nineties realists, but he's more interested in documenting history than teasing out shadows or reacting against contemporary nostalgia. And what he finds, outlined in his history *The Nineties* and embodied in his famous essay collection *Sex, Drugs, and Cocoa Puffs*, centers heavily on this apathy.

Klosterman offers up as the decade's quintessential movie the Ben Stiller–directed comedy-drama *Reality Bites*. It stars Winona Ryder as a filmmaker in the midst of a love triangle with Stiller and Ethan Hawke (and movies today are better *how*?). The two are archetypes of the time: Stiller is the charming Reagan-era executive in a suit who seems to have everything under control, while Hawke is a shaggy-haired product of grunge who can't hold down a paying job.

The choice between the two should be obvious, yet the movie flips our expectations, with Ryder ultimately choosing Hawke, unable to resist his jaded apathy. In this, *Reality Bites* reeks of the disenchantment that so characterized its time, the rebellion against what was then considered a productive adult life.[6]

---

6   *Reality Bites*, directed by Ben Stiller (Universal Pictures, 1994), 99 minutes.

Yet before we surrender the nineties to the slackers, let's consider this bit of subtext: Ryder probably wouldn't have stayed with Hawke. Eventually she would have gotten tired of him, demanded he get health insurance already, and come to see her fascination with his flip ways as just a phase she was going through. And that's just it: nineties slackerism was always just a phase. It was more style than substance, useful if you wanted to smoke cigarettes with the cool kids outside the mall. And while it was an important trend, while it undoubtedly influenced its native decade, it can't fully cut through to the substance of what the nineties were and why they seem better than what we have today.

*

If the slackers had a moment during the nineties, then it's curious how annoyingly hard everyone else seemed to be working. The nineties were part of the longest peacetime economic expansion in American history, which began under George H. W. Bush and continued until the dot-com bubble burst in 2000. Both output and worker productivity increased across nearly the entire economy. The stock market was booming; small businesses were thriving; innovators were scrambling to juice dollars out of this newfangled internet thing.

It was the first real consumerist revolution since the 1950s. This is why when so many of us think of the nineties, what comes to mind isn't slackers but *stuff*, towering heaps of *stuff*: Pokémon cartridges, Magic cards, Tamagotchis, Moon Shoes, Velcro sneakers, Super Soakers, Gameboys, Pogs, Beanie Babies, VCRs, CDs, Fruit by the Foot, Warheads, Foxtails, NordicTracks, Surge cans, floppy disks, pieces of the Aggro Crag, Pendants of Life, yo-yos, Discmans, pagers. The '60s had their music and political causes; the '80s had their patriotism and renewal; but my decade had an infinity matrix of Koosh Balls stretching into oblivion, available in purple, orange, and green.

What's more, it was *good* stuff. That's not to say there wasn't plenty of junk—I'm still baffled by the appeal of Pogs, little cardboard bottle caps with stylized designs that boys would collect. But most nineties merchandise was pretty imaginative and fun if you were a kid.

More than any decade, the nineties seemed to understand that children respond to creativity. They don't care about blaring noises or immersive graphics so much as concept, variety, imagination. Perhaps because innovation was needed to move product, perhaps because its ethos placed such a shine on youth, the nineties seemed determined not to insult the intelligence of children. Kids were approached on their own terms.

This applied to nowhere so much as children's TV. Back then, networks like Nickelodeon and the Disney Channel were fiercely competing for the youthful attention span. Out of this came an explosion of wild, dart-at-the-wall, dear-God-let's-hope-this-works television.

The best example of this was *Legends of the Hidden Temple*. That statement can land in the current zeitgeist with a groan, given how thoroughly the popular Nickelodeon game show has been milked for every droplet of nostalgia it can muster. But then there's a reason you can't go to a millennial Halloween party without running into at least one couple dressed as the Silver Snakes. A kind of *American Gladiators*-meets-Indiana Jones hybrid that aired from 1993 to 1995, what made *Legends* so iconic was its final round, which saw teams of children running through an insanely complicated, Mayan temple–themed maze trying to retrieve lost artifacts all while so-called Temple Guards, half-naked dudes in Indian costumes, jumped out and scared the crap out of them. It felt like an especially immersive video game brought to life. The show was hosted, naturally, by a giant talking stone head named Olmec and an explorer named Kirk Fogg who swung out on a rope.[7]

7　*Legends of the Hidden Temple*, created by David Stanley and Scott Stone, directed by Charles Ciup and Glenn Weiss, aired on Nickelodeon, 1993–1995.

Legends felt like something a team of unusually bright nine-year-olds would think up on a federal holiday. It was, in a word, creative, and in this it was a hallmark of its decade. Contrast *Legends* with much of the tweenage-sitcom drivel that's come to dominate Nickelodeon ever since and you'll see the point. It's almost axiomatic that *Legends* couldn't get made in the year 2024. The suits would worry that a show that relied for plot exposition on a talking rock might not click with the target demo. The activists would whine about white children appropriating such Indigenous cultural touchstones as an obstacle course. And the SWAT teams would descend the second any one of the little darlings was hauled away by a grown man wearing feathers.

It took a more bohemian and less troubled decade to produce *Legends.* The best we moderns could do was a watered-down reboot that aired in 2021 on the CW network that both featured and was aimed at adults (read: weeping millennials). Shamelessly derivative, inexplicably boring, with no raison d'être except to try to alchemize nostalgia into dollars, it was canceled after only one season.[8]

***

It isn't easy to pinpoint what made an entire decade so attractive to an entire generation. But if I had to chalk up nineties nostalgia to one factor, even just one word, it would be: creativity. Out of its more relaxed attitude, its ability to care just a little less, came a striking degree of experimentation.

Legends of the Hidden Temple splayed the youthful imagination across a soundstage. *Seinfeld* and even *Friends* showed the sitcom could be more than just family-based morality tales with happy endings. Video games like *Half Life* and *System Shock* 2 placed a

---

8   Denise Petski, "'Legends of the Hidden Temple' Canceled by the CW After One Season," *Deadline*, June 3, 2022, https://deadline .com/2022/06/legends-of-the-hidden-temple-canceled-the-cw-after-one -season-1235038265/.

premium on atmosphere and immersive storytelling that's rarely seen today. Educational game shows like *Where in the World Is Carmen Sandiego?* and computer game franchises like the Super Solvers revolutionized so-called edutainment and made learning fun. Hip-hop took off and grunge was invented. David Foster Wallace wrote *Infinite Jest*.

Another key factor was that the nineties were when we achieved, as Kurt Andersen put it, "just the right amount of technology."[9] It was when we hit that high point on the X-Y axis between interconnectedness and mental calm. The internet was there if you wanted to shop online or look up something, but it was housed in a desktop behemoth in the living room corner; it couldn't follow you around in your pocket, vibrating and buzzing until you wanted to hurl it into a volcano. Technology was still subordinate to us rather than the other way around. If you had a weird idea, you didn't have to worry about it being judged to death by a dreadfully conformist Twitter mob. You could play with it, put it out there, see where it went.

In this, the nineties seemed like the decade when we could have it all: creativity and consumerism, technology and humanity, bohemia and a responsible mainstream, the kind of liberal conservatism (or was it conservative liberalism?) that was embraced by both President George H. W. Bush and President Bill Clinton. It was a delicate balance, to be sure, but we seemed to have found it, and there was nothing to suggest it would ever slip away.

***

Why do we feel nostalgic? Why do we long for the town where we grew up or a close childhood friend—or a seemingly simpler time?

---

9   Kurt Andersen, "The Best Decade Ever? The 1990s, Obviously." *New York Times*, February 6, 2015, https://www.nytimes.com/2015/02/08/opinion/sunday/the-best-decade-ever-the-1990s-obviously.html.

The conservative writer Anthony Esolen posits that nostalgia is not merely a pining for the past; it's a kind of contextualization, a desire to position ourselves in a time and place where we feel like we belong. Why does Odysseus long to go home? Not just because it's in the past but because it's *home*—Ithaca is the place that shaped him and thus fits him like a glove.[10]

Against a thoughtful conservative like Esolen stands (predictably) the medical community, which for centuries took a dimmer view of nostalgia. They used to diagnose it as a disorder, tied up with more serious conditions like trauma and depression.

Both of these definitions have a point (though I'm far more inclined to Esolen's). Yet let's also allow for a narrower, more thuddingly obvious meaning: sometimes we long for the past because the past really was better. And this is the case with nineties nostalgia. That creativity, that ease of being, that relief from concerns over nuclear war and stagflation, as well as China and TikTok (but I repeat myself)—let's resolve the motion before this house: the nineties were a better time.

But let's also not dismiss Esolen quite so easily. It wasn't just that the nineties were a great time to be alive; it's that they were perhaps a slightly more human time too. They were a period when, in spite of all the commercialization and crassness, we felt just a little more at ease as people, a little closer to the way life was meant to be lived, a little less haunted by social media and political insanity. It was a kind of interbellum period, sandwiched between the Cold War and '60s culture wars, and the war on terror and culture wars of today. It was a time of relative peace.

We millennials will never get those days back, alas, though being in my generation does have its upsides. Every single one of us still knows why Apple Jacks don't taste like apple. And it's a secret we'll take to the grave.

---

10 Anthony Esolen, *Nostalgia: Going Home in a Homeless World* (Washington: Regnery Gateway, 2018).

CHAPTER 2

Spaceship Earth's Melted Plastic

The year was 2019 and the annual Army-Navy football game had kicked off to roaring crowds in Philadelphia. Yet the normally headline event was about to be overshadowed by a dire specter: *racism.*

During a live broadcast, a crowd of both Army and Navy fans flashed the "okay" hand symbol at the camera. You've probably made this gesture before: you place your index finger and thumb together while extending your other three fingers. It means the opposite of flipping the bird: *okay. All good. Cool man.*

Apparently it also means: *the master race will crush the vermin mongrels beneath its jackboot.* Clips of the fans making the okay sign raced across Twitter where the mob delivered its verdict: *racist! The gesture was racist!* The blowback against the soldiers and sailors was so fierce that officials at West Point and the Naval Academy launched official investigations into their conduct.[1]

The okay sign dates back to ancient Greece where it was (ironically) a symbol of love. It's been used more recently not just in everyday life to express approval but in the Hindu and Buddhist religions, as well as in yoga where it symbolizes harmony and perfection. Yet it wasn't until our more enlightened time that it was abruptly discovered to be a bat signal for Nazis.

The origins of the Great Okay Hand Panic are well known: in fact, they were reported in most of the articles that covered the controversy at the time. In 2017, a pack of actual white supremacists got together on the online message board 4chan and cooked up a hoax: they would start a rumor that a commonly used gesture was racist in order to troll the liberal media. The entire thing was a rope-a-dope. There was no serious connotation of bigotry attached to the hand signal nor had there ever been.[2]

Yet their prank went off swimmingly. The Army and Navy fans were tarred as bigots (they were later exonerated, having been merely playing a popular game, trying to sneak the gesture into as many TV shots as possible[3]). The Anti-Defamation League listed the okay

1   Kevin Bohn and Greg Clary, "Army and Navy launch internal investigations into controversial hand gesture captured on video," CNN, December 16, 2019, https://www.cnn.com/2019/12/15/politics/navy -internal-investigation-hand-gesture-video/index.html.

2   Morgan Sung, "4chan trolling turned the OK sign into a symbol of hate," *Mashable*, September 26, 2019, https://mashable.com/article/ok-hand -gesture-hate-symbol-anti-defamation-league-white-sumpremacy.

3   "Results of Investigation Into Hand Gestures," West Point Public Affairs, Release number 54-19, December 20, 2019, https://www.westpoint.edu /news/press-releases/results-of-investigation-hand-gestures.

sign as a "symbol of hate."[4] The hacktastic Southern Poverty Law Center darkly noted that the gesture was almost always accompanied by a smirk (maybe because—and I'm just drawing out of a hat here—the person is signaling everything is okay?).[5] A Chicago school spent $53,000 reprinting its yearbook after the original was found to feature photos of students making the sign.[6] The Chicago Cubs banned a fan permanently from their games after he made the gesture in the background of a broadcast (a picture accompanying an NBC News report literally pixelated the man's hand).[7] A lawyer who flashed the sign during the Senate confirmation hearings for Supreme Court Justice Brett Kavanaugh was dragged all across Twitter (it turned out she was a Jewish Mexican American descendant of Holocaust survivors).[8]

What happened here was remarkable. Prominent journalists and bigotry hall monitors had given the 4chan jokers everything they'd wanted. They'd kowtowed to actual racists, allowing themselves to

---

4   Bobby Allyn, "The 'OK' Hand Gesture Is Now Listed as a Symbol of Hate," NPR, September 26, 2019, https://www.npr.org/2019/09/26/764728163 /the-ok-hand-gesture-is-now-listed-as-a-symbol-of-hate.

5   David Newert, "Is That an OK sign? A White Power Symbol? Or Just a Right-Wing Troll?" Southern Poverty Law Center, September 19, 2018, https://www.splcenter.org/hatewatch/2018/09/18 /ok-sign-white-power-symbol-or-just-right-wing-troll.

6   Ewan Palmer, "Chicago High School Yearbook Had Photos of Students Flashing White Supremacist Signs so Board Spent $53K to Print New Ones," *Newsweek*, May 22, 2019, https://www.newsweek.com /chicago-school-ok-sign-yearbook-white-supremacy-1432360.

7   Elisha Fieldstadt, "Chicago Cubs ban fan who flashed 'white power' symbol on air behind black reporter," NBC News, May 9, 2019, https ://www.nbcnews.com/news/sports/cubs-fan-banned-wrigley-field-after -flashing-white-power-symbol-n1003681.

8   Mahita Gajanan, "A Kavanaugh Supporter Was Accused of Making a White Power Symbol. She's a Descendant of Holocaust Survivors," *Time*, September 4, 2018, https://time.com/5386860 /zina-gelman-bash-white-power-symbol/.

be trolled because it afforded them an opportunity to signal outrage. And in decline-era America, outrage is an opportunity we cannot pass up. So it was that a perfectly harmless hand signal was tossed onto the ever-growing heap of things we're no longer allowed to say or do.

***

Reflect on the Great Okay Hand Panic for too long and you might find yourself reaching for the Zoloft and Everclear. Or you might just think about Disney World.

I went to Disney World a few times as a kid and the blissful memories will be with me forever: the blazing summer heat, the $34 soggy chicken sandwich at the Pinocchio restaurant, the heat again, still the heat, the sweat mixing with sunscreen on my back to form some new chemical compound that was probably turning me into an X-Man, the heat. . . .

Okay, so maybe don't go in August. But there's one Disney experience I always look back upon with pleasure: Spaceship Earth. You know that giant golf ball that looms over the Epcot Center theme park? The one that looks like it's awaiting the arrival of some Brobdingnagian Tiger Woods? There's a ride inside that thing. Spaceship Earth straps you into a slow-moving car and takes you on a tour showing how people have shared information throughout the ages. From the earliest cave paintings to the modern smartphone, it's a strictly objective look at the history of communication brought to you by the fine people at AT&T.

I always enjoyed Spaceship Earth when I was a kid, and as I grew older, I came to realize it was more than just a way to kill time while that one family member was taking forever in the bathroom. Spaceship Earth was a time capsule. It was a perfect summary of a neoliberal ethos that had prevailed throughout the second half of the twentieth century and reached its zenith (when else?) in the 1990s. That ethos was the belief that more communication and more interconnectedness are always good. They're so good, in fact, that they might just save humanity. Shrink the world through technology and you'd bring people together. Bring people together and you might finally close the book on all those bloody wars and ancient enmities. Why would anyone take up arms against his fellow man when he could see him onscreen and spam him with eggplant emojis? As the narrator on Spaceship Earth puts it, "we stand on the brink of a new renaissance."

At the vanguard of that renaissance is, of course, YouTube, which allows you to watch a video of Spaceship Earth for free, which means you no longer have to pay to ride it.[9] Just one of the many delicious ironies of the communication revolution, brought to you by the absolutely wonderful human beings at AT&T.

But before we get ahead of ourselves, it's worth noting that during the 1990s this techno-optimism was very much in the air. Bill Gates and Steve Jobs were regarded as titans. Bill Clinton signed the Telecommunications Act, which deregulated the phone and cable companies.

Today, we can't deny that all this technological development has borne fruit. Yet ride Spaceship Earth in the year 2024 and it can feel like an anachronism, even a joke. Everyone knows the communication revolution, brought to you by those nigh-Galahad-esque paragons of virtue and wisdom at AT&T, has not brought us together in global brotherhood. What it's done is to make it so we can't use the word "brotherhood" without wondering whether we're about to be canceled for misogyny.

---

9   Walt Disney Imagineering, "Spaceship Earth," 1982, Epcot Center, Disney World. Note: AT&T was Spaceship Earth's sponsor from 1984 to 2004, which covered the years I used to visit Disney World. Today, the ride has no sponsor.

Somehow, the promise of mass communication collapsed into a flame war. From Spaceship Earth to the Great Okay Hand Panic in just a few decades. How did that happen anyway?

***

In the beginning, there was the internet chat room. And God saw that it was good.

Actually He didn't, I suspect, given what was to come afterward and the reputation chat rooms had at the time. In the halcyon days of the 'net, chat rooms were regarded as seedy, the kind of places where creeps in trench coats went to lease nondescript vans. Log into a chat room and you might be abducted by a stranger. It wasn't clear how, but you might.

The first publicly accessible online chat room was created by CompuServe in 1980. In the ensuing decades, these fora would proliferate and evolve, coming to specialize in just about every type of conversation. Were you a quantum physicist looking for love with a fellow subscriber to the Copenhagen Interpretation? Chances are a chat room had you covered.

In the beginning, there was the chat room, and then there was the blog. In certain respects, the blog felt like a regression from the chat room, in that it didn't allow for a multiplicity of people to dialogue with each other, specializing instead in entries from a single blogger or at most a group. Yet the blog was vitally important in its own right. Whereas the chat room revolutionized conversation, the blog revolutionized opinion.

Once upon a time, a newspaper opinion columnist was a tough gig to get. If you wanted to be the next David Ignatius (and all the cool kids did), you had to put in your time as a journalist, start as a cub reporter on the metro desk covering sewage maintenance timetables and pothole repair graft, then maybe do a stint overseas to expand your horizons.

Or you at least had to go the William F. Buckley route and start your own magazine. Editors in the pre-internet age had an arcane belief that writers needed some experience in the world before they were ready to opine on it. Today, we rightly understand this view to be racist, but back then it was relatively common.

The blog changed all that. Suddenly any unemployed stiff sitting at home in his pajamas could have an authoritative soapbox from which to sound off—and I don't mean that derisively, as I zip up my *Star Wars* footies. One of the earliest conservative blogs was cheekily named Pajamas Media (today abbreviated as PJ Media). The blog effectively circumvented the old gatekeepers: political opinions weren't just for the well-connected (or even the showered and shaved) anymore.

As the 1990s became the 2000s became the 2010s, as elite journos and editors seemed increasingly out of touch with a war-battered and recession-fleeced nation, as DIY blogging services like WordPress and Blogger flourished, the angry blogger became a force in his own right. Conservative blogs challenged the left-leaning establishment media, while progressives like Ezra Klein and Matt Yglesias assailed that same establishment media for not covering the Bush administration hard enough. Klein and Yglesias would go on to found the website Vox.com and become media elites in their own right, showing just how disruptive the new blog-based ecosystem could be.

Yet what no one yet knew was that these two forms of media, the chat room and the blog, were about to get a room and conceive the Antichrist.

***

When Twitter was first launched in 2006, it was not immediately clear that it was a portal to hell that would unleash demons into our world and cast all we knew into a darkness thicker than iron. At first, everyone just seemed confused.

"Entering the brave new world of Twitter. What the heck is this anyway?" tweeted Congressman Paul Ryan.[10] "First tweet. What happens next?" tweeted Congressman Jim Himes.[11] Senator Barbara Mikulski helpfully reported, "Hi all just had a heartsmart lunch."[12]

Yet what Twitter had done, even if it wasn't clear at its inception, was to take the dark side of the chat room's open conversation and collide it at warp speed with the dark side of the blog's punchy commentary. Now, not only could you accuse someone you'd never met before of being an assclown, you could do so in real time and in front of the entire world. You could even do it to the president—Barack Obama joined Twitter in 2015 and every subsequent heir to George Washington has had an account.

In this sense, Twitter initially seemed like the ultimate in democratic communication. If you were on Facebook, your conversations in those days were limited to your so-called "wall" with your so-called "friends" who were mostly fellow students at your college. If you were on AOL Instant Messenger, you could only chat with your "buddies," whose entrances were heralded by that earsplitting sound of a door creaking open, which even today functions as a millennial Pavlov's bell.

These platforms placed guardrails on your ability to communicate. What Twitter did was to demolish those guardrails in favor of a no-holds-barred mass dialogue. Everyone was chucked into the same bear pit. A former chairman of the Federal Reserve would see his tweets posted in boxes the same size as those of a fourteen-year-old who thought this whole Marxist-Lernerism thing had gotten a bad rap. And unless the Fed chair set his tweets to private, anyone, not just those he

---

10   Paul Ryan, "Entering the brave new world of Twitter. What the heck is this anyway?" Twitter, February 4, 2009.

11   Jim Himes, "First tweet. What happens next?" Twitter, April 16, 2009.

12   Barbara Mikulski, "Hi all just had a heartsmart lunch," Twitter, April 22, 2010.

followed, could see them and publicly reply to them. The playing field was completely level. For Americans, who revel in the little guy standing up to the powerful, this seemed like a godsend—those powerful were even marked by blue checks, amulets of status that doubled as beacons for trolls.

As Twitter evolved, several important trends began to emerge. The first was that its sheer accessibility and popularity meant it contained essentially unlimited opinion. You could type, say, "refrigerator crisper" into its search box and find someone taking every imaginable position on the refrigerator crisper. You could find people in favor of refrigerator crispers, people against refrigerator crispers, and people insisting refrigerator crispers were just a false flag operation.

Linked to this was another trend: because opinion was virtually unlimited, if you wanted more followers and retweets, you had to stand out. You had to say something extreme or vitriolic. You had to call the refrigerator crisper a trick of the Jew or suggest nuclear weapons should be used against refrigerator crispers. And others would then have to follow suit if they wanted their time in the sun, either vehemently attacking you or vehemently doubling down on what you'd said. This guaranteed that fringe and absolutist views worked their way into the mainstream.

Yet paradoxically, while Twitter contained unlimited opinion, its incentives were skewed toward conformity. You needed to push the envelope, yes, but you needed to push it on a "trending topic" everyone else was already talking about, or at least a subject that was of visceral interest to a particular subculture. That was the only way to get noticed and reap those precious likes and followers. This is how the Twitter mob was born: hordes of tweets frantically trying to milk attention out of a popular topic. So while Twitter was legion, it was also uniform, organized into a handful of feeding frenzies.

And while a mob can be a consequence of too much democracy (see: Revolution, the French), it soon became clear that even Twitter's democratic promise was just a mirage. Despite its immense volume of hot takes, at the platform's peak, well under a quarter of Americans had Twitter accounts and just 10 percent of those accounts were responsible for 80 percent of all tweets.[13]

The freewheeling conversation, the sense that Twitter could give you an accurate read of public opinion, was a farce—and all the more so because users tended to tailor their feeds based on their interests and points of view. In reality you were talking to the same four hundred people over and over again. And those four hundred people tended to be more privileged than the average American, as a study from the Pew Research Center found.[14] Politicians, celebrities, and elite journalists were not only more likely to tweet than your average car mechanic, they were often required to by their jobs. There's also the matter of the car mechanic having better things to do than launch hot takes into the sun all day.

Rather than the vox populi, Twitter became more like Sector T, a vast and strange and distorted nebula where up was down and normal was marginal and fetishists floated past screaming into oblivion. In such an environment, where all the incentives had been warped, you might even find yourself believing the okay sign was the new *"Sieg heil!"*

Then there was the fact that half the time you didn't even know who was calling you an assclown. A sizable portion of Twitter accounts are either anonymous or run by automated bots. And even when you do know who you're talking to, that anonymity is still a factor: you're engaging with a name and a two-dimensional avatar, not a real-life person in the flesh. Such anonymity is one of the most consequential

---

13   Stefan Wojcik and Adam Hughes, "Sizing Up Twitter Users," Pew Research Center, April 24, 2019, https://www.pewresearch.org /internet/2019/04/24/sizing-up-twitter-users/.

14   Wojcik, "Sizing Up Twitter Users."

features of Twitter as well as online life more generally, and it's worth exploring at greater length.

∗∗∗

The thinker Adam Smith is best known for debuting the economic concept of the "invisible hand," which regularly tickles free-market thinkers while getting in slap fights with Bernie Sanders. But Smith was also the most perceptive philosopher we've ever had on the subject of human sympathy.

In his work *The Theory of Moral Sentiments*, Smith notes that we have no superhuman ability to feel others' pain. What we can do is to use our imaginations to invest ourselves just a little in their plights, to make the external personal. If you see me fall down and twist my ankle, you immediately conjure up what it must be like to fall down and twist your own ankle. You perhaps recall a time in your life when you fell down and twisted your ankle. And inspired by this offloading of my pain onto yourself, you rush in to help (please?).

Smith saw such sympathy as both nature and nurture, both innate to us and learned from those around us. He also saw it as conducive of morality, since it requires us to make value judgments based on the motives behind the sympathetic action, the circumstances and norms in which it takes place, and other factors. Your sympathy for my twisted ankle would naturally be dimmed if I was on the run from the police or had been jogging in the middle of the road holding up traffic for miles. Likewise, your sympathy for me might be heightened if you knew I was a father who needed a functioning ankle to hold down a job in rhythmic gymnastics. It's this merger of the self with others that fine-tunes our moral equipment, tempers our passions, and enables us to participate in society.[15]

---

15 Adam Smith, *The Theory of Moral Sentiments* (New York: Uplifting Publications, 2009, originally published 1759).

This is why I don't always agree when conservatives rail against empathy (which is roughly what Smith means by sympathy). Empathy is a poor basis for the law or defense policy, but you also can't relate to the world, let alone be a good person, without it. And what seems all the more salient today is that in order to fully sympathize with another, you have to interact with them in the flesh. It's far more difficult to muster up sympathy when you see someone twist their ankle on a screen or read about it in a news report. The distance and even invisibility diminishes and even extinguishes the effect.

Twitter's signal achievement has been to strip our national conversation of its sympathy. If you're chatting with me in a bar, you're forced to look at me, take me in, acknowledge me as a fellow person, *sympathize* with me, all of which leads you to perhaps temper your views and even listen to mine (again, please?). Not always, of course: passersby still yell at each other and barfights break out. But this is how discourse is supposed to take place: in a greater latticework of human relations.

On Twitter, not only does the anonymity, or at least the impersonality, make that sympathy difficult to muster, the full-contact nature of the dialogue means the result is often something darker. When I was on Twitter, I was forever getting really, *really* emotionally invested in meaningless spats between meaningless pundits, one of whom was invariably Rick Wilson. Even after I'd log off, I'd still seethe over the audacity of some two-bit hot take artist whom I wanted humiliated, smashed. The reason was that I knew him only as a smug face and a string of idiotic opinions. Whereas if I'd met him in person, I might know him as a smug face and a string of idiotic opinions who also had a facial tic like my favorite uncle and was working the grill at the neighborhood cookout. And then we'd get to talking. Everything would be okay.

There are admittedly limits to this critique. If impersonal discourse is always bad, then that rules out newspaper columns, pamphlets, a certain book on national decline, the printing press, the entire history of written thought. For millennia, people knew their king or emperor only as a selfie on a coin. Impersonal contact is never ideal but it's sometimes how the world works and it was hardly invented in 2006.

Likewise is in-person contact no guarantee of sympathy and thus rationality and peace. The famous Melian Dialogue in ancient Greece saw delegations from Athens and Melos meet up and engage face-to-face in one of the most eloquent and honest conversations about war in human history. Athens then proceeded to invade Melos and kill or enslave its entire population.[16]

What is new, however, is the notion of the *town square* as an impersonal forum, that the space in which we discuss our future ought to be a cold, reductive, invective-encouraging feed. Yet this is what Twitter— "our new digital town square!" as its dead-eyed denizens shriek—has done. Twitter is where public figures go to talk, whether we like it or not. News is broken there; major announcements are made. And while Twitter is believed to be losing users, they're often leaving for other products that imitate the Twitter model, like Threads and Truth Social. Estimates vary but Twitter as of 2024 is still believed to have hundreds of millions of monthly users.

The United States is supposed to be a liberal nation in the sense that we believe in the power of speech and debate to enable the best ideas to rise to the top. Yet when our forum for achieving this is so distorted, when it incentivizes demonization and mob action over inquiry and consensus, is it any wonder we're in such a dire state?

* * *

---

16   Thucydides, *History of the Peloponnesian War,* Book 5, Chapters 84–116 (New York: Penguin Classics, 1972). Originally written in the late fifth century BC.

Politics, culture, religion—all of this is downstream from the ability to organize ideas into words, and that ability itself is downstream from a guarantee that we can express ourselves freely and accurately. It's why the totalitarian Party in George Orwell's *Nineteen Eighty-Four* takes as its paramount goal the destruction of language—it understands that if you destroy words, you destroy the ability to communicate thoughts, and eventually even to think those thoughts in the first place.[17]

And while the availability of words matters, the atmosphere in which those words are exchanged matters too. "The medium is the message," as Marshall McLuhan famously said, and right now the message being sent by our medium is: *drag him*. Is it any wonder, then, that as our speech has grown more hostile, our politics has grown more hostile too? That some of our members of Congress even resemble emissaries from Sector T's bizarre subcultures? There's the QAnon nut . . . the obtuse millennial socialist . . .

Back in 2023, Elon Musk announced he was changing Twitter's name to X, thus instantly solving all of its problems. Musk as Twitter CEO has given hope to conservatives, who complain that the platform is biased against them and warn about its left-wing censorship. They're right about this, starting with the platform's appalling censorship of the Hunter Biden laptop story in 2020. But if you're on the right, there's a deeper critique to be made here. It is that Twitter isn't just illiberal but, by dehumanizing us, by encouraging hysteria and unreason and the mob, it's unconservative too.

***

I live in greater Washington, D.C., and at least in my experience it's the only place in the country where you can be at a happy hour and

---

17   George Orwell, *Nineteen Eighty-Four* (London: Secker & Warburg, 1949).

a debate on porn will spontaneously break out. You'll be sitting there trying to unwind after work when someone, usually from a think tank with a name like the Center for Family Insolubility, abruptly pivots to the nation's debilitating fertility crisis. Presumably this doesn't happen in New York or L.A., but D.C. is *special*. And whenever I find myself in one of these discussions, usually with young men, there's a question I always ask.

Did you see your first naked woman in person or on a screen?

Once they get over the shock of hearing this—this is D.C., remember—almost everyone says on a screen. And the younger the men are, the more unanimous the survey. The ice then having been broken, the men start sharing war stories . . . *Pamela Anderson in a '99 Maxim shoot . . . Cindy Crawford on a Kazaa download . . .*

Therein another withered frontier of the communication revolution: the ubiquity of online porn.

It isn't just that pornography exists online in the way that recipes and memes do. It is that porn has been the single most important driver of internet growth. Online porn solved once and for all the problem of the man in the trench coat slinking out of the seedy theater. You no longer needed to risk exposure (so to speak) to view sex; you didn't even need to leave your couch. Your lizard brain, ever snarling in the background of especially the male psyche, could be sated in a matter of seconds.

Today, the number of web searches seeking out porn is about one in seven.[18] And when you consider the total volume of online searches in the modern world—about 8.5 billion every day—the demand for porn is staggering. There has never been a flesh market, a brothel, a peep show in the history of the world like America's most accessible public utility.

---

18   Tim Harford, "Does pornography still drive the internet?" BBC, June 4, 2019, https://www.bbc.com/news/business-48283409.

The largest porn site on earth, XVideos, is also the eleventh most visited website in the world, putting it up there with service providers like Google and content empires like Netflix. The second largest porn site, the better-known and Canadian-based Pornhub ("want to get busy, eh?"), is the thirteenth most visited website.[19] Pornhub claimed in 2019 that it hosted eleven petabytes of data, or enough pornographic content to play nonstop for seven thousand years.[20] And while the porn industry's total value remains a murky quantity, one estimate puts it at $97 billion.[21] If porn were a country, its GDP would be larger than Guatemala's. Its parliament debates would also be awesome.

And this is before you count all the content that isn't pornographic per se but once upon a time might have been classified that way: the Instagram models, the flesh from off a billboard, the prostitutes on *Game of Thrones* played by actual porn stars. Yum! A feast. Except then you'll be watching some HBO show and realize your eyes are glazing over during the sex scenes. You're fast-forwarding through shots of naked people—what the hell is wrong with you?—because you want to get back to the story rather than watch the protagonist thrust and gasp against her friend *again* to ever so subtly drive home the point that *they banged.*

---

19   Joel Khalili, "These are the most popular websites right now—and they might just surprise you," Techradar, October 31, 2023, compiled using data from Similarweb, https://www.techradar.com/news/porn-sites-attract-more-visitors-than-netflix-and-amazon-youll-never-guess-how-many.

20   Eric Spitznagel, "Where the Filthy Things Are," *Popular Mechanics,* October 29, 2019, https://www.popularmechanics.com/culture/web/a29623446/pornhub-porn-data-storage/.

21   "Things Are Looking Up in America's Porn Industry," NBC News, January 20, 2015, https://www.nbcnews.com/business/business-news/things-are-looking-americas-porn-industry-n289431.

This sense of sex as banal, as unnecessary intermission, is every bit as distorting as Twitter's debasement of our speech. Sex is premised on mystique, on longing for the unseen to become seen, with desire forged not just in the flesh but in the imagination. Yet with all its stigmas torn down, with Spaceship Earth blaring it from every corner, that mystique has been dispelled. Sex is everywhere. And what we're discovering is that if sex is everywhere, then sex is nowhere.

Across the board, Americans are having less sex than they used to, but the decline is particularly steep among the young. According to a study in the *Archives of Sexual Behavior*, the number of adolescents reporting no sexual activity between 2009 and 2018 rose from 28.8 percent to 44.2 percent among young men and 49.5 percent to 74 percent among young women. And while it might seem like they're turning to porn, that actually isn't the case. All forms of sexual activity among teens, including solo masturbation, have decreased.[22]

Celebrate the decline in teenage sex all you like, and as a parent I'm tempted to join you. But then this sudden embrace of abstinence lands aside more ominous trends. Birth rates in the United States have fallen below replacement level, meaning fewer than two births per woman, betokening a smaller population and a younger generation unable to pay off the golf tabs of the old. Sperm counts among young men are falling too, by as much as 50 percent over the last half-century, according to one review of the medical literature.[23] Erectile dysfunction is also believed to be, shall we say, on the rise, and anecdotal evidence

---

22 Debby Herbenick, et al., "Changes in Penile-Vaginal Intercourse Frequency and Sexual Repertoire from 2009 to 2018: Findings from the National Survey of Sexual Health and Behavior," *Archives of Sexual Behavior* 51, pp. 1419–33 (2022).

23 Hagai Levine, et al., "Temporal trends in sperm count: a systematic review and meta-regression analysis of samples collected globally in the 20th and 21st centuries," *Human Reproduction Update* 29, no. 2, March–April 2023, pp. 157–76.

suggests more and more men under the age of forty are reporting problems with ED.[24]

Is all of this linked? There's plenty of research that connects porn
use to both ED and a decreased enjoyment of sex—that porn establishes
false expectations of sex is pretty much undisputed—which it stands to
reason could lead to less sex overall. (Though we should be fair and note
there are other likely factors behind our sexual decline too, from the
post-pandemic withering of social life to the post-#MeToo breakdown
in gender relations.)

Yet there's also a common sense angle at work here. Stripped of
its mystery—dare we say its sacredness?—sex becomes just another
pleasure, and a rather involved and potentially risky one at that. And
then you can't even escape it. Plaster Cheez-Its on every billboard in the
country and eventually the national appetite for Cheez-Its will decrease.
And that's a shame. Because Cheez-Its are delicious.

***

Back when sexual openness could still conceivably be called counter-
cultural, there was a lively debate among feminists as to the merits
of pornography. Most feminists supported porn, viewing it as both
a career option for women and a means of liberation, a way for them
to seize control of their own bodies. In the minority were thinkers
like Andrea Dworkin, who worried that porn would essentially sub-
jugate the feminine. As laid out in her 1981 book *Pornography: Men
Possessing Women*, Dworkin saw porn as dehumanizing rather than
elevating, turning women into objects of abuse for men and disposable
tissues for the consumer.[25]

---

24   Giulia Rastrelli, et al., "Erectile dysfunction in fit and healthy young men:
     psychological or pathological?" *Translational Andrology and Urology 6*,
     no. 1, pp. 79–90.

25   Andrea Dworkin, *Pornography: Men Possessing Women* (New York:
     Putnam, 1981).

Regardless of which side is right, the fact is that this was a debate, as debates on the left so often are, about power structures. And beyond the identity politics, there's another question that needs to be asked.

What if the real issue is one of limits?

The premise of the sexual revolution waged in the 1960s was that sex needed to be unleashed in all its forms: straight sex, gay sex, extramarital sex, group sex, kinky sex, political sex, literary sex, pornographic sex. A rising sexual tide would lift all boats—that was how the thinking went. Instead, what appears to have happened is that by elevating pornographic sex, we've eclipsed all the other types. Sex was not a rising waterline; it was a sluice gate opening between pools. And when all the water gushed into pornography, it drained out of the real world. And then—this is the devilish bit—pornographic sex eventually eclipsed even itself. It became so omnipresent that it lost its appeal. We tuned it out and ended up with a national dry spell.

Ultimately what the average sixties sexual revolutionary was after wasn't a policy or an ethic so much as a gauzy feeling, the free and thrilling mélange of knowing that flesh was out in the sun and taboos were melting away. "Cunnilingus is cool," declared one subversive 1960s button, "fellatio is fun." Now that the sexual revolution has been refracted through the communication revolution, the result is that for many fellatio is *not* fun—or at least not worth the trouble. And getting people to think that truly takes some doing.

* * *

Spaceship Earth, like so much else at Disney World, from the Mickey Mouse figurines to the chicken patties, is made of plastic. There's nothing wrong with that per se—plastic is a very underrated commodity!—but it does feel apropos. Just as the ride is a plastic simulation of an interconnected future, so too has the internet become a plastic version of reality. It might feel exciting and bright but ultimately it replaces that which we ought to value with flashy yet soulless artificiality.

What do online discourse and internet porn have in common? This inherent fakeness. Twitter is counterfeit speech and porn is counterfeit sex. Both can be enjoyable at first but at some point you realize you are *not* having a human conversation; you are *not* making love; you are not your Twitter avatar or that one porn star in that video you keep watching; the degree of separation between you and the former is significant and between you and the latter is absolute. You're sitting there by yourself with one hand on your computer mouse and the other covered in an orange mist from a nearby Doritos bag. It's all just a carbon copy and it leaves you wanting more.

It seems axiomatic but it's worth stating: the false is no substitute for the true. And if we're looking for yet another divide in this country—and when are we not?—one line very much worth drawing is between the real and the fake, the realm God created and the realm man created. And what to think of the realm God created? Just picture me giving the okay sign.

CHAPTER 3

The Smartphone Surveillance State

There is a certain bar in Washington, D.C., that today is one of the more upscale establishments on Capitol Hill. Yet back in the mid-2000s, it was a proper dive, with all the hallmarks that once entailed—beer served in plastic pitchers, bathrooms that probably did inspire the first *Saw* movie, lines of the underaged waiting patiently to get into said bathrooms so they could wash the X's off their hands and order Yuenglings.

I would go to that grimy dive with my friends when I was in college and I would *dance*. And by dance, I mean shift my body in a faintly epileptic fashion on the fire hazard of a dance floor. It was always packed, that dance floor, and ominously there was only one exit. The things you do when you're nineteen that later strike you as clinically insane are many and usually not worth revisiting.

I bring up this one because, despite its seediness, there was, at least for me, very little risk of any kind of scandal breaking out. More typical was that I'd get bumped like a pinball between bigger guys who were dancing with their backs to me all while my glasses fogged up and my shirt clung to my back and my beer splashed onto my shoes and I thought, *this is fun, right? Other people have told me this is fun. . . .*

But the bigger reason there was very little risk of a scandal breaking out is that no one in those days worried their lives could be ruined by a picture taken on a phone. Someone might post a photo to Facebook of you "dancing," sure, but then that kind of thing was expected, even encouraged. And Facebook circa 2006 was more like a glorified yearbook, limited to your real-life classmates. If a photo of you did go up, chances are almost no one from outside your college would see it.

Today, this is no longer true. Anyone who dares to venture any-where more public than a Kohl's fitting room faces a potential gauntlet of paparazzi, a matrix of phones as numerous as there are people, each one harboring the capacity to bring your behavior to the atten-tion of the world. All it takes is one photo. One photo of you drinking underage. One photo of you kissing someone you shouldn't. One photo of you even just blinking weirdly in the flash. And then onto TikTok and Instagram and Twitter it goes, where, why, yes, as it turns out, the mob *does* have time to spend on it.

This happens all the time. To take just the world of sports, there was Urban Meyer, the briefly tenured and very much married coach of the Jacksonville Jaguars, humiliated after he was photographed at an Ohio bar with a woman dancing provocatively against him.[1] There was former Washington Commanders quarterback Dwayne Haskins, who was

---

[1]   John Reid, "Urban Meyer video at bar in Ohio goes viral. Here's the reaction on social media," *Florida Times-Union*, October 3, 2021, https://www .jacksonville.com/story/sports/nfl/2021/10/03/social-media-reacts-urban -meyer-bar-video/5979948001/.

snapped in 2020 partying with strippers (the news coverage at the time zeroed in on the real scandal: he wasn't even wearing a mask!).[2]

In fairness, the odds that you'll ever go viral are slim (it also helps if you refrain from cheating on your wife in public). But then two important things have changed: first, those odds, however narrow, are much greater than when I was in college; and second, if you do become the next Hester Prynne, your scarlet letter will stick to you in perpetuity. Once, Europeans headed to America to escape their sins, and Americans headed west. No more. The internet is both everywhere and forever, a permanent and instantly accessible rap sheet.

And even if you don't become the next international punch line, the potential for abuse just within your network of friends and classmates is substantial. We still call this "cyberbullying," a term that reeks of the days of MySpace and Muse, but what it looks like in 2024 is teenagers leaving vicious comments on each other's Instagram posts. Or a photo of a girl supposedly looking fat summoning down waves of hate and shame. Or, as is all too common, a boy asking a girl for naked selfies and then sharing them with only seventy of his closest friends.

There's a reason a survey from the UK Royal Society for Public Health found that the young consider Instagram to be the worst form of social media for their mental health—and Instagram is just pictures![3] There's also quite a bit of research suggesting that online life is a driver of FOMO, or fear of missing out, whereby you see photos of a party and feel self-conscious because you're not there. And if social media

---

2   Samantha Previte, "Dwayne Haskins under fire after maskless strip club photos leak," *New York Post*, December 22, 2020, https://nypost.com/2020/12/22/dwayne-haskins-under-fire-after -maskless-strip-club-photos-leak-out/.

3   "#StatusOfMind," Royal Society for Public Health, May 19, 2017, https://www.rsph.org.uk/static/uploaded/d125b27c-0b62-41c5 -a2c0155a8887cd01.pdf

can cause FOMO, it stands to reason it can inspire the opposite effect, making people at parties feel self-conscious because they *aren't* missing out, because they're at a place where Things Are Happening and their every move might end up captured forever online.

I've spoken with more than one youngster (there is no greater font of wisdom than a thirty-five-year-old advising a thirty-one-year-old) who's wondered whether all this surveillance has conditioned them to be more cautious and withdrawn. It's an understandable fear. Why ask out a girl if the risk isn't just rejection but school-wide humiliation? Why act out in any way if it could plant an ugly black smudge on your social record?

In 2019, a tempest spun through a teapot after a video emerged of Congresswoman Alexandria Ocasio-Cortez boogying on a rooftop at Boston University back when she was a student there. The vitriol aimed at her seemed surreal: the woman is a literal socialist and *this* is why we're attacking her? The fact that she once took a little time to dance (and rather well, I might add)?[4]

The same goes for Sanna Marin, the former Finnish prime minister, who was caught on tape dancing at a nightclub and later at a private party. That she did this during a dire pandemic and Russia's invasion of Ukraine might offer some clue as to why she needed to cut loose just a bit.[5] And what does it say about her critics that it cast them in the role of the reverend from *Footloose*?

---

4   Tiffany May, "Alexandria Ocasio-Cortez Dancing Video Was Meant as a Smear, but It Backfired," *New York Times*, January 4, 2019, https ://www.nytimes.com/2019/01/04/us/politics/alexandria-ocasio-cortez -dance-video.html.

5   Sanya Mansoor, "Finland's Prime Minister Is Under Fire After a Video of Her Partying Leaked Online," *Time*, August 18, 2022, https://time .com/6207085/sanna-marin-prime-minister-video-dancing/.

There's a lovely passage in Ian Fleming's James Bond novel *Live and Let Die* where 007 finds himself reflecting on the caprice of everyday life:

> You are as linked to the ground mechanic's careless fingers in Nassau just as you are linked to the weak head of the little man in the family saloon who mistakes the red light for the green and meets you head-on, for the first and last time, as you are motoring quietly home from some private sin. There's nothing to do about it. You start to die the moment you are born. The whole of life is cutting through the pack with death. So take it easy. Light a cigarette and be grateful you are still alive as you suck the smoke deep into your lungs.[6]

Not bad, that, and especially that phrase "motoring quietly home from some private sin." Because at least today, our sins are no longer private—or at least they're at constant risk of being publicized. We live in a world where our sins are increasingly the business of that world. And because the world itself is sinful, it's more than happy to gossip and even inflict cruelties on the basis of those sins, sins begetting more sins.

If this sounds like a standard of justice not fit for human beings, then just be glad you didn't have to see me dancing. Welcome to the smartphone surveillance state. Try not to look silly as I snap a photo for Insta.

***

6   Ian Fleming, *Live and Let Die* (New York: William Morrow, 2023, originally published 1954).

When Instagram first launched in 2010, I turned up my nose like a caricature of a Frenchman. *Why should I sign up for another social media platform?* I sniffed. *I can already post my photos on Facebook!*

Man, did that take not age well. Jump ahead fourteen years and my Facebook feed has become one long *Star Wars* screen crawl of pet food ads and decade-old memes. And while Instagram is trending in that direction too—perhaps because it was bought by Meta, née Facebook—the internet's most famous photo album still has plenty of cultural cachet among the young.

It's on Instagram that we find a key tenet of the smartphone surveillance state: we don't just get caught up in others' dragnets; we feed it ourselves. In North Korea, struggling farmers do not send belfies to the regime in the hopes it will get them noticed (and fed). But in the United States, most of the intrusive photos and videos that swirl about the internet aren't taken by some clandestine lurker in a dark dive. They're posted willingly by the person in the photo or video.

Of course, we don't think of it this way. We're just living our best life, showing the world how glamorous we look on a sun-kissed Bermuda beach with a glass of champagne in one hand and a nonchalant brush-off to our battalions of haters from the other. This is the promise of Instagram: whereas Twitter turned everyone into an opinion columnist, Instagram turned everyone into a lifestyle model. Everyone can now perform their vacation through the keyhole of the camera lens, neatly obscuring the bank account we just overdrafted to afford the champagne and the category 5 hurricane currently bearing down on Bermuda.

This is why Instagram doesn't feel like surveillance: it's both consensual and heavily curated. *We* decide what *we* post and *we* can take it down anytime *we* like. As opposed to at the mall where we know we're being watched by a distant camera whether we consent or not.

But then, doesn't it start to feel just a little like surveillance when we scroll past hundreds of photos of hundreds of people on our feed? Or realize we know more about some earlobe model than we do about our own uncles (even if what we know is carefully controlled by said earlobe model)? A mall cop can get in trouble if he's caught stalking a shopper using his surveillance equipment; an Instagram addict not so much.

If anything, the average Instagrammer puts the mall cop to shame. More than 95 million photos and videos are shared on Instagram per day, with more than 50 billion having been uploaded since the app launched.[7] There is no totalitarian regime in history that ever had access to that volume of information. And while we don't know how many photos on Insta are of actual people (as opposed to tiny dogs and misattributed quotes), we do know that a photo is 38 percent more likely to be liked if it shows a person's face.[8]

Back when I was active on Facebook, I could post what I thought was the wittiest joke, the most penetrating insight—and get half a dozen likes. Yet a half-hearted selfie of my mug looking crestfallen after the Patriots lost would grant countless boosts to my self-esteem! Similar incentives are placed on the demand side—if you're scrolling through Instagram and you come across a photo of someone, it registers as the easiest kind of pleasure: our brains process pictures much faster than they do words.

Instagram thus incentivizes us to both upload photos of ourselves and seek out and react to those photos. And while much of this is just

---

7   Nikolina Cveticanin, "Unfiltered Instagram Statistics You'll Want to Share With All Your Followers," DataProt, June 8, 2023, https://dataprot .net/statistics/instagram-statistics/.

8   Saeideh Bakhshi, et al., "Faces Engage Us: Photos with Faces Attract More Likes and Comments on Instagram," Georgia Institute of Technology and Yahoo Labs, 2014, https://www.researchgate.net /publication/266655817_Faces_engage_us_photos_with_faces_attract _more_likes_and_comments_on_Instagram.

harmless fun, there are very dark consequences to living under surveillance, especially for young women (about a third of Instagram users are females between the ages of thirteen and thirty-four[9]). Depression, anxiety, body image issues, low self-esteem, bullying, FOMO, and deteriorated mental health have all been credibly linked to Instagram.[10]

The keyhole is a particular problem here. If you believe the Bermuda model really is that glamorous, you're going to think your own life and body are inadequate by comparison. The CDC warned in 2023 that 30 percent of teenage girls admitted to having recently contemplated suicide. And while there was no established causative link to online life, that number was up 60 percent over a decade ago, back when the peer pressure from Instagram was far less severe.[11]

And for those of us who are parents, this ought to be all we need to know. It's out with the torches and pitchforks and into the town square, where we form up and storm Instagram headquarters, incapacitating the guards and breaching the inner sanctum—*keep moving!*—until we reach the throne room and the chair slowly turns around revealing the real power behind the smartphone surveillance state . . . and it's a mirror.

There's no question the tech companies can wield a heavy hand, from Twitter censoring conservative opinions to Facebook vacuuming up our personal data. Likewise, Instagram's almighty algorithms play a role in determining what we see in our feeds. But it's still voluntary at the end of the day. The ultimate authority on these platforms is us,

---

9   Stacy Jo Dixon, "Distribution of Instagram users worldwide as of January 2023, by age and gender," Statista and Kepios, August 29, 2023, https://www.statista.com/statistics/248769/age-distribution-of -worldwide-instagram-users/.

10 Amanda MacMillan, "Why Instagram Is the Worst Social Media for Mental Health," *Time*, May 25, 2017, https://time.com/4793331 /instagram-social-media-mental-health/.

11 "Youth Risk Behavior Survey: Data Summary and Trends Report." Centers for Disease Control, 2021, https://www.cdc.gov/healthyyouth /data/yrbs/pdf/YRBS_Data-Summary-Trends_Report2023_508.pdf.

the users (I sometimes think those who fume the loudest about big tech are just trying to avoid that mirror). We're the ones who post the selfies. We mete out the likes. We create the cultural expectation that every sixteen-year-old needs an Insta. We allow our sixteen-year-olds to sign up for Insta (difficult though it admittedly is for parents to hold firm in the face of social pressure).

And we form the mobs that are the smartphone surveillance state's final adjudicator. That influencer in Bermuda had no idea her sunglasses had been "culturally appropriated" from the San tribe of African bushmen. But she'll learn. Oh, she'll learn.

***

I have, at many points in my life, been fortunate to associate with thoughtful libertarians. These are the people who wake up cold in the dead of night worrying the Department of Homeland Security has just usurped more power. And then you wake up the next morning and find the Department of Homeland Security really has usurped more power. Libertarians as a rule are skeptical of government, and as a rule that will bear itself out every time.

Another agency the libertarians hate is the National Security Agency, or NSA, which is responsible for collecting intelligence from phone calls, social media, and the like. The problem, as any libertarian will pop out of a manhole to tell you, is that the NSA does not limit itself to matters of national security where it has probable cause. As whistleblower and former NSA employee Edward Snowden revealed in 2013, the NSA can snoop on just about anything. It harvests and stores massive amounts of phone metadata—who you've called, when, from where—and has been granted expansive warrants by a secret court that allow it to access this information more or less at will.

So, no surprise that libertarians are mildly irritated with the NSA. Yet libertarians also tend to draw a thick line between the public and private sectors, and then turn their fire only on the former. They might decry the NSA, but less so the smartphone surveillance state or the social media that enables it. Instagram is consensual, after all, whereas a spook tapping your phone calls is very much not.

I agree with this to a point: I think the lack of accountability from agencies like the NSA is disturbing and marvel at how a country with a robust Bill of Rights has ended up with such an intrusive security apparatus. I also think the line between public and private is real and helpful, even if it's sometimes more blurred than libertarians think.

Yet I don't think accepting this libertarian frame means we have to limit our scrutiny to one side of the line. Such a limitation can be hobbling, setting off-limits all manner of valuable critiques because their targets happen not to come at the end of a badge and barrel. Government might have a monopoly on the use of force, but that doesn't mean abuses, horrors, inefficiencies, and just plain annoyances don't crop up in the private sector. And when it comes to surveillance, ask yourself this: is your life more likely to be ruined by a government spook or a photo that an individual took on his phone? Is your daughter more likely to feel anxious over the NSA or the 'gram?

There's also the matter of one feeding the other, of so-called private surveillance enabling the worst impulses of government. To take just one example, you probably have a tech-obsessed friend with an Amazon Ring doorbell, which comes with a built-in camera that keeps an eye on his front porch. Yet Amazon also coordinates with police departments and sometimes provides them with footage taken on Ring cameras without a warrant or the consent of the owner. And even when legal avenues are pursued, the sheer scope of Ring surveillance can make for wandering eyes. In 2022, an Ohio man who had done nothing wrong was ordered by police to turn over footage from a Ring camera *showing the inside of his home.*[12]

12   Alfred Nf, "The privacy loophole in your doorbell," *Politico*, March 7, 2023, https://www.politico.com/news/2023/03/07/privacy-loophole-ring-doorbell-00084979.

In George Orwell's *Nineteen Eighty-Four,* it is indeed the government, the Party and its agitprop manifestation Big Brother, that surveils and oppresses the people through its vigilant telescreens. Against them is set Winston and Julia, two Party members who embark on an illegal affair in the countryside beyond the state's watchful eye. (It's often debated whether Winston and Julia love each other or whether their sex is just a mutual expression of defiance. I think it's clear they do love each other, which makes the Party's eventual annihilation of their bond through torture all the more tragic and total.)

Today, we clink our glasses over having turned "totalitarian" into a dirty word. Yet what would happen now if Winston and Julia were caught on camera and the footage went viral? We would share the video on social, comment on it, critique it. We would snipe about their physical attributes, maybe even bully Julia for the way she looks. Articles would run not just in bottom-scraping gossip rags but newspapers desperate for clicks. The fact that Winston and Julia were white would be harped upon endlessly, as though that proved anything. TikTok influencers would post parody videos. And all this would happen courtesy not of the Party but the free will of private individuals amid our glorious age of reason.

The difference would be torture by other means. And then we might just destroy their love too. Because as with Winston's brutalization by the Party, who could ever go through something like that and not be changed forever?

***

In 2012, the fast-food chain Chick-fil-A made waves when its CEO Dan Cathy announced he supported the "biblical definition of the family." This wasn't exactly breaking news: that Chick-fil-A restaurants are closed on Sundays should have been a subtle clue to the company's leanings. But the left, as the left is programmed to do, erupted in contempt. One of those angered was a man whose name I won't share here but who decided it was time to make a courageous stand against bigotry.

He recorded himself pulling up to a Chick-fil-A drive-thru window and confronting the employee there about her company's leanings.

The video, which the man then idiotically uploaded to YouTube, sees him mansplain to a female service worker how "Chick-fil-A is a hateful corporation" that supports "hate groups." The employee, meanwhile, is the very picture of restraint, giving the man a free water, saying she can't comment, eventually warning that he's making her feel uncomfortable. In response, the man sneers, "I don't know how you live with yourself and work here. I don't understand," adding, "you deserve better." The Morlocks of Christian bigotry having been vanquished back to the underground, he drives away.

It's impossible to watch the video and not conclude the man is a massive douche. But then we all act like douches now and again, and what happened next should shake even the stoutest of conservative constitutions. The video went viral, the man was identified, and death threats were sent to his company. His employer ordered him to quit; when he instead proposed a public apology, he was fired. He quickly lined up interviews at other companies, but in every single case the video was discovered and any offer was withdrawn. Two and a half years later, he, his wife, and his children were homeless and living on food stamps. The man was battling suicidal thoughts.[13]

You might say the Douche of the Drive-Thru deserved his fate. You might also note that he's since gotten back on his feet, is living in Costa Rica, and calls the experience a "gift" that's "humbled" him. You might further add that the drive-thru employee, ever the model of composure, has said she's forgiven him.

---

13 "Former CFO on Food Stamps After Controversial Viral Video About Chick-Fil-A," ABCNews.com, March 25, 2015, https://abcnews.go.com/Business/cfo-food-stamps-controversial-viral-video/story?id=29533695#:~:text=Adam%20Smith%20is%20now%20on,viral%20and%20destroyed%20his%20career.

All's well that ends well, right? Yet something about the sheer bloodlust and reductionism of this ordeal is difficult to shake. An entire life was once again flattened onto a sympathy-sapping screen and then condensed into just ninety seconds of bad behavior. I'm not in the habit of making excuses for white progressives, least of all white progressives who can't appreciate the deliciousness of Chick-fil-A Polynesian sauce. But it seems that amid this puritanical surveillance state of ours, we've forgotten some key values: charity, forgiveness, love, modesty, privacy, and self-restraint.[14]

---

14 "His first protest ever cost him his career, reputation and sense of self," CBC Radio, December 21, 2018, https://www.cbc.ca/radio /outintheopen/reputation-1.4589616/his-first-protest-ever-cost-him -his-career-reputation-and-sense-of-self-1.4596546#:~:text=In%20 The%20Open-,His%20first%20protest%20ever%20cost%20him%20 his%20career%2C%20reputation%20and,he%20was%20doing%20 something%20positive.

CHAPTER 4

The Sound of Silence

A few nights ago, I did the unthinkable. I managed to watch TV without scrolling on my phone at the same time.

It was an absolutely grueling sacrifice and one I'm not eager to repeat anytime soon. For two entire episodes of *How I Met Your Mother*, I took in the wacky hijinks of Ted and Robin and the gang without ever splicing my attention over to Wikipedia so I could look up the name of that third extra sitting at the bar table in the background or checking Twitter to see if anyone had written a "we need to talk about . . ." piece about Barney's dishonest seducing of a barista. Instead I just *sat* there, thoughts unrealized on a second screen. My teeth clenched. This must have been what it was like when Khalid Sheikh Mohammed was waterboarded 183 times.

Several years ago, *The Onion* published a satirical article with the headline "Americans demand new form of media to bridge entertainment gap while looking from laptop to phone."[1] These days, we seem unable to pass the slightest amount of time without being stimulated by a screen. And preferably multiple screens, mind you; just the TV won't do. The quintessential evening for the all-American couple used to be dinner with some wine; now we sit on opposite sides of the couch in the pallid glow of a Hulu original while staring at our phones. In fact, we should resurrect Norman Rockwell so he can paint that very scene.

Back in 2018, iPhones began automatically updating their users on how much screen time they were logging every week. Every Sunday morning, perhaps in the spirit of repentance, a notification would pop up informing you that you'd spent an average of two or three or four hours each day photosynthesizing in front of your demon-brick. At first my iPhone also helpfully informed me whether this was an increase or decrease—as in my screen time was up 23 percent over the previous week. But after a while, and as my phone time began to spike, this ceased. "You averaged four hours and thirty-two minutes of screen time last week," it would say clinically, like a doctor who had given up hope. *Get him off the methadone. He's beyond help now.*

For me, the main culprit was YouTube. I had long ago logged off of Twitter, outgrown Snapchat, and express-mailed my Social Security number straight to China so as to not need TikTok. But YouTube? I could scroll through those algorithm-handpicked influencer videos all day. "Ben Shapiro responds to Ana Kasparian responds to Jordan Peterson responds to something called a Vaush responds to Andrew Tate responds to a newsreel video of FDR from 1934 responds to some dude playing *Call of Duty* responds to the Swedish Chef"? Yes, please!

---

1   "Americans demand new form of media to bridge entertainment gap while looking from laptop to phone," *The Onion*, July 30, 2014, https://www.theonion.com/americans-demand-new-form-of-media-to-bridge-entertainm-1819576756.

Surely there's some wisdom to be had in there. Or maybe just fast food for thought.

I would watch YouTube when I was eating lunch, walking down the stairs, even brushing my teeth. And I was psychologically incapable of doing any work without an ambience video playing in the background on a TV, usually either a coffee shop from Calm Café or the (genuinely impressive) landscapes and score of the video game *Skyrim*.

You would have thought I was scared to death of being alone. There have always been extroverts among us, of course, but the need to constantly be accompanied not by a real person but a technological device is a problem unique and endemic to our time. It's enough to bring out that old reactionary itch. What was it like to live without your phone constantly nagging you? What does the world sound like without YouTube's and Slack's endless interjections? Before our attention spans were shredded to ribbons, could you hear the call of a bird and discover therein a kaleidoscope? What does a bird even sound like anyway? Maybe I can find an instructional video on YouTube . . .

***

Ah, the smartphone vibration. How many exquisite forms you take.

There's the single note used by most apps on the iPhone, that one dull shake, thoroughly amoral in its outlook yet almost taunting in its vanilla blandness, like the voice of Ben Stein. You hear it and you know it's not necessarily bad, maybe just another CNN alert reporting on the progress of racial reparations on the International Space Station. But then, it's also the l apps. It *could* be CNN . . . or it *could* be Slack or Google Chat or WhatsApp—and you're not just going to ignore your coworkers, *right*? The understatement of the single note is wrought with imperative—and even worse is that it rarely arrives alone. Where there's one, there's usually about twelve more, landing in rapid succession like an Uzi being fired. The boys from accounting are at it in #watercooler again, rather than, you know, taking care of their kids on the weekend.

Then there's the double note, reserved at least on iPhones for SMS text messages. This is the most familiar vibration: hmmmm*hmmmmm*. And while it's usually not accompanied by several more like the single note, that's only because its evil takes a different form. There's a tone of melancholy to the text vibration, its second pulse trailing off like a lament into the wind. The effect is of a maiden standing on a cliff above a crashing sea singing forlornly in the hopes that her long-lost husband will return home. You hear that and you think: *My wife is trapped in a desert*. It's a siren song of pure blackmail, and it usually works.

Then there's the single, demanding, almost violent note that iPhone uses for its system updates. *HMMMM*. Message: *you're getting more photo options you don't need and f**k you*.

I live in an area of great ornithological diversity, but I could never write a credible guide to bird calls. Yet the coos and caws of my phone? Just call me Charles Darwin. And that's no coincidence. According to psychologists, the vibration of the smartphone has a triggering effect on the human brain, causing our heart rates to increase and even our skin to tingle. It also inevitably leaves us wanting more.[2] Here is the very sequence of substance addiction: anticipate the hit to come, take the hit, find it couldn't fully placate the urge, anticipate the next hit, and so on. (Oscar Wilde said of the cigarette, "It is exquisite and it leaves one unsatisfied." Of checking our phones, that's exactly half-true.)

---

2   Sammy Caiola, "Dinging, buzzing, vibrating cellphone is causing anxiety and so is its silence," *The Sacramento Bee*, April 27, 2017, https://www .thegazette.com/health-wellness/dinging-buzzing-vibrating-cellphone-is -causing-anxiety-and-so-is-its-silence/.

The average American looks at his smartphone 144 times per day,[3] and what's remarkable is that some of those glimpses aren't even prompted by a vibration. We prompt the vibrations ourselves, switching on our screens in the hopes we missed a buzz.

We also experience what's called a "phantom vibration," a buzz that's entirely imaginary.[4] I remember when I was single, I might text a girl I'd met the night before and then nonchalantly put my phone back in my pocket. *I don't care whether she texts me back!!!* I'd scream to myself. Except I did care, and I would think of little else until she did. And if she didn't, I would soon start to feel vibrations that weren't there. *Was that an imaginary ripple up my leg or was she just glad to see me?* Invariably the former, alas, and one of the many pleasures of being married is that I no longer have to put up with this.

It's quite a drug, one that hallucinates itself into existence for you. I've savored many a cigarette in my life but I've never faked to myself the aroma of tobacco smoke or a spring in my step from the nicotine. And surely part of the issue here is that our vibrating, shrieking, hectoring phones are narcotics, enticing us back with the promise of fleeting fulfillment.

But if our smartphones are akin to death sticks, then the endless noise they produce is the equivalent of a smoker's cough: a nettlesome, distracting, *stressful* by-product. Check just about any poll on the subject and you'll find that Americans are deeply stressed out, both because of how they perceive their country and how they perceive their own lives. Admittedly they have good reason to feel this way (and reading books about national decline probably isn't helping). But part of the

---

3   Alex Kerai, "Cell Phone Usage Statistics: Mornings Are for Notifications," Study by Reviews.org, 2023, https://www.reviews.org/mobile/cell -phone-addiction/#:~:text=89%25%20of%20Americans%20say%20 they,minutes%20of%20receiving%20a%20notification.

4   Sammy Cailoa, "Dinging, buzzing, vibrating cellphone . . ."

problem is that they're forever being reminded of all this, that they can't escape an endless injection of negative or at least demanding notifications directly into their legs.

Once upon a time, Spaceship Earth regaled us with tales of how the communication revolution would make our lives easier. Today, the American Psychological Association warns that our smartphones are a leading cause of stress.[5] And it's here that a romanticized cultural trope has collided with reality. Back in the 2000s, the show *The West Wing* valorized a certain class of overworked paper pushers who dashed from one caffeinated meeting to the next, their workdays never really ending, their professional lives blending with their personal ones. Today, a good many of us live with similar stress and blurred boundaries thanks to our noisy phones. And rather than LARPing Josh Lyman, I think we'd just like a moment of peace.

***

Quick: What was the most revolutionary year of the last century or so? I bet I can predict your answer.

If you're the sort who likes to burn your draft card while simultaneously fantasizing about the bourgeois doing compulsory labor, then 1968 might be your jam. If you prefer to sit at the *Risk* board long after your college roommates have gone to bed moving around the plastic pieces and referring to yourself as "The Colonel," then 1989 may be for you.

Some of the neoliberal stripe have even suggested these two revolutionary years are linked, that the liberation movement of the sixties that

---

5   "APA's Survey Finds Constantly Checking Electronic Devices Linked to Significant Stress for Most Americans," American Psychological Association, 2017, https://www.apa.org/news/press/releases/2017/02 /checking-devices.

reached its zenith in 1968 was only fully realized come the fall of the Berlin Wall and Soviet totalitarianism in 1989. Turn 68 upside down and you get 89. The palindrome knows all.

But I would argue there was another revolutionary year, one at least as important as those two, one that often gets overlooked: 2007.

In January 2007, at the Macworld Expo in San Francisco, Apple CEO Steve Jobs emerged out of a walk-in closet filled with identical black turtlenecks and introduced a little handheld novelty he called the iPhone.[6] Technically, it wasn't an original idea. The PalmPilot had already been on shelves for over a decade, while the first ever smart-phone, the IBM Simon Personal Communicator, had debuted all the way back in 1992. And so out came the tech dinosaurs, snarling at this new entry in an old genre. Microsoft CEO Steve Ballmer mocked the iPhone's steep price tag as well as its lack of an external keyboard (yes, this was seen as a disadvantage back then: *our research shows what people want is tiny buttons, dammit!*).[7]

But then, in fairness to Ballmer, the iPhone really was outrageously expensive (it still is) and it hardly caught on because of its on-screen keyboard. It caught on because of the software: the open-ended app store that allowed developers to innovate with incredible freedom; the melding of the iPod into the iPhone so you could listen to your music; how thoroughly idiotproof the operating system was (even I have yet to injure myself on one).

The Revolution of 2007 was to shake the tech sector to its founda-tions. Dashboard-mounted GPS systems were tossed in the trash; the

6   Kerry J. Byrne, "On this day in history, Jan. 9, 2007, Steve Jobs introduces Apple iPhone at Macworld in San Francisco," *New York Post*, January 9, 2023, https://nypost.com/2023/01/09/on-this-day-in-history-jan-9-2007 -steve-jobs-introduces-apple-iphone-at-macworld-in-san-francisco/.

7   "Ballmer Laughs at iPhone." YouTube, Uploaded by smugmacgeek, September 18, 2007.

digital camera industry was wiped out forever. Yet the single most revolutionary thing the iPhone did was to place the internet into our back pockets. Again, more specialized smartphones had done this before, but it wasn't until the iPhone that this particular superpower was granted to the more casual consumer.

I remember well my first friend who bought an iPhone back in college: having once been an avid talker, suddenly he couldn't even watch a movie without whipping out his smaller screen to check IMDB. He seemed perpetually distracted, and this had a profound impact on me. When I bought an iPhone 3GS a year later, I vowed to never end up like that.

Yet most of us did end up like that to one degree or another. Because so much can be found online, the temptation to check is overwhelming. Our every synapse can be instantly gratified. This is why the chief legacy of the Revolution of 2007 is one of decompartmentalization. What the iPhone did, more than anything else, was to take activities and pastimes that had once been grounded in set places and erase their boundary lines. Everything was suddenly everywhere. Nothing was rooted anymore.

Now, not only could you bring up annotative information while watching TV, you could also watch TV not on your TV. Your iPhone could bring traditional channels, as well as YouTube's cavernous library, wherever you wanted to take them. "Surfing the web" had once been the province of a glowing desktop computer in the living room corner whose CPU whirred like a jet engine and looked like the evil tower from Minas Morgul; now you could do it while speeding down I-95. Your job had once been largely confined to your office; now your email—and later your Slack messages—could follow you to happy hour. Shopping had once meant a trip to a store (remember those?); now you could order everything you needed from Amazon while out on a walk.

As an aside, it's worth both acknowledging the benefits of this decompartmentalization—reading the news during a long stay in a waiting room, for example—and asking whether the human mind can handle it. We already know our smartphones have rewired our psyches, diminishing our memories, for example, so we don't remember facts so much as where to look them up. How is the exploding of everything out of its proper context affecting us? This is the problem with revolutionaries: as Chesterton understood, they so rarely ask why a fence is in place before they tear it down. It is also the problem with the dinosaurs from *Jurassic Park*.

Yet if we had to distill down all this decompartmentalization to a single by-product, it would be the noise. My friend back in 2008 was distracted for a reason. The clamor of the big city, that constant barrage of stimuli that every urban dweller is familiar with, has been exported across the globe and into the quietest alcove of the home. Everyone now has a portable Times Square in his pocket, hooting with bright lights to see and brands to check out and movies to watch and headlines to read. And it very nearly is everyone: 92 percent of Americans own smartphones, far more than have houses, children, or jobs.[8] That's quite a revolution; it's also quite a racket.

***

Why do fewer and fewer Americans believe in God? There are many reasons for our nation's declining faith, but one of them is surely that it's more difficult to *hear* anything that might be construed as spiritual.

Perhaps the most conservative clergyman in the Catholic Church today is Robert Cardinal Sarah, who hails from the West African nation

---

8 Jon Bortin, "Cell phone statistics 2024," *Consumer Affairs*, September 28, 2023, https://www.consumeraffairs.com/cell_phones/cell-phone -statistics.html.

of Guinea. In 2017, Cardinal Sarah published a book called *The Power of Silence* in which he warned that we're increasingly living under a "dictatorship of noise." "In modern society, silence has come into disrepute," he writes, "this is the symptom of a serious, worrisome illness." He adds, "The real questions of life are posed in silence."

There's some tension in the good cardinal's denunciation of noise. The Catholic Church is one of the last proponents of the traditional family, yet anyone with four boys darting about the living room knows that such a life is hardly quiet. Cardinal Sarah also cites the monastery as a model of quiet reflection—good, perhaps, for the monks, but the rest of civilization does require some din.

Yet Cardinal Sarah is on point when he notes that the contemplative life is being abolished by modern noise, and in particular the noise generated from our smartphones. Not only that, but those who strive for the opposite, those who dare to shut their mouths from time to time, are increasingly held up as suspect. Amid a cacophony of vibrations and alerts and opinions, Sarah says, "the silent person becomes someone who does not know how to defend himself. He is subhuman."[9]

We've all seen this before. What happens if a public official stops for even a second to think after being asked a question? *JOE Q. MCGILLICUDDY STUNNED INTO SILENCE BY BRAVE REPORTER!* I used to work in radio where the personalities would quip that they had a "fear of dead air." What they meant was that if they were on-air and paused for even a second, they worried untold listeners would grow impatient and lunge for the dial, tuning them out and sinking their ratings. Our own expectations have now largely gone the same way. With everyone conditioned toward constant sound, a moment to think can come off as bizarre and humiliating. With every

---

9   Robert Sarah, *The Power of Silence* (San Francisco: Ignatius Press, 2017).

public statement just a screen-flick of the thumb away from oblivion, this fear of dead air is perhaps even understandable.

Cardinal Sarah is concerned with heavenly matters, as well he should be, but even if you don't believe in God, that doesn't mean you should write off the contemplative. It is there that we shed our stress and find inner peace, which is a prerequisite not just for spiritual experience but rational thought. Critical thinking isn't possible without some measure of quiet. Crashing music distracts us too much. Screaming pundits poison our deliberations.

Yet even when we might seek out that quiet, the political forces around us increasingly reflect our world of noise. I recently walked into a building and saw a banner hanging from the ceiling: "BLACK LIVES MATTER, SILENCE IS VIOLENCE." The thing is, the building was a library. And a university library at that, which should come as a surprise to no one. I was half-tempted to start screaming at the top of my lungs lest I perpetuate racial injustices by the reference desk.

Yet it's here that we see how noise has become institutionalized, and how politics is shaped by it. To be silent today isn't just to be at odds with the times; it's to be enabling of evil. Do you need a few minutes to ponder the Black Lives Matter agenda? Too bad. Get back on Twitter. Every second you think prolongs a genocide. That we can't hope to have a considered discussion in the face of such agitprop is the entire point.

Woodrow Wilson, America's worst president, said, "A conservative is a man who just sits and thinks, mostly sits." Of course, the world would be a better place today had Wilson spent more time sitting and thinking, rather than joining World War I and stomping all over our civil liberties. Yet it's this Wilsonian spirit of trumpet-blasting action, of rushing past the contemplative toward the online barricades, that suffuses so much of our political culture, including among supposed conservatives.

Wilson was, at least in theory, a fan of leagues and nations. Yet the final mark against our noisy techno-culture is that it isn't a sign of community at all but of isolation. It prevents us from focusing on each other, hearing each other, getting to know each other. It's conducive to neither the contemplative nor the social life. It's past time to admit that sitting on opposite sides of the couch staring at our phones is a practice characterized not by silence but oppressive noise.

CHAPTER 5

The Return of X-Files Politics

I've sometimes wondered, in this age of misinformation and paranoia, whether I could invent a conspiracy theory at random and
people would believe it.

Let's say I were to propose that the government was secretly stock-
piling barrels of oil inside maple trees to prepare for an invasion of Peru.
In this case, the conspiracy is very close to random: oil was in the first
news headline I read this morning, a maple tree was the first thing I saw
when I looked out my window, and Peru was chosen by closing my eyes
and running my cursor over a map of the world.

Now let's take this and run with it. Let's say the Peruvians have
been secretly plotting to kidnap our children and put them to work in
their salt mines. Worried about a first strike, the American government
decided to disperse the oil needed for an invasion across the country
so it couldn't be destroyed in a single attack. And since maple trees are
sufficiently trusted as to be present at Bohemian Grove meetings, it was
decided they should be the repositories.

It all makes sense, you see. And anyone who disagrees is a fed.

When I began this chapter, I seriously considered floating my Peruvian plot on a few 4chan boards to see how far it would get. But then I'm sure no one ever imagined a silly conspiracy theory about a pizza parlor harboring Satanists would see a gunman walk into said pizzeria and start shooting.[1] Or idle nonsense about Donald Trump being a Russian plant would bewitch the political establishment for years.[2]

So I withdrew my bit of fiction. I didn't want to accidentally trigger the overthrow of the United States government (since they still owe me a tax refund).

Conspiracy theories are a dangerous thing in this year of our edgelord 2024. Need more proof? Take yourself back to just after January 6. Of course, if you watch CNN, you constantly go back to just after January 6, since they somehow find ways to work January 6 into the weather reports. But everyone else should now do the same. There was a palpable dread at the time that the riot at the Capitol building had been just the opening act, that a civil war was coming, or at least something akin to Northern Ireland's Troubles. And its distinguishing feature, what would make it so quintessentially American, was how *weird* it was going to be.

The guy in the Viking helmet who appointed himself speaker of the House for a hot second had set a tone. The factions in Spain's civil

1   Faiz Saddiqui and Susan Svrluga, "N.C. Man Told Police He Went to D.C. Pizzeria to Investigate Conspiracy Theory," *Washington Post*, December 5, 2016, https://www.washingtonpost.com/news/local/wp/2016/12/04/d-c-police-respond-to-report-of-a-man-with-a-gun-at-comet-ping-pong-restaurant/.

2   Jessica Taylor, "Hillary Clinton Says She Was Right About 'Vast Russia Conspiracy'; Investigations Ongoing," NPR, June 1, 2017, https://www.npr.org/2017/06/01/530941011/clinton-says-she-was-right-about-vast-russia-conspiracy-investigations-ongoing.

war had cool names like the Carlists and the Falangists; we were going to have the MyPillow Militia and the Fighting Frogs and the Incel Airborne and the Sons of Q. "For Robert Mueller!" leftist black-masks would scream as they charged into battle against Sidney Powell's private army of Christian nationalists. "It is a curious conflict to study," future historians would aver, "in that everyone involved appears to have been a complete moron."

January 6 stands out among American political violence because it was so informed by the conspiratorial. The entire raison d'être for the riot, that the election had been stolen from Donald Trump, was itself a conspiracy theory, and from there it only got stranger. It was as though the wall between Reddit and reality had been torn open and all the internet's lurid phantasms had come pouring out. And then the Antrim County vote tabulators would descend in their flying saucers while Ray Epps stood atop a hill and shouted to both his MAGA stooges and his #Resistance guerillx handlers: "HOLD THE LINE! HOOOOOOLD THE LIIIIIIIINE!"

***

America has long been fertile ground for conspiracy theories. This is the home of the Roswell alien cover-up and the Area 51 alien cover-up, the idea that John F. Kennedy was killed by the government and the idea that Elvis was kept alive by the government, the faking of the moon landing and the discovery of aliens on the moon, fluoride in the water and chemtrails in the sky.

We've been like this practically since day one. During the presidential campaign of 1800, Thomas Jefferson was accused of siring an African harem and John Adams was alleged to be establishing a royal bloodline. The supposedly tranquil early nineteenth century was rife with paranoia about Freemasons, shadowy bankers, and Catholic influence. After he lost the 1824 election, Andrew Jackson spent the next four years grumbling about a "corrupt bargain"—that is, a stolen election—which became a central issue in the 1828 presidential contest. When New England in the nineteenth century experienced several tuberculosis outbreaks, locals reasonably hypothesized this was due to vampire attacks.

A proud history, to be sure, and in the 1980s a former rock deejay from North Carolina had an idea. Art Bell had been hosting a political radio show called *Coast to Coast AM*, yet he'd grown bored. Rather than lean further into political commentary, Bell decided to take his show in a different direction. He began dabbling in conspiracy theories and the paranormal—UFOs, ghosts, Satanism, crop circles—opening his phone lines to anyone who'd had an experience that couldn't be conventionally explained. The formula made him a household name, and *Coast to Coast AM* became the uncontested king of overnight radio, syndicated on hundreds of stations across the United States and Canada.[3]

Just as Rush Limbaugh capitalized perfectly upon the Clinton presidency and the backlash to decades of left-wing counterculture, so too did Bell seize upon his own cultural moment. Despite a Democrat being in the White House, the 1990s were a time of reaction against government. The Waco and Ruby Ridge raids saw federal agents horrifically botch standoff situations, killing people and inviting scorn. The Oklahoma City bombing in 1995 was carried out by an anti-government extremist named Timothy McVeigh and intended to ignite a greater war against the feds.

And, of course, there was the best TV show from that period—don't you dare start humming the *Friends* theme—*The X-Files*. Created by

---

3   Sam Roberts, "Art Bell, Radio Host Who Tuned in to the Dark Side, Dies at 72," *New York Times*, April 17, 2018, https://www.nytimes .com/2018/04/17/obituaries/art-bell-radio-host-who-tuned-in-to-the -dark-side-dies-at-72.html.

Chris Carter and starring David Duchovny and Gillian Anderson as two FBI agents who investigate the paranormal, the series spent a glorious eleven seasons pulping script out of every ghost and ghoul and goblin on offer. The premise of *The X-Files* was more or less that every conspiracy theory was true, and that the government had been covering up all of it. The show's tagline, "The Truth Is Out There," might have been printed on the 1990s' collective welcome mat. This was a time when it was okay to imagine that shadowy G-men were injecting sterilants into your ranch dressing.

It was in this climate that Art Bell's radio show became an institution. Yet if the ghost-hunting nineties are starting to sound like our own conspiratorial times, it's here that we approach a key difference. Bell famously didn't screen his callers but neither did he necessarily agree with them. His role was of the mildly skeptical moderator, the calm therapist who talked your story out of you without necessarily validating it. He sought not a polemic in favor of the paranormal but a forum for it, an open town hall where everyone with a poltergeist in his attic or an alien lobotomy on his medical record could discuss his experience. For the audience, the appeal was similar to sitting around the campfire and listening to ghost stories.[4]

In this, Bell both captured the moment and helped shape it. With the exception of the notable fringe—McVeigh and those right-wing militias, Heaven's Gate and its UFO cult—people weren't especially apocalyptic during the 1990s. There was no mainstream urgency about these conspiracies, no sense that the government needed to be taken down yesterday. The center might have tilted libertarian but it held.

---

4   Thomas Genoni Jr., "Peddling the Paranormal: Late-Night Radio's Art Bell," *Skeptical Inquirer, Skeptical Briefs* 8, no. 1, March 1, 1998, https://skepticalinquirer.org/newsletter/peddling-the-paranormal -late-night-radios-art-bell/.

Yet exceptions can end up mattering greatly, and one of those exceptions was a Texan and radio host by the name of Alex Jones. For all the incredibly unorthodox impact Jones would later have on American politics, during the 1990s he was a fairly garden-variety conspiracy theorist. He was furious over the deaths at Waco, and when Timothy McVeigh struck in 1995, he surmised that Oklahoma City had been a federal operation.[5]

Jones began with a public access TV program, only to switch to radio and take a gig at (fittingly) KJFK FM in Austin, Texas. There he honed what would become his model, talking obsessively about the New World Order and its conspiracies and false flags. Unlike Bell, Jones was both furious about all this and explicitly political. He wasn't a man of the right per se, but he was obsessive in his trashing of Bill Clinton, and when his incendiary diatribes allegedly began to cost the station advertisers (though Jones disputes this was ever the case), he was fired.[6]

Jones would rebound with a show broadcast on the internet, which was also syndicated on dozens of radio stations. It was there that on September 11, 2001, Jones would first label the terrorist attacks a government plot. For a nation both emotionally and physically scarred, this was a leap too far; the order of the day on a.m. radio wasn't baseless conspiracy-mongering but the tough-minded patriotism of a Sean Hannity. A majority of Jones's stations dropped him. Yet Jones's willingness to question the official 9/11 narrative found him an audience online. Thanks to the internet, he became a leading light of the 9/11

5   Alexander Zaitchik, "Meet Alex Jones," *Rolling Stone*, March 2, 2011, https://www.rollingstone.com/culture/culture-news/meet-alex -jones-175845/.

6   Lee Nichols, "Media Clips: Psst, It's a Conspiracy: KJFK Gives Alex Jones the Boot," *Austin Chronicle*, December 10, 1999, https://www .austinchronicle.com/news/1999-12-10/75039/.

Truther movement, a phenomenon of the aughts whose cultural significance is often forgotten.[7]

Jones had already founded a news website in 1999 called Infowars, which would become a leading source for 9/11 Truther conspiracy theories. And credit Jones with this much: his understanding of the media landscape was prescient. It was right there in the name: Infowars. More than anyone else, Jones grasped that there was to be a fight over information, and that the internet had made it possible for alternative narratives to challenge the mainstream line. As the news ecosystem expanded, as many Americans came to see their media less as objective journalists and more as ideological gatekeepers trying to throttle the flow of information, Jones began to make some sense.

Yet what set Jones apart more than anything else was that aforementioned anger.[8] His show was no *Morning Edition* for crop circle enthusiasts. It was more like a training camp for those who wanted to resist the New World Order. Jones railed against his targets, his voice cracking and his face filling in with continents of splotchy red. "I DON'T LIKE THEM PUTTING CHEMICALS IN THE WATER THAT TURN THE FRIGGING FROGS GAY!!" Jones roared in one now-infamous monologue, before punching his desk repeatedly.[9] "GENITALS—I DON'T CARE IF YOU'RE BLACK OR WHITE—ARE A THIRD THE SIZE OF A 1960S MALE!!" he declared in another.[10]

Masculinity was key to the Jones persona. The feds were forever trying to feminize you, emasculate you, make you weak, and so the solution was

---

7　Zaitchik, "Meet Alex Jones."

8　David Leffler, "Alex Jones Is Mad as Hell," *Austin Monthly*, October 2020, https://www.austinmonthly.com/alex-jones-is-mad-as-hell/.

9　"Alex Jones's Most Unhinged Meltdowns." YouTube, uploaded by The Young Turks, November 22, 2022.

10　"Alex Jones: Genitals are Shrinking." YouTube, uploaded by Indisputable with Dr. Rashad Richey, May 20, 2022.

to defy them by beefing up as much as possible. Jones regularly bragged on-air about his workout routines and posed shirtless. He peddled vitamin supplements and elixirs that allegedly increased male potency.[11] This couldn't have contrasted more with the soft-spoken Art Bell. Jones's message was: They're coming for you so you'd better be ready. Where one was curious, the other was training in the mountains with a Kalashnikov.

But it was with the rise of Donald Trump that Jones truly felt the sunlight on his face. On December 2, 2015, two months before the Iowa caucuses, Jones scored the coup of his career when Trump appeared on his show.[12] As Trump became the GOP frontrunner and won the nomination and the presidency, Jones was assimilated, at least to a degree, into the right-wing media ecosystem. Roger Stone, natty political maverick and Trump advisor, was a frequent guest on Jones's show and even joined him live on election night to quaff champagne when Trump won.[13]

Trump was key to Jones's success and the proliferation of conspiracy theories more generally, sometimes through his actions, sometimes through no fault of his own. Because he was such an unavoidable and unorthodox figure, because he was willing to entertain fringe bugaboos when other politicians wouldn't, he became a projection board for conspiracy theorists of all stripes: for QAnon populists, he was battling an elite cabal of human traffickers and child molesters; for Antifa militants, he was ushering in a new age of fascism; for white nationalists, he was here to dismantle the Jewish establishment. The sea change was undeniable: what had once been discussed amid eerie bumper music on overnight radio

11 James Hamblin, "Testosterone Wars," *The Atlantic*, June 22, 2017, https ://www.theatlantic.com/health/archive/2017/06/testosterone-wars/531252/.

12 "InfoWars: Alex Jones Interviews Donald Trump—December 2, 2015." YouTube, uploaded by Factbase Videos, November 4, 2017.

13 Kirk, Michael, et al. *United States of Conspiracy. Frontline*, PBS, January 20, 2021.

had been infused with anger and spilled into the mainstream of national politics.

***

What is the American mainstream anymore? What constitutes our shared culture? Is it faith, freedom, and the flag? A commitment to the Enlightenment principles of our founding documents? Some kind of vague post-Christian moral consensus? The imperial grandeur of our military? One nation under McDonald's? Collective bitching about the last season of *Game of Thrones*?

This is a harder question to answer than it once was, and one reason is that so much of our lives has migrated online. This has provided space for a multiplicity of odd subcultures to organize and thrive where once they would have been shunned. When it comes to conspiracy theories, the internet has had two profoundly important effects.

The first has a fancy name: epistemic closure. And while it has a precise and complex philosophical definition, in more popular parlance it refers to the closing off of a dialogue.[14] Let's say you believe in X. You can now go online and find dozens of other people who also believe in X. You can hang around with these X devotees and discuss X at length. And since those who don't believe in X either don't show up to your carefully tailored Reddit or are immediately downvoted into oblivion when they do, you end up taking X for granted. You come to believe the arguments for X are so overwhelming as to negate the arguments against X. You come to assume that anyone with any sense must believe in X because those you regularly interact with believe in X. Your little online community is thus extended like deceptive canvas over the entire sky. That's epistemic closure.

---

14 Patricia Cohen, "'Epistemic Closure'? Those Are Fighting Words," *New York Times*, April 27, 2010, https://www.nytimes.com/2010/04/28 /books/28conserv.html.

The second consequence has been to prioritize the absolute. As we've seen, the incentives online are tilted toward absolutism—more Jones than Bell. The result is that people who believe in X end up *really* believing in X. They watch as the lukewarm are swatted down by the true believers; they race to outdo each other in the purity of their beliefs. They come to see those who don't believe in X as dupes and then idiots and then enemies. X gradually develops into an unfalsifiable proposition, even an entire worldview.

The result is that rather than one common culture, or even a plurality of similar but distinct local cultures, we end up with myriad subcultures, all believing they're larger and more important than they really are, all closed off from facts and realities that are inconvenient to them. It's in such an environment that conspiracy theories don't just thrive but end up seeming more real than reality itself. This is how your aunt comes to believe that Donald Trump is working with Q to bring back Jesus: not only is Alex Jones telling her as much but she's found a walled-off online community that believes just the same.

In his essay "Fairy Tales," G. K. Chesterton writes, "I think poets have made a mistake: because the world of the fairy-tales is a brighter and more varied world than ours, they have fancied it less moral; really it is brighter and more varied because it is more moral."[15]

Why do we believe in conspiracy theories? Perhaps because they have the same appeal Chesterton identified in fairy tales. They blend reality and fantasy into a brighter package. They enchant our world, taking the banality of our day-to-day lives and suffusing them with intrigue and whimsy. How much more thrilling is an overcast day if there's a plot churning in the background! How much more interesting is a curtain if there's a man lurking behind it!

---

15   G. K. Chesterton, "Fairy Tales," *All Things Considered* (New York: Simon & Schuster, 2014, originally published in 1908).

Conspiracy theories are also, as Chesterton saw fairy tales, bracingly moral. To believe in Q is to see yourself on the side of light, to be battling not just an evil power but the most evil power imaginable, one that rapes children. For a species that seeks both patterns and binaries, this is a heady brew. For one living in a time when authentic morality tales are few and far between, it perhaps even fills an important need.

It also really, *really* doesn't help that we have a shadowy government that feeds the conspiracy theorists by doing unbelievably idiotic things and then trying to cover them up. Remember Alex Jones ranting about how the feds want to make you gay? The Pentagon in 1994 actually—seriously—considered developing a bomb packed with a chemical that would have turned enemies into raging homosexuals (whether Kim Jong-un was exposed has yet to be confirmed).[16] As for conspiracies of child-molesting cabals, that right there is just nonsense, pure drivel that needs to be denounced by good people of all . . . and who is this Jeffrey Epstein over here? Who was just caught at the center of a human trafficking ring? With every A-list Washingtonian and New Yorker in his Rolodex? Who mysteriously died in jail before he had to testify in a courtroom?

You might think Q had a point.

But even if conspiracy theories grow out of a germ of truth, we can't downplay the harm that conspiracy culture is doing, turning our fellow countrymen into mortal enemies. The hatred conspiracy theories engender might be dispelled when we emerge from our online beehives, when we see our neighbors raking the leaves and our sympathy kicks in. But trust in a society is a valuable thing, and because we're losing it, because we're increasingly wondering whether Joe down the street

---

16 Dan Glaister, "Air force looked at spray to turn enemy gay," *The Guardian*, June 13, 2007, https://www.theguardian.com/world/2007/jun/13/usa.danglaister.

is subletting his basement to a Chinese virology lab, it's making any kind of sane politics difficult.

Rather than smearing our fellow Americans, what we need to do is go back to smearing foreigners. The damned Peruvians might think they've got the jump on us, but just *wait* until they see this meme I'm about to post.

CHAPTER 6

The Final Frontier Is Now Closed

Right now, there is a fight raging inside the space program as to whether America should next return to the Moon or travel to Mars. This is no small matter. The United States might have pioneered space travel with the Apollo program, but we haven't set foot on the lunar surface since 1972, and we've never put a man on the fourth planet. Now, we can't even agree on which one should come first.

Those who favor the Moon tend to be the small-c conservative sorts, the buttoned-up Red Foremans who favor practicality over wild-eyed idealism. They've vested their hopes, naturally, in NASA and its Artemis program, which seeks to return astronauts to the Moon by 2024. No hippie-dippie dreamers they, their goals are relatively modest: a few research stations on the lunar surface, a limited defense presence, perhaps a mining operation for the element helium 3, which could be key to the development of nuclear fusion. But no antigravity shopping malls by the Tycho crater, boys, at least not yet. Let's keep it in our pants here.

By contrast, the Mars enthusiasts are a bit wilder. They have absolutely no problem pulling over the van at some music festival and lighting up a joint with no regard for the morrow, and also no problem trying to terraform a planet that's on average 140 million miles away from Earth. Red Planeteers place their faith in private-sector daredevils like Elon Musk whose company SpaceX hopes to soon be Mars-bound. They view Mars not just as a worthy goal but an expansion of mankind's horizons. Citizen of the world? Get back, Davos man. Man's real home is among the stars.

Thankfully there have yet to be any reports of sabotage between the two camps, no defaced planetariums. Yet the divide is very real, and as the science journalist Lewis M. Andrews writes, "What makes the conflict between the Moon and Mars enthusiasts so difficult to resolve is the lack of room for compromise."[1] Author David W. Brown explains further, "The tools necessary to do anything useful in the two environments are very different and require, for the most part, very different technologies—including, crucially, an entirely different landing vehicle to navigate the Martian atmosphere."[2]

Think of it as a culture war inside the space program. And while in theory we might do both, letting NASA handle the Moon while Musk sends us to Mars, limited resources, necessary collaboration, and the extraordinary discrepancies between the two missions make this about as difficult to reconcile as the fight over woke trigonometry.

And that's before you get to idiots like me who are scientifically illiterate but insist on weighing in anyway. What if we went to Venus?

---

1   Lewis M. Andrews, "The culture war inside the space program," *Spectator World*, September 1, 2022, https://thespectator.com/topic/the-culture-war-inside-the-space-program/.

2   David W. Brown, "For NASA, it Should be Mars or Bust," *Wall Street Journal*, December 18, 2020, https://www.wsj.com/articles/for-nasa-it-should-be-mars-or-bust-11608306732.

Hear me out on this one. To be sure, Venus swirls with toxic clouds of sulfuric acid and its surface is subjected to pressures ninety times stronger than Earth's gravity. But the Soviet Union managed to land a handful of probes there. And if the commies could do it, then surely these colors can't run.

In the excellent sci-fi TV show *The Expanse*, man has colonized both the Moon and Mars, while Venus ends up concealing an evil life form called a "protomolecule" that tears open a gate to another side of the galaxy and nearly wipes out humanity.[3] But then, that's exactly why we need to go there: to make sure this kind of shit doesn't happen.

My meddling in the space program might be an affront to science, but it comes from a good place. Growing up, I set my sights on neither the surface nor the stars, but those bodies in between, the planets, so like our own home yet so different both from Earth and each other, and so diverse in weight, chemical composition, and color. Who can gaze upon Saturn, with its marigold streaks and mighty rings, and not be flooded with wonder? Who can look upon Neptune, the blue enigma at the outer precinct of our solar system, and not feel a fascination with the unknown that ices into a creeping dread?

The planets are poetic, both because some of them look like they could support human life and because most of them swirl with malign forces that would pitilessly crush the likes of us. (Also, while it's good to have a culture war inside the space program, where was this militancy two decades ago? When Pluto was unplaneted, there should have been blood.)

All the more reason, then, to explore the surfaces that mankind could potentially inhabit. Yet as any remedial science student knows,

---

3   *The Expanse*, created by Mark Fergus and Hawk Ostby, produced by Naren Shankar, et al., aired on Syfy and Amazon Prime, based on the novels by James S. A. Corey, 2015–2022.

this doesn't happen anymore. Our last manned moon landing was more than fifty years ago, while any plans to land on Mars have likewise been postponed. That's not to say we don't have a presence on either celestial body: NASA has sent five robotic explorers to Mars, which regularly send back breathtaking photographs of its dusty red landscape, while China has sent a rover to the far side of the Moon.

But the enchantment of landing a fellow human has for decades eluded us. Interplanetary exploration can feel like an artifact of the Cold War, all grainy video footage and thwacking Kennedy accents—except unlike, say, nuclear bomb drills in which the surface of a desk is presented as an impenetrable shield against atomic radiation, few seem to know why our pioneering of the final frontier has seen us turn back and flee for the safety of the earthly homestead.

***

The first reason we haven't been back to the Moon is the sheer cost of getting there. The Apollo program, which ran from 1961 to 1972 and saw twenty-four astronauts fly nine missions to the Moon, cost about $257 billion in today's dollars.[4] And while the federal government is overall much bigger than it was back then, its expansion has been driven not by scientific research but entitlement programs. The costs of Social Security, Medicare, and Medicaid have all ballooned, and entitlements are considered "mandatory spending," meaning their funding is automatic and isn't voted on by Congress. NASA has not enjoyed such default status. While the space agency was about 4 percent of the federal budget in 1965, it was 0.5 percent in 2020.[5]

---

4   Casey Dreier, "An Improved Cost Analysis of the Apollo Program," *Space Policy* 60, May 2022.

5   "Space Data Insights: NASA Budget, 1959–2020." *The Space Report*, Space Foundation, 2020, https://www.thespacereport.org/uncategorized /space-data-insights-nasa-budget-1959-2020/.

Another reason we haven't been back to the Moon is that we have some of the worst politicians ever to set foot on terra firma. Seriously. It may be one reason lawmakers are so reluctant to invest in new space technology is they're afraid we'll use it to blast them into outer orbit.

Members of Congress spend more time than ever trying to get reelected, and thanks to the influx of big money into politics, they're also spending more time than ever raising dollars. All this has incentivized low-risk budget items with high potential returns, which members can then brag about on the campaign trail and on the phone with donors. If you dump more money into the Pentagon, you can assure your constituents you're "keeping America safe" and "giving our military men and women a raise," even if you're really just padding the bureaucracy. If you secure more funding for the Robert C. Byrd LGBTQ+ Succotash Museum in your home state, you can demonstrate brick-and-mortar results and make your district feel like it's receiving special attention.

Whereas if you promise $100 billion for another Moon mission, you might strike a soaring chord in older voters who remember the Apollo launches, but ultimately NASA is a line item clouded in uncertainty. We *might* put another man on the Moon, we *might* open a Burger King on Venus (we must), but these things are going to take time and may ultimately not succeed. They don't put a chicken in every pot; they don't help drain the swamp; they don't even contribute to other ham-handed political clichés that ought to be banished from the English language. NASA missions require patience, and patience is the enemy of our instant gratification–obsessed legislators who have all the attention span of a Chihuahua on amphetamines.

In addition to the political consequences, there's another type of risk involved in spaceflight: the risk to human life. The fittingly numbered Apollo 13 mission saw an oxygen tank explode onboard and nearly kill the crew. Three years earlier, the Apollo 1 mission was aborted after a cabin fire ignited during a launch rehearsal and killed three astronauts.

Once upon a time, space crews felled in the line of duty were exalted as heroes. The explosion of the space shuttle *Challenger* in 1986, which claimed the lives of all seven crew members, is today remembered less as a NASA snafu than as a moment of bittersweet glory, whose tone was set by President Ronald Reagan when he hailed the fallen astronauts as having "slipped the surly bonds of earth to touch the face of God." The *Challenger* crew were martyrs who had sought out the heavens in the name of all mankind. How bold, how pioneering, how fundamentally American.

Whereas today, if a space shuttle were to explode, social media's first responders would rush in. Ululating trolls would demand scalps; names of obscure NASA bureaucrats would be dragged through the mud; fourteen government bodies would announce simultaneous investigations. And while the hordes wouldn't *necessarily* call for an end to the shuttle program, the incentives they set loose would point in that direction. The margin for error today is simply smaller than it used to be. The patient sense of collective purpose is no longer there.

Yet another reason we haven't been back to the Moon is that NASA's focus has been gradually shifted toward the more earthbound challenge of climate change. That hardly makes it unique: just about every government department has been gradually shifted toward the more earthbound challenge of climate change. Yet under Barack Obama, a shift in priorities for NASA in particular began to materialize. During the Obama administration, the Constellation spaceflight program was canceled along with its Orion spacecraft and Ares rockets, vaporizing any hope of returning to the Moon in the short term.[6]

---

6   Tarik Maliq, "NASA grieves over canceled program," NBC News, February 2, 2010, https://www.nbcnews.com/id/wbna35209628#:~:text=NASA%20and%20President%20Barack%20Obama's,astronauts%20back%20to%20the%20moon.

The result was that while NASA's overall funding during the Obama years remained fairly consistent, its distribution underwent a major change. Exploration and space operations, the ostensible reason NASA was created in the first place, saw its funding within NASA decrease by 7.6 percent, while earth sciences, which these days translates into the study of climate change, saw a budget hike of 41 percent.[7]

This was consistent with Obama's liberalism, which emphasized both environmental sustainability and—brace yourself: there be crazy in them thar hills—diversity. In 2010, Obama's NASA administrator Charles Bolden told Al-Jazeera that his "perhaps foremost" goal as assigned by the president was "to find a way to reach out to the Muslim world and engage much more with dominantly Muslim nations to help them feel good about their historic contribution to science, math, and engineering."[8, 9]

I'm sure the world's Muslims were immensely grateful to have American space bureaucrats lecturing them about Avicenna and Averroes. Why NASA was ever delegated either of these agendas is beyond me. It was also beyond forty-nine former NASA astronauts and engineers, who in 2012 sent the agency an open letter challenging its "unbridled advocacy" of climate change politics. Among them were seven astronauts who had worked on the Apollo program.[10]

---

7   Jeffrey Mervis, "Earth science is not hard science, congressional Republicans declare," Science.org, March 13, 2015, https://www.science.org/content/article/earth-science-not-hard-science-congressional-republicans-declare (graphic prepared by office of Senator Ted Cruz).

8   "Talk to Al Jazeera—NASA administrator Charles Bolden." YouTube. Posted by Al Jazeera English, July 1, 2010.

9   Byron York, "Obama's new mission for NASA: Reach out to Muslim world," *Washington Examiner*, July 4, 2010, https://www.washingtonexaminer.com/opinion/beltway-confidential/916283/obamas-new-mission-for-nasa-reach-out-to-muslim-world/.

10   Gus Lubin, "49 Former NASA Scientists Send a Letter Disputing Climate Change," *Business Insider*, April 11, 2012, https://www.businessinsider.com/nasa-scientists-dispute-climate-change-2012-4.

A pivot came after the election of Donald Trump, who soared into Washington on a giant eagle with an AR-15 in its talons determined to send Americans back to the stars. The Trump administration blunted the growth of NASA's earth sciences division and created the all-important Space Force. Trump also spiked Obama's airy-fairy pledge to establish a presence on Mars by 2030 in favor of a more achievable and concrete lunar colony by 2024 (you didn't think Trump would pass up a chance to take sides in a culture war, did you?).[11]

All this means it's possible that space is one glimmer of hope in this book's unyielding gauntlet of doom. Yet as we go to press, the 2024 Moon landing has already been postponed.[12] And it remains the case that for a good half-century, America's interplanetary dreams have all but dissolved into space dust.

***

When we first went to the Moon, it wasn't just a momentous achievement for scientists and space nerds. It was a truly national undertaking akin to the war effort two decades earlier. The boys might not have been shipped off, the factories weren't churning out ordnance, but in the 1960s Americans in unison turned their gazes skyward.

Writer Peter Van Buren recalls, "What I remember was a country that saw a single good thing happen together. While in 2022 the majority of young people say they want to be a YouTuber, kids then

---

11   Alexandra Witze, "Can NASA Really Return People to the Moon by 2024?" *Nature*, July 8, 2019, https://www.washingtonexaminer .com/opinion/beltway-confidential/916283/obamas-new-mission -for-nasa-reach-out-to-muslim-world/.

12   Joey Roulette, "NASA to push back moon mission timelines amid spacecraft delays," Reuters, January 8, 2024, https://www.reuters .com/technology/space/nasa-push-back-moon-mission-timelines-amid -spacecraft-delays-sources-2024-01-09/#:~:text=NASA's%20second%20 Artemis%20mission%20is,will%20need%20to%20be%20replaced.

wanted to walk in space."[13] That contrast between social media and the stars shouldn't escape us. Whereas back then the national eye was trained in a single direction, upward, today it has been focused much closer to home.

The end of the Cold War robbed us of a competitor that was likewise seeking out the stars. Disruptions like 9/11 and the Great Recession necessarily called us back to earthly matters. And as the consequences of these events became clear, as the promise of millennials' glory days evaporated, social media was there to refract our stories and experiences and grievances into a zillion parts. Not the cosmos but the individual became the new subject of fascination. Lunar craters? We can look at those on Google Images. We'd found ourselves a new final frontier and it was not space but the self.

Whereas once we'd learned an entire vocabulary that was centered on space travel—"lunar module," "atmospheric reentry"—now we have terms like "mental health day," "living my best life," and "sharing my truth." The former might be grounded in science while the latter were lifted from a particularly bad crop of corporate motivational posters. But the fact that such a parlance exists in the popular mind suggests this is more than a momentary fascination; it's a national culture, like the one that grew up around the Moon landing.

Americans in the 2020s seem captivated by themselves in the way that Americans in the 1960s were captivated by the moon. We step out onto the tarmac and wave goodbye to our friends and family whom we love but—let's just be honest—are holding us back from living our best lives before setting off on our inward journey with a mighty blast of self-absorption that propels us past our altruism and our societal

---

13   Peter Van Buren, "When the moon brought America together," *Spectator World*, January 25, 2023, https://thespectator.com/topic /when-the-moon-brought-america-together/.

responsibilities, until, *shreep*, that moment of perfect airlessness when we're free, truly free, alone in the vast and beautiful void of subjective truth and self-esteem.

I don't mean all this quite as scornfully as it might sound. The human heart is a worthy subject, and plenty of writers have explored it with sensitivity. Yet it's simply true that man today is less keen to explore both foreign jungles and distant planets, while he is more than willing to go over his own feelings with a carefully calibrated tricorder. And why should a culture of the self care at all about the stars? Space is the opposite of therapeutic: it's cold, inhospitable, demanding of sacrifice for the good of the species.

Once upon a time, interest in space travel was so pervasive that it came with its own choir of pessimists. Among them was the philosopher Hannah Arendt, who worried that man's quest to the stars was less a swaggering triumph than a kind of planetary cry for help. Americans had been so atomized, so stripped of any allegiance to family and community and nature, that they'd sought out transcendence in the cosmos. They'd become alienated from Earth itself, yet by settling on other worlds they would only instead diminish themselves into objects of control, inhabitants of a cold and mechanized habitat created and engineered not by God but by other men.[14, 15]

You can see her point. For all of its romance, life inside a Moon colony sounds pretty dreary. It also sounds like an exercise in enormous uncertainty. W. H. Auden in his poem "Moon Landing" ridiculed the first moonwalk as a "huge phallic triumph" that only hubristic

---

14   Hannah Arendt, "Has man's conquest of space increased or decreased his stature?" "Symposium on Space," *The Great Ideas Today*, Encyclopedia Britannica. 1963 edition.

15   Hannah Arendt, *The Human Condition, Second Edition* (Chicago: University of Chicago Press, 2018, originally published 1958).

men could cheer, and worried it would usher in a disruptive new age.[16] In C. S. Lewis's exquisite novel *Perelandra*, humanity travels to Venus (finally), only to discover a new Eden with man cast in the role of interloper and corruptor.[17]

The common theme is that man is native to Earth, alien everywhere else, and causes unwelcome disruptions both to himself and others when he travels between worlds. Yet compelling though these concerns are, it's worth pointing out how little any of this has come to pass. We haven't despoiled the Moon—we haven't even been there in decades. There's been no radical Space Age—the real game changer has been the Information Age.

We have become more alienated as individuals, but then our response has been to turn the individual into its own frontier. And while you might argue that we could focus on both interstellar aspirations *and* TikTok likes, I can't help but think one has distracted from the other. Imagine that tomorrow we landed a man on the Moon: would it attract more attention than Meghan Markle's "shout your truth" interview with Oprah in 2021? You laugh, but you had to think about it for a second, didn't you?

***

The Expanse really is one of the greatest TV shows of the 2010s. Based on the novels by James S. A. Corey, it slowly builds a compelling and believable sci-fi vision: With Earth overpopulated, man successfully settles on the Moon, is in the process of terraforming Mars, and mines the asteroid belt for resources. Yet as is the case with any human venture, greed and tribalism assert themselves. At the start of the series,

---

16 W. H. Auden, "Moon Landing," *The New Yorker*, September 6, 1969, https://www.newyorker.com/magazine/1969/09/06/moon-landing.

17 C. S. Lewis, *Perelandra* (New York: Scribner, 1996, originally published 1943).

Earthers, Martians, and Belters are on the brink of war. Toss in that mysterious "protomolecule," which might be a biological weapon or even alien life, and you'll burn through six episodes before you notice you forgot to shower.[18]

Yet there's an unavoidable meta effect to watching *The Expanse*, one that sums up our own condition rather well. Here you are, sitting in front of a TV, watching a prestige show about celestial habitation—when we haven't been back to any of those celestial bodies in decades. We can communicate our reactions to their gorgeous CGI renderings instantly on social media but we can't set foot on their real-world inspirations.

It is fair to worry that by exploring Mars we could neglect Earth, or that our own planet fits us in a way that others simply never will. The headlines a hundred years from now practically write themselves: *Martian teens four times as likely as Earthlings to experience depression! Tensions develop between the United States and New New Brazil over competing lunar colonies! I spent three days on Europa: here's why it turned me vegan!*

Yes, I regret to inform you that the *Guardian* still exists in the year 2124. But even if space voyages bring about a new set of problems, is that really a reason not to do it? We don't lament the Age of Discovery because explorers and settlers confronted dangers in the Americas. As a denizen of the New World, I wouldn't be here if a motley collection of religious extremists and gold-digging buccaneers hadn't set sail across the Atlantic.

It is natural for man to long for his home. But it's also natural for him to seek out those ominous squiggles on the map labeled "monsters be here." Odysseus embarks on his famous voyage because he longs for Ithaca and his family. Yet the rest of us read his adventures because we're fascinated by the lumbering Cyclops and Circe's eroticism and

---

18   *The Expanse*, Mark Fergus and Hawk Ostby.

the secret of the sun-god's cattle. A peripatetic life might not be for everyone, but it is for some. And our species is forever in the debt of those who gave in to that domestic restlessness.

In 1890, the federal government declared that America's western frontier was closed, there being no land left that hadn't been claimed. Today, we've effectively closed our final frontier even though we still have so very much of it left to explore. Mars? The Moon? The only answer is: yes.

CHAPTER 7

To Live and Die in the USA

I wouldn't mind traveling to a Moon colony one day (even if it sounds a bit depressing). But first I'd like to visit the glorious Republic of Estonia.

Estonia is a largely coastal nation, bordered to the north and west by the sea and to the east by Lake Peipus, which separates it from Russia. Its story during the twentieth century is the familiar Eastern European one: it was brutalized first by the Soviets, then by the Nazis, then by the Soviets again, then by the Soviets a few more times for good measure. Upon independence in 1991, Estonia embarked upon what many consider to be the most successful transition of a former Soviet republic to liberal democracy. Bucking the Eastern European stereotype, today it's ranked as one of the least corrupt countries on earth.[1]

---

1   "Corruption Perceptions Index," Transparency International, 2023, https://www.transparency.org/en/cpi/2023.

Estonia also bears another enviable distinction, which is why I'd like to go there: its people consistently rank as drinking among the most booze in the world.

The average Estonian in 2022 drank just over eleven liters of absolute alcohol, or about three gallons of the good stuff. That translates into 160 bottles of beer or twenty-one bottles of wine, depending on your taste.[2] Estonia's taste—its signature drink, the Guinness to its Dublin—is a spiced-and-vanilla liqueur known as Vana Tallinn. It's so delicious that historically it's been used by Estonians as currency.[3]

Clearly this is a country very much not in decline. Yet, during the 2010s, tragedy struck: alcohol consumption in Estonia fell off significantly. That was before COVID-19, however, and also before the great booze war of 2019 between Estonia and its neighbor Latvia. Have you not heard of this landmark engagement? It began when Estonia, tired of locals crossing the border for a cheaper drink, slashed its alcohol tax by 25 percent. Latvia then responded in kind, chopping its own tax rate by 15 percent.[4] (Don't ever tell me tax cuts never did any good.)

For an aspiring hooch tourist like myself, what's not to love? Estonians drink because their winters are harsh and long. They drink because it's woven into their cultural fabric.

---

2   "Alcohol consumption in Estonia has been steadily increasing since 2019," *Estonian World*, June 7, 2023, https://estonianworld.com/life /study-alcohol-consumption-in-estonia-has-been-steadily-increasing -since-2019/.

3   Summer Rylander, "Estonia's Signature Spirit Is So Popular It Was Used As Currency," *Food & Wine*, June 25, 2021, https://www.foodandwine .com/cocktails-spirits/estonian-spirit-vana-talinn#:~:text=Vana%20 Talinn%20Is%20Estonia's%20Most%20Popular%20Spirit.

4   Lillo Montalto Monella and Chris Harris, "Will a booze tax war in the Baltics leave Latvia & Estonia with a bad hangover?" *Euronews*, July 27, 2019, https://www.euronews.com/2019/07/27/money-before-man-baltic -booze-war-threatens-latvia-estonia-with-health-hangover.

And on average they still live a year longer than Americans.

***

Estonia, it's worth pointing out, is not the only global heavy drinker. Check the numbers and you'll find other hiccupping offenders: the Czech Republic, Australia, Finland, Lithuania, Germany, France, Spain, and Ireland all consistently rank as being in no condition to drive. America, by contrast, is almost always middle of the pack, not in the same league as its European barmates. (This is because, as with many things, America tends to span extremes that balance each other out. A Packers fan in northern Wisconsin tends to drink *a lot*, while a Southern Baptist from Alabama tends to drink very little.)

Yet with the exception of Lithuania, all of the countries listed above also boast higher life expectancies than the United States. An Irishman can expect to live to the golden age of eighty-two, compared to just seventy-six in the city on a hill.[5] (Imagine getting outlived by the people whose favorite means of therapy is singing songs about funerals.)

The problem is only getting worse. Between 2019 and 2021, American life expectancy fell by 2.7 years to its lowest age since 1996.[6] That means in just two years, a full two and a half decades of progress on human longevity was wiped out. And the familiar bogey COVID-19 can't get all the blame. Americans did die from the coronavirus at a horrendous rate, but then many Europeans did too, and European countries haven't seen the same backslide on life expectancy that we have. Not just in Europe but in nations all over the world, life expectancies

---

5   "Life expectancy at birth, total (years) – Ireland." The World Bank, 2021, https://data.worldbank.org/indicator/SP.DYN.LE00.IN?locations=IE. All national life expectancy values taken from the World Bank database.

6   Elizabeth Arias, et al., "Provisional Life Expectancy Estimates for 2021," NVSS Vital Statistics Rapid Release, Centers for Disease Control, Report No. 23, August 2022, https://www.cdc.gov/nchs/data/vsrr/vsrr023.pdf.

have bounced right back to where they were before the pandemic. In the United States, this has yet to happen.[7]

In fairness, America has long been in the cellar when it comes to life expectancy among first-world nations. This is the land of pancakes smothered in butter for breakfast and bacon doughnut triple cheese-burgers for dinner, of the constitutional right to own a gun that can shred a watermelon in two seconds flat and of cars so big they make us feel invincible enough to try hitting ninety-five on that mountain pass.

And may it ever be this way. You can have my Aunt Jemima/Land O'Lakes hybrid condiment when you pry my plate from my cold, sticky hands. Still, there's no question America is going in the wrong direc-tion on life expectancy. And what could be a more urgent indicator of decline than that we're literally dying sooner than we used to?

***

The leading cause of death in the United States is, of course, the Burger King Triple Whopper with Cheese (the second leading cause of death is suicide after hearing those Burger King "YOU RULE!" commercials). The CDC reports that about seven hundred thousand Americans died of heart disease in 2021, up significantly over 2019 and even 2020, while from 2010 to 2019, the heart disease rate actually fell by 10 percent.[8]

Heart disease is linked to another woeful reality: the obesity rate continues to pop buttons from sea to shining sea. In 2021, more than 42 percent of American adults were estimated to be obese, while seven in ten adults were either overweight or obese. Twenty percent of children,

---

7   Selena Simmons-Duffin, "'Live free and die?' The sad state of US life expectancy," NPR, March 25, 2023, https://www.opb.org/article/2023/03/25/sad-state-of-us-life-expectancy/.

8   "Heart Disease Facts." Centers for Disease Control, 2021, https://www.cdc.gov/heartdisease/facts.htm.

about 14.7 million, were also considered obese.[9] (Those numbers are likely a bit skewed, as they rely on the flawed body mass index standard, which has counted many a perfectly healthy football lineman as obese.[10] Still, a quick trip to the water park shows the stark reality.)

After heart disease, the second leading cause of death among Americans in 2021 was cancer, a complex ailment that can correlate with any number of unhealthy behaviors (or none at all). Curiously, COVID-19 was only the third most deadly killer, though from the news coverage you'd have thought it was the gold medalist.[11] The only bad PR McDonald's risked that year was if one of its executives was caught not wearing a mask.

Before we continue, let's hand out the participation trophies. In 2021, a total of zero deaths were caused by not listing your pronouns in your Twitter bio! Zero deaths were caused by Jordan Peterson! And—this is interesting—zero deaths were caused by the opinions of J. K. Rowling! We'd like to thank everyone for playing and wish them better luck next year.

Back on the trail of the grim reaper: about 43,000 people in 2021 died in car crashes. That doesn't sound like much compared to the heart disease and cancer tolls, but it's up 10.5 percent over 2020, which itself was up 6.8 percent over 2019, and is the highest

9   "Overweight & Obesity Statistics." National Institute of Diabetes and Digestive and Kidney Diseases, US Department of Health and Human Services, 2021, https://www.niddk.nih.gov/health-information/health-statistics/overweight-obesity.

10 Kathy Katella, "Why You Shouldn't Rely on BMI Alone," Yale Medicine, August 4, 2023, https://www.yalemedicine.org/news/why-you-shouldnt-rely-on-bmi-alone#:~:text=One%20reason%20is%20that%20a,be%20misleading%20in%20some%20cases.

11 "What are the leading causes of death in the US?" USA Facts, data from the Centers for Disease Control, October 6, 2023, https://usafacts.org/articles/americans-causes-of-death-by-age-cdc-data/.

automobile death rate since 2005.[12] Given that the roads are supposed to get safer as cars become more crashproof, this is a distressing trend.

Then again, what could be more American than wrapping your Ford F-150 around a palmetto tree? As Hunter S. Thompson put it, "Old elephants limp off to the hills to die; old Americans go out to the highway and drive themselves to death with huge cars."[13] As of 2019, we were 2.3 times more likely to die on the road than those in other high-income countries.[14]

Gun violence is a problem that grabs headlines, but this is thanks largely to a handful of disturbing mass shootings that are relatively rare and not representative of the whole. Still, nearly 49,000 gun deaths were recorded in 2021, the highest number on record. And it's worth pointing out that the majority of those were suicides: about 26,000 people killed themselves with a gun in 2021, compared to 21,000 murders (the remaining 2,000 were either accidents, involved law enforcement, or featured inconclusive motives).[15]

Yet gun violence receives inordinately more press than another much more potent killer. In 2021, more than 106,000 deaths were caused by drug overdoses—five times the homicide rate and more than

---

12   "Newly Released Estimates Show Traffic Fatalities Reached a 16-Year High in 2021." National Highway Traffic Safety Administration, May 17, 2022, https://www.nhtsa.gov/press-releases/early-estimate-2021-traffic-fatalities.

13   Hunter S. Thompson, *Fear and Loathing in Las Vegas* (New York: Vintage, 2013, originally published 1972).

14   Merissa A. Yellman, et al., "Motor Vehicle Crash Deaths—United States and 28 Other High-Income Countries, 2015 and 2019," Morbidity and Mortality Weekly Report, Centers for Disease Control, July 1, 2022, https://www.cdc.gov/mmwr/volumes/71/wr/pdfs/mm7126a1-h.pdf.

15   John Gramlich, "What the data says about gun deaths in the US" Pew Research Center, data from the Centers for Disease Control, April 26, 2023, https://www.pewresearch.org/short-reads/2023/04/26/what-the-data-says-about-gun-deaths-in-the-u-s/.

twice the gun fatality rate—the lion's share of them from opioids like fentanyl. Overdose deaths rose an astonishing 30 percent between 2019 and 2020, and another 15 percent from 2020 to 2021.[16]

The opioid crisis rages on, scattering its corpses across the rubble of postindustrial America. And it's here that we arrive at an important and very gnarled root of the life expectancy problem. If you crack open a couple of beers, there's at least a chance you might do it with friends. Yet heroin, and its evil cousin fentanyl, are the opposite of a social habit. That's not to say addicts won't shoot up together; it's not to say slaves to other substances won't isolate themselves. But no one throws a house party and brings out a platter of needles for the guests. The opioid, perhaps uniquely, is a solitary drug. And it is *the* drug of twenty-first-century America.

One of the few writers to ever attempt to chronicle heroin addiction was the American beat poet William Burroughs. Burroughs was an unapologetic libertine, and his novel *Junky* sees the title character cruising the subway, robbing strangers, doing whatever it takes to feed the monster inside of him. Yet what's most arresting is how disjointed it all is. Characters walk in, sell the protagonist Lee some "junk," and vanish; Lee's wife makes a brief appearance only to never be heard from again. (In real life, Burroughs accidentally killed his wife in Mexico during a game of William Tell, one cause of death still thankfully rare among Americans.) Other people in the novel exist only as props, there to either abet or obstruct Lee's next high. As Burroughs writes, "Junk is not, like alcohol or weed, a means to increased enjoyment of life. Junk is not a kick. It is a way of life."[17]

---

16 "Drug Overdose Death Rates." National Institute on Drug Abuse, June 30, 2023, https://nida.nih.gov/research-topics/trends-statistics /overdose-death-rates.

17 William Burroughs, *Junky* (New York: Grove Press, 2012, originally published 1953).

With a heroin addiction, everything and everyone else shrinks before the towering need to consume more lest you become "dope sick" and suffer the brutal symptoms of withdrawal. In towns roiled by opioids, the crime rate, and in particular break-and-enter robberies, often goes up, the reason being that opioid devotees will do anything to feed their habit, even if it means smashing into a home and stealing money. This is also why junkies withdraw from their kith and kin, especially those who won't provide them with cash or who call them out on their destructive behavior. Other people become mere props to addiction. Then there's the fact that heroin dulls your energy levels, emotional responses, and sex drive, further diminishing your need for, and desire for, others.

What's most striking about opioid abuse is the utter desolation of it all. An alcoholic might stumble into a bar and guffaw too loudly, but at least he's being social in a distorted sense, even if everyone around him keeps motioning for the check. Not so with heroin. In fact, Burroughs juxtaposes the two substances directly: "As I began using stuff every day, or often several times a day, I stopped drinking and going out at night," he writes. "When you use junk, you don't drink."[18] You don't do much else either.

＊

In January 2020, a mysterious plague began rampaging across China. Yet one Dr. Anthony Fauci adjusted his sunglasses, took a long sip from his daiquiri, and told an interviewer, "This is not a major threat to the people of the United States."[19]

---

18   Burroughs, *Junky.*

19   Kyle Smith, "Anthony Fauci's Misadventures in Fortune Telling," *National Review*, April 20, 2021, https://www.nationalreview.com/2021/04/anthony -faucis-misadventures-in-fortune-telling/.

Two months later, the entirety of the political and scientific establishment would execute a U-turn so gnarly you could almost smell the rubber. Suddenly, the coronavirus—remember when we called it that?—wasn't just a threat to the public; it was *the* threat to the public. It was such a threat that all other concerns had to be subordinated to its prevention: schools would be closed, businesses would be shuttered, Gretchen Whitmer would be taken seriously.

It was akin to one of those changes of heart you see on social media where a frothing zealot for one cause abruptly becomes a frothing zealot for the opposite cause. It was also an example of something that should never happen in public policy: total convergence, the redirection of everything toward a single goal. Life is too complicated, and the needs of politics too various, to ever be captured in one cause or policy or idea. Yet from March 2020 through a good span of 2022, everything—*everything*—was about mitigating COVID-19.

What this meant in practice was that isolation became the sine qua non of American life. A new vocabulary grew up around this reality: social distancing, flattening the curve, remote learning. You were told to stay inside and binge-watch John Oliver in your jammies if you knew what was good for you—*unless* you were one of those precious few deemed an "essential worker." In that case, you were allowed to work grueling hours in a delivery van or a hospital so the gentry of the pandemic, the yuppies who screamed in panic every time the Uber Eats guy rang the doorbell, might live.

The hypocrisies and cruelties of this period were many and I'm not keen to revisit them here. We think we live in this deeply knowledge-driven society, but here was the whole of the American elite forgetting one of the oldest anthropological truths in existence: man is a social animal. Aristotle could have told them that 2,300 years ago. For like $12 million in NIH grants.

The result of converging everything under a single imperative of quarantine was predictably that Americans became lonely. And it was around then that the death rate really began to climb.

Think about all those causes of death listed above: heart disease and suicide and car crashes and opioids. Each in its own way is characterized by loneliness. That's true of the guy flying down the highway in a Toyota Camry, ferrying no one else and thinking of no one else. It's true even of the man who has a heart attack: during COVID-19, he likely wasn't going out much to exercise; his gym was closed for the sake of his health. Nearly twice as many people died in 2020 from heart disease than from COVID-19,[20] and while public health officials rushed to hypothesize that the coronavirus was exacerbating cardiovascular problems, the more established causes seem to be both patients delaying care because they were told to stay at home and a more sedentary and isolated lifestyle.

So it was that in May 2023, after more than three years of on-and-off isolation, Joe Biden's surgeon general Vivek Murthy emerged to make an announcement: there was a new health crisis afoot. It was an "epidemic of loneliness."[21]

You don't say.

So to recap: the government says there's no emergency. Then the government says you must isolate because there is an emergency. Then

20   Sherry L. Murphy, "Mortality in the United States, 2020," National Center for Health Statistics, Centers for Disease Control, NCHS Data Brief No. 427, December 2021, https://www.cdc.gov/nchs/data/databriefs/db427.pdf.

21   Vivek Murthy, "New Surgeon General Advisory Raises Alarm about the Devastating Impact of the Epidemic of Loneliness and Isolation in the United States," US Department of Health and Human Services, May 3, 2023, https://www.hhs.gov/about/news/2023/05/03/new-surgeon-general-advisory-raises-alarm-about-devastating-impact-epidemic-loneliness-isolation-united-states.html.

the government says your isolation is itself an emergency. You can't win with these people. You'd get better health information from licking trans fats off an asbestos ceiling and seeing what happens.

Completely valid exasperation aside, it's hard to argue with Murthy when he says, "Loneliness is more than just a bad feeling. When people are socially disconnected, their risk of anxiety and depression increases." Murthy estimates that "at any moment, about one out of every two Americans is experiencing measurable levels of loneliness."[22] Loneliness, he notes, is linked to depression, anxiety, and suicide; it's also linked to a vastly increased risk of heart disease and stroke. In general, Murthy notes, "lacking social connection increases risk of premature death by more than 60%."[23]

There's a reason suicides and pickled livers and drug overdoses are called "deaths of despair." And there's a reason having an active social network is so strongly correlated with a longer life. Even the informal accountability that exists between friends—*I want to be as ripped as you are, bro; you sure you should fly that plane after doing those keg stands, bro?*—can help keep you on the straight and narrow.

***

"I have no friends." That was the opening line of a video posted in 2019 to LinkedIn by a British man named Mark Gaisford, which quickly went viral. "I know a lot of people," Gaisford clarified, "but it's mostly through networking and work and everything to do with

---

22   Vivek Murthy, "Surgeon General: We Have Become a Lonely Nation. It's Time to Fix That," *New York Times*, April 30, 2023, https://www .nytimes.com/2023/04/30/opinion/loneliness-epidemic-america.html.

23   Vivek Murthy, "New Surgeon General Advisory . . ."

work." "I don't take them out for dinner and I don't go on long country walks with them. I don't do stuff with them that friends do."²⁴

Even more candid was a video posted by the YouTuber Akta, who admitted she too once had no friends. After a typically catty high school row where her friends voted to throw her out of their social group (it's good to see young people still invested in democracy), Akta became a recluse and focused on her studies. Come university, she met plenty of people to sit with in the cafeteria, but they were more superficial hang-out props than real friends—she felt stressed out by them, not fulfilled.²⁵

Akta is one of those individuals who can post a deeply revealing video to randos on the internet but struggles to converse in a room full of real people (I have the opposite problem). And thankfully both her and Gaisford's stories have happy endings: Akta developed a good circle of friends after graduating while Gaisford went to a meet-up at the local pub. Yet search for "I have no friends" on YouTube and the results are endless: "I'm 23 and I have no friends," "25 years old: I have NO friends," "Being ugly and having no friends at 46: my experience."

What's striking is how many of these loners come off as charming, how many you wish you could meet and take out for a beer. Social anxiety has existed across history; it's not just another quarantine by-product. And the scope of the problem is further complicated by how you define the word "friend." My wife is forever calling me out because I use the term so elastically, referring to some guy I emailed once as a "friend" like he was standing next to me on the wedding

---

24 Garren Keith Gaynor, "Man's painfully honest video goes viral: 'I have no friends,'" *New York Post*, December 18, 2019, https://nypost.com/2019/12/18/mans-painfully-honest-video-goes-viral-i-have-no-friends/.

25 "18 years old: I have no friends." YouTube. Posted by Akta, August 22, 2021.

altar. Whereas she, descendant of Irish immigrants that she is, is much stingier with that honor.

Friendship as a concept really is relative, depending on how open a person is and how comfortable he feels around others. But then, it isn't *that* relative, whether between individuals or even time periods. And according to a study by the Survey Center on American Life, a full 12 percent of Americans in 2021 reported having zero close friends, up from only 3 percent in 1990. Half of all Americans said they had three or fewer close friends, up from 27 percent three decades earlier. And while 33 percent in 1990 reported having ten or more close friends, social butterflies had dwindled to only 13 percent in 2021.[26]

Scan the comments or reply tweets on these videos and surveys and even more unvarnished accounts of the friendship bust emerge. *How do I make a friend? How does that even happen? I went to a pottery class but everyone else already knew someone. Is there some secret to it? I stay inside and play video games all day. I have no idea how to talk to a woman. I haven't left my apartment in three days. If I died tomorrow, I don't think anyone would notice.*

For this to happen anywhere would be concerning. For it to happen in the United States, one of the most wonderfully extroverted societies in the world—one of the great pleasures of this place is the impromptu conversations you have with strangers in elevators—seems like a desecration of our national character.

Imagine you're thinking about taking your life or shooting up heroin or just driving like a maniac (now imagine you aren't from New York so you don't drive like a maniac as a matter of course). If you

---

26　Daniel A. Cox, "The State of American Friendship: Change, Challenges, and Loss," May 2021 American Perspectives Survey, Survey Center on American Life, June 8, 2021, https://www.americansurveycenter.org /research/the-state-of-american-friendship-change-challenges-and-loss/.

have friends who are checking up on you or a social engagement that evening, it doesn't guarantee you're going to pump the brakes either figuratively or literally. But it does make it more likely.

There is no more powerful motive toward life and away from making the ultimate mistake than friendship and love. There is no better health measure than the sociality we were denied for so long and now seem to be denying ourselves. I'm sure the Estonians would heartily agree—they're just too drunk to say anything.

CHAPTER 8

Drinking Alone

In 1995, a social scientist at Harvard University named Robert Putnam published an article in the *Journal of Democracy*. It was, by his own account, not expected to make much of a splash. Putnam saw it as just another commentary the likes of which academics publish all the time and are usually read by their fellow academics and at most one family member.

But this article was different. It became an international sensation, even netting Putnam an invitation to Camp David to meet President Bill Clinton.

The article was called "Bowling Alone,"[1] and five years later Putnam would expand it into a book with the same title. The book became an even bigger sensation, a global bestseller that was translated

---

[1]   Robert D. Putnam, "Bowling Alone: America's Declining Social Capital," *Journal of Democracy* 6, no. 1, January 1995, pp. 65–78.

into nine languages and turned Putnam into a kind of guru of communitarianism. The Irish prime minister, or Taoiseach, told him that *Bowling Alone* was the most important book he'd ever read. (An Irish journalist later qualified this by saying the Taoiseach had hardly read anything at all.)[2]

Bowling Alone catapulted Putnam into the kind of celebrity usually reserved for fantasy academics like Robert Langdon. How did he achieve this kind of fame? He placed his finger precisely on the zeitgeist.

In *Bowling Alone*, Putnam identified something called social capital, meaning the groups and associations that individuals form when they gather in service of a common goal and the relationships and trust that blossom as a result. Think of everything from churches to labor unions to the YMCA to the book's eponymous bowling clubs. Such social capital had been the backbone of the American postwar period, as the return of the GIs saw an explosion of civic energy. Yet since the 1960s, it had slipped into decline. We no longer seemed as interested in spending time with our fellow Americans. Rather than head down to the lanes on Wednesday evenings with the boys, we were now Bowling Alone.

This trend toward isolation was by no means unique in American history: Putnam says we were similarly lonely at the start of the twentieth century. Rather than continue indefinitely on a trajectory, our communitarianism and individualism have tended to yin and yang with the self-corrections that define any liberal society. It would also be wrong to view that more community-focused time as a golden age. Travel back to the early 1960s and you'd find commentators worried about *too much* communitarianism, which they saw as eclipsing the

2   Robert D. Putnam, *Bowling Alone: The Collapse and Revival of American Community*, second edition (New York: Simon & Schuster, 2001, originally published 2000).

individual, subsuming him into his social roles while he secretly yearned to break his chains.

Yet Putnam also convincingly documents the wreckage of our more contemporary shift away from community: weaker social bonds, he finds, mean children do worse in school, governments have a harder time finding consensus, the poor are more likely to turn to crime and drugs (sound familiar?). In order to become successful and happy adults, individuals need not just strong families and schools but social groups to provide them with structure, mentorship, and just someone to talk to. The interest in *Bowling Alone* showed that people were experiencing this in their own lives, and so found all the more resonant the idea that it was a national phenomenon, that it wasn't just happening to them.

Bowling Alone might have started an international dialogue, but since it was published there's been no real swing back of the pendulum. Our social capital has not been revitalized; instead, we've skidded even further toward isolation. Those institutions that were once the stuff of American social life—city clubs, softball leagues, labor unions, church groups—have only continued to dwindle. It's a problem that ties in directly with the loneliness crisis. Even if we wanted to be social, where would we go to do it? Even if we wanted authentic community, where would it come from?

***

Why has our social capital plummeted? COVID-19 is a major cause, of course, along with the displacement of authentic social life by the internet. But there's another important reason at work: our community groups have lost the trust of the public. Let's take a look at two especially vivid examples: the Boy Scouts and the Catholic Church.

For any boy of the twentieth century, the Boy Scouts were an unavoidable fact of life, something you either participated in or knew several friends who did. Back in 2010, Gallup found that about four in ten adult men reported having been a Scout.[3] You would often see the Scouts around town, hanging the flags from the telephone poles on Memorial Day, cleaning up public parks, hiking down trails in their khaki uniforms with their green merit badge sashes dangling from their belts.

Yet Bowling Alone has taken its toll on the Scouts too. Scout membership peaked in the early 1970s, and while you wouldn't know it from the often-rowdy meetings in the local church hall I used to attend, the falloff has been significant. There were 6.5 million registered Boy Scouts and Cub Scouts in 1972[4] and only two million in 2019. The pandemic year of 2020 saw a stunning further 43 percent slice in Scout memberships.[5]

That number may yet rebound a bit, but there are real reasons to think the Scouts are in serious, even existential trouble. The organization has gone woke, allowing girls to join, emphasizing gay rights, and introducing a new merit badge called Citizenship in Society that promotes a distinctly left-wing idea of diversity[6]—all of which has driven away

3   Byron Johnson and Jon Clifton, "Younger Generations Less Likely to Join Boy Scouts," Gallup Daily Tracking, April 20–October 4, 2010, https://news.gallup.com/poll/145187/younger-generations-less-likely-join-boy-scouts.aspx#:~:text=Fewer%20men%20in%20their%2020s,Daily%20polling%20April%2020%2DOct.

4   Ben Wattenberg, "Active Leisure—Boy Scouts of America," *The First Measured Century*, PBS, 2000, https://www.pbs.org/fmc/book/7leisure4.htm.

5   Rebecca Klapper, "Boy Scout, Cub Scout Membership Drops by 43% From 2019 to 2020," *Newsweek*, June 30, 2021, https://www.newsweek.com/boy-scout-cub-scout-membership-drops-43-2019-2020-1605652#:~:text=Membership%20in%20the%20Boy%20Scouts,provided%20to%20the%20Associated%20Press.

6   "Citizenship in Society," Boy Scouts of America Merit Badge Series, https://filestore.scouting.org/filestore/merit_badge_reqandres/CitizenshipSociety_ScoutReqs.pdf.

conservative parents, the Scouts' target demo. Most devastating of all, in 2019, the Church of Latter-day Saints, one of the Boy Scouts' strongest allies, withdrew all of its members over concerns of woke indoctrination, slashing the Scouts' membership overnight by 18 percent.[7]

The Boy Scouts have also suffered one of the worst sex abuse scandals ever to rock American public life. The Scouts reportedly kept "perversion files" that dated back to the 1940s, documenting scoutmasters and other adult leaders known to molest children. Rather than being removed and reported to the police, these predators were kept on the job or shuffled between troops where predictably they struck again.

As a result, the Scouts were whacked by a cudgel of lawsuits, including a class-action suit that included more than eighty thousand men who claimed they'd been molested in the organization as boys. That number is almost certainly inflated, as is usually the case with class-action suits, but the victims are very real and so was the cover-up. In 2020, the organization filed for bankruptcy, and while they've since exited amid a reorganization and a whopping $2.46 billion settlement with the victims, they've burned through significant resources and credibility in the process.[8]

Beyond even the molestation scandal, you might say in our heavily polarized times that the Scouts have fallen into the chasm between the two sides of the culture war. Conservatives are annoyed over that newfound wokeness, while the left views the organization as retrograde in any event. "Let the Boy Scouts die out, already," pronounced the liberal

7   Brady McCombs and David Crary, "Mormons pulling 400,000 youths out of struggling Boy Scouts," Associated Press, December 17, 2019, https://apnews.com/article/4415256925664852096cb7d57abe1df8.

8   Dietrich Knauth, "Boy Scouts' record $2.46 bln sex abuse settlement upheld by judge," Reuters, March 28, 2023, https://www.reuters.com/legal/judge-affirms-boy-scouts-americas-246-bln-sex-abuse-settlement-2023-03-28/.

New Republic in early 2020[9] (something people have been saying about the *New Republic* for years).

Yet while still acknowledging the horrors perpetrated within Scouting, it's worth noting exactly what the critics are proposing to euthanize. The Boy Scouts is one of the largest youth organizations in America. It is perhaps the last national organization that emphasizes traditional male pastimes like camping, hiking, and boating, and teaches self-sufficiency skills like first aid, knot-tying, and wilderness survival. It's a lifeline to many young boys who feel alienated and disoriented, or who just otherwise wouldn't have enough to do.

If it were to die off, what would the critics replace it with? The DMV? TikTok?

Even more portentous is the Catholic Church. I grew up Catholic so my papist bias may shine through here, but even the most ablaze Calvinist and lip-curled atheist must admit the extensive role played by the Church in our public life. It's the largest nongovernmental provider of schooling and health care in the country; it's the largest charitable organization with its extensive network of food banks and homeless shelters; it provides opportunities for civic participation with everything from the Knights of Columbus to Catholic Relief Services to Sunday altar serving.

All this is now fading away. Caught in between the culture wars à la the Scouts—the left assails it for opposing gay marriage while traditionalists chafe at Pope Francis for cracking down on the Latin Mass—with membership dwindling and parishes consolidating, the twenty-first century presents existential challenges for the rock of Saint Peter. Many of these wounds, of course, are self-inflicted. The largest conspiracy

---

9   Matt Farwell, "Let the Boy Scouts Die Out Already," *The New Republic*, February 21, 2020, https://newrepublic.com/article/156648 /let-boy-scouts-die-out-already.

to conceal molestation in the history of mankind has wrought what it will, emptying the pews in Catholic heartlands from New England to Ireland. The endless waves of Church wrongdoing can exhaust even the most devout of Catholic psyches. Growing up in the Catholic Church, the biggest obstacle to a faith in God was our society's rampant secularism. The second biggest obstacle was the Catholic Church.

But again it's worth asking: What alternative do the critics propose? What will fill the void as the Church in North America continues to downsize?

Once upon a time, the French writer Alexis de Tocqueville praised the United States for its voluntary associations, its community groups that brought people together and set them to work solving societal problems. Tocqueville saw such civic life as uniquely American and an essential guarantor of our liberty. He thought it strengthened our democracy and prevented an overbearing state from becoming the main implement of social reform.[10] Where the British might appoint a lord or the French a bureaucrat, the Americans tackled problems through genuine community.

Today, what we have is more like the nightmare of the conservative sociologist Robert Nisbet. Those mediating communal institutions are giving way, leaving just lonely individuals and the engorged and distant state that sends them checks in the mail.[11]

Here is a dilemma of the modern condition: We have more transparency than ever before, more capacity to hold the Scouts and Church to account than ever before, yet we remain just as human as ever before. Transparency has enabled us to look under the hood of just about every institution, while human nature has guaranteed we almost always find

---

10   Alexis de Tocqueville, *Democracy in America* (New York: Signet, 2010, originally published 1835–1840).

11   Robert Nisbet, *The Quest for Community: A Study in the Ethics of Order and Freedom* (Washington: ISI Books, 2010, originally published 1953).

wrongdoing, even hideous venality, when we do. Yet, if this pattern continues, every institution will end up discredited. Society itself will wither away.

We've got the moralizing zeal, but we don't have the constructive civic-mindedness needed to reform and when necessary rebuild the institutions we find lacking. That zeal, on the back of the existing trend toward Bowling Alone, will lead not toward renewal but isolation.

* * *

Read Tocqueville long enough and you might start to think that whereas Britain was once called a nation of shopkeepers, America is a nation of volunteers. It's a tradition that dates back to the 1730s when the country's first volunteer fire department was founded in Philadelphia at the encouragement of one Benjamin Franklin.

Volunteering was seen not just as necessary to stop the local smithy from going up in flames but as a means of accruing knowledge and character. As Franklin said, "You tell me, and I forget. You teach me, and I remember. You involve me, and I learn."

More recently, volunteer life has fallen into a state of crisis. The problem naturally came to a head during the pandemic: between September 2020 and September 2021, fewer than a quarter of American adults reported any kind of formal volunteer service, down from 30 percent in 2019.[12] But it also can't be blamed on the lockdowns alone—the problem had been building for decades. In 2002, the average number of hours worked by volunteers was fifty-two, while by 2017 it was

---

12   Erin Schneider and Tim J. Marshall, "At Height of Pandemic, More Than Half of People Age 16 and Over Helped Neighbors, 23% Formally Volunteered," data prepared by the US Census Bureau and Americorps, January 25, 2023, https://www.census.gov/library/stories/2023/01/volunteering-and-civic-life-in-america.html.

down to forty, by 2019 it was twenty-six, and come 2021 it was just twenty-five.[13]

The volunteer rate is trapped in a kind of feedback loop with Bowling Alone. As parishioners flock out of churches, those churches shut down and consolidate, robbing potential future volunteers of opportunities. Organizations like Scout troops and charities rely on volunteers as well, and without that willingness to step up and serve, they too can end up closing their doors for good.

The wreckage has been especially palpable among volunteer fire departments. The total number of volunteer firefighters across the country dropped 17 percent between 1984 and 2020.[14] The main culprit is a lack of young people signing up, which has resulted in a reduced and rapidly graying firefighting force.

This has led many to fault millennials for ruining fire departments just as it's led many to fault millennials for ruining everything (*Business Insider* once blamed us for ruining napkins!), but one fireman interviewed by NPR said the real problem was too much complexity and bureaucracy. "The big difference between then and now—if we joined tonight we could ride the truck tomorrow," he said. "It was none of this stuff. You got to do all the in-house training before you can ride."[15]

13 Leslie Lenkowsky, "Americans Are Volunteering Less. What Can Nonprofits Do to Bring Them Back?" *Chronicle of Philanthropy,* February 14, 2023, https://www.philanthropy.com/article/americans-are-volunteering-less-what-can-nonprofits-do-to-bring-them-back.

14 Frank Morris, "Volunteer fire departments that the US relies on are stretched dangerously thin," NPR, February 1, 2022, https://www.npr.org/2022/02/01/1077371659/volunteer-fire-departments-that-the-u-s-relies-on-are-stretched-dangerously-thin/.

15 Adam Bearne, "Volunteer firefighters are getting older. It could be a life-or-death issue," NPR, June 23, 2023, https://www.npr.org/2023/06/13/1181131195/volunteer-firefighters-older-shortage-younger-workers-fire#:~:text=Leaning%20on%20older%20volunteers%20has,and%20our%20ability%20to%20respond.%22.

The dwindling volunteer spirit can also be seen in another important metric: the military enlistment rate. The armed forces aren't volunteers in the strictest sense—they receive a salary and can turn their service into a lucrative career if they so choose—yet few organizations demand greater sacrifice from those who join. The individual is subsumed into the larger unit, setting aside his ambitions and needs in the name of national service. And the military, as PBS puts it, has reached "crisis levels of low recruitment."[16] The Army, Navy, and Air Force all fell well short of their 2023 recruitment goals by a combined forty-one thousand enlistees.[17]

The problem is one of both demand and supply. On the demand side, like the Scouts and the Church, the military has damaged its credibility. Where once it fostered courageous leadership, now it has a reputation for losing fruitless wars in faraway lands. Where once it was officered by men like Dwight Eisenhower and George Patton, now it seems led by political timeservers. Only 9 percent of Americans ages sixteen to twenty-one said they would consider enlisting in 2022.[18] And on top of that—this is the supply side—most Americans would be ineligible to serve anyway. Thanks to rising obesity, mental health issues, and other problems, only an estimated 23 percent of Americans

16 Ali Rogin and Andrew Corkery, "Why recruiting and confidence in America's armed forces is so low right now," PBS, August 13, 2023, https://www.pbs.org/newshour/show/why-recruiting-and-confidence -in-americas-armed-forces-is-so-low-right-now.

17 David Vergun, "DOD Addresses Recruiting Shortfall Challenges," DOD News, US Department of Defense, December 13, 2023, https ://www.defense.gov/News/News-Stories/Article/Article/3616786 /dod-addresses-recruiting-shortfall-challenges/.

18 Ben Kesling, "The US Army Expects to End Up 15,000 Recruits Short This Year," *Wall Street Journal*, July 18, 2023, https://www.wsj.com/story /the-us-army-expects-to-end-up-15000-recruits-short-this-year -b5e9de86.

ages seventeen to twenty-four qualified for military service in 2020, according to the Department of Defense.[19]

The recruitment drought is perhaps the direst consequence of America losing its volunteer spirit: without a robust military we can't defend our homeland (at least not without conscription). And as volunteerism has sagged, other essential functions have fallen away as well. Whether you favor a strong welfare state or a thinner safety net, every society needs charities to help the poor. Yet to take just one example, food banks in 2023 saw both volunteers and donations dwindle compared to previous years.[20] This tracked with a 2022 report by the group Giving USA that found Americans were donating the lowest portion of their disposable incomes to charities since 1995.[21]

Again, this feels not just like a warning light but a diminishment of the American character. Between 2009 and 2018, the United States ranked as the most generous country in the world when it came to charitable giving.[22] Such generosity has long been in our marrow, and rightly so: a rich nation can only be a good nation if it's animated by a spirit of noblesse oblige. Yet just when that charity is most needed, just

---

19   Jim Garamone, "After Tough Year, Military Recruiting Is Looking Up," DOD News, US Department of Defense, December 22, 2023, https://www.defense.gov/News/News-Stories/Article/Article/3625464 /after-tough-year-military-recruiting-is-looking-up/.

20   April Rubin, "Food bank demand high but donations fall," Axios, November 23, 2023, https://www.axios.com/2023/11/23 /food-banks-insecurity-donations.

21   Ivana Saric, "Americans are giving to charity at lowest level in nearly 3 decades," Axios, June 22, 2023, data from Giving USA, https://www .axios.com/2023/06/22/charitable-giving-donations-income.

22   "Why Americans Donate: What Motivates People to Give and What Causes Do They Give to?" UN World Food Program USA, November 14, 2023, data from CAF World Giving Index, https://www.wfpusa.org /articles/why-americans-donate-what-motivates-people-to-give-and -what-causes-do-they-give-to/.

when food banks are experiencing heightened demand amid rampant inflation while having to pay more themselves for the groceries they distribute, we're volunteering and donating less.

And again, it all ties together. Fewer parishioners in pews mean fewer contributions to Catholic Charities. Fewer Boy Scouts mean fewer food bank volunteers. And fewer of all of the above means less social capital and a pendulum that never seems to swing back.

* * *

So Americans are joining less, volunteering less, enlisting less. Yet at least before the pandemic we had a veritable ironwork of civic solidarity: the office happy hour.

The late, great American bard Toby Keith put it this way:

> Been a long day, no break
> We made it to the middle of the week
> And I'm thinking that I'm probably gonna need
> To get to know you casually
> Just having fun, two for one
> Watch a good time get a little better
> Ain't no ball and chain for the suits and skirts
> Just drinks after work[23]

And who could disagree? We might not be chucking heavy balls at military formations of white pins, but we could always head to some moldering dive with a name like O'McLanahan's accompanied by Joe from the next cubicle over and that one chick from accounting for a few half-priced Miller Lites until closing.

---

23 Toby Keith, "Drinks After Work," *Drinks After Work*, Show Dog-Universal Music, 2013.

Then came the pandemic. It wasn't just that the bars shut down; it was that the offices did too. Many of us were working from home, cut off from our coworkers, and as it turned out, that only made us want that Miller Lite all the more.

When COVID-19 first arrived, there was a brief debate as to whether governments should shut down the liquor stores. "Why should Total Wine stay open when the schools are closed?!" some cried. The answer was that an inability to obtain booze could force alcoholics into withdrawal and kill them. So in most states, after briefly shutting down, the liquor marts reopened. They wouldn't close again for the duration of the lockdowns.

This was the right call, but it had staggering consequences. Given that the gym and the Dave and Buster's had gone dark, there simply wasn't anything else to do. Alcohol sales in stores were 54 percent higher in March 2020 than they were in March 2019, according to Nielsen data.[24] Online sales of alcohol through services like Drizly increased by a whopping 243 percent over the previous year.[25]

As the pandemic wore on, our drinking plateaued a bit, but remained high. A Columbia University study found there were 20 percent more alcohol sales between March and September 2020 than over the same period in 2019.[26] A Rand Corporation study in the autumn

---

24 Nicole Caldwell, "How Alcohol Sales Have Shifted During COVID-19," *Newsweek*, data compiled by Nielsen, July 22, 2021, https://www .newsweek.com/how-alcohol-sales-have-shifted-during-covid-19-1564524.

25 Joseph V. Micallef, "How The COVID-19 Pandemic Is Upending The Alcoholic Beverage Industry," *Forbes*, data compiled by Nielsen, April 4, 2020, https://www.forbes.com/sites/joemicallef/2020/04/04/how-the -covid-19-pandemic-is-upending-the-alcoholic-beverage-industry/.

26 Joao M. Casteldelli-Maia, et al., "The concerning increasing trend of alcohol beverage sales in the US during the COVID-19 pandemic." *Alcohol* 96, November 2021, pp. 37–42, https://pubmed.ncbi.nlm.nih .gov/34245809/.

of 2020 found that the average frequency of drinking had risen by 14 percent compared to before the pandemic, and that women in particular were imbibing more.[27] A Harris poll from the summer of 2021 found that close to one in five Americans had reported "heavy drinking" over the previous thirty days.[28]

So it was that we were no longer even Bowling Alone; we were Drinking Alone. Those precious remaining beachheads of communal life had been shuttered by fiat. Stuck at home and robbed of the social support structures that might have helped us cope with a frightening pandemic, many of us turned to the bottle. This was the final frontier of our lonely atomization and it exacted a grim toll. According to the National Institutes of Health, alcohol-induced deaths increased 26 percent in 2020, and continued to rise in 2021.[29]

Drinking Alone is a social phenomenon, and we should distinguish it from drinking alone. If you want to have a beer or five by yourself after work, far be it from me to stop you. I'm a writer for goodness' sake—half the reason I'm about to end this section of the book is so I can go pour myself a tumbler of shimmering Irish.

But then, to come full circle, this is something that distinguishes Americans from those Europeans who imbibe more than we do and live

---

27   Michael S. Pollard, "Alcohol Consumption Rises Sharply During Pandemic Shutdown; Heavy Drinking by Women Rises 41%," Rand Corporation, September 29, 2020, https://www.rand.org/news /press/2020/09/29.html.

28   "New Survey Provides Insights into Drinking Behaviors During the Pandemic." Data compiled by Harris Poll for Alkermes, Inc., September 22, 2021, https://investor.alkermes.com/news-releases/news-release-details /new-survey-provides-insights-drinking-behaviors-during-pandemic.

29   "Alcohol-related deaths, which increased during the first year of the COVID-19 pandemic, continued to rise in 2021," National Institute on Alcohol Abuse and Alcoholism, April 12, 2023, https://www.niaaa .nih.gov/news-events/research-update/alcohol-related-deaths-which -increased-during-first-year-covid-19-pandemic-continued-rise-2021.

longer. To generalize for a moment: Euros do almost all their drinking socially, out with friends or over dinner with family. I've talked to more than one European who's been utterly baffled by American solo booze culture, the yuppie who heads home after work and pours himself a solitary glass of wine. Isn't sociality the entire point of getting drunk?

And maybe that helps explain the disparity between the mortality rates: alcohol isn't good for you but isolation *especially* isn't good. Either way, here in the United States, Drinking Alone was being used to fend off a very real darkness. It was the lubricant for a lonely America that had seen its institutions closed down, its public spaces roped off, and its sense of community withered into an arid isolation.

***

In March 2022, the *New York Times* noticed something interesting. In cities all across the country, even in cities where crime had otherwise fallen or at least remained flat, carjackings had skyrocketed.

In Philadelphia, the number of carjackings from 2019 to 2021 nearly quadrupled; in Chicago, there were an astonishing 1,900 carjackings in 2021. In Washington, D.C., carjacking has become a kind of crime au courant, with vehicles lifted in broad daylight from posh neighborhoods once thought safe.[30] An Exxon gas station across the Potomac not far from where I live made national headlines when a man whose car was being jacked pulled a gun on the perps and killed one of them.[31] (Things change quickly when you cross that Virginia line.)

---

30   Campbell Robertson, "'I Honestly Believe It's a Game': Why Carjacking Is on the Rise Among Teens," *New York Times*, March 1, 2022, https://www.nytimes.com/2022/03/01/us/car-theft-teens-pandemic.html.

31   Walter Morris, "Driver Shoots 2 Carjacking Suspects in Alexandria, Killing 1," NBC Washington, May 13, 2022, https://www.nbcwashington.com/news/local/northern-virginia/motorist-shoots-2-1-fatally-in-attempted-carjacking-in-alexandria/3051035/.

What's even more interesting is what happens after these vehicles are lifted: often the cars aren't stripped for parts or sold. They're found abandoned a couple of neighborhoods away, a pointless joyride for the lulz. The culprits are largely teenagers who will sometimes post a video of the offense to TikTok and watch the likes roll in.

This is something new in the history of modern crime, and the culprit is widely understood to be the pandemic, and its shuttering of after-school life. For years, these kids didn't have sports leagues to attend; when the *Times* ran its article, some of them were still "learning" from home. Without social networks, they were finding release on the streets.

And while there's obviously a chasm of difference between jacking an Acura and opening a Bud Light on the couch—the Acura has more flavor, for one—this outbreak of carjackings stems from the same withered branch as Drinking Alone. Both are disordered attempts to shake off boredom. Both are the dark consequences of losing our communal structure.

And while both have little precedent in this century, both might have been predicted by a student of history. After a plague brutalized ancient Athens during the Peloponnesian War, the historian Thucydides noted that "the catastrophe was so overwhelming that men, not knowing what would happen next to them, became indifferent to every rule of religion or of law." The sickness was "the beginnings of a state of unprecedented lawlessness" over which "no fear of god or law of man had a restraining influence."[32] Writing about the Plague of Cyprian six centuries later, Pontius of Carthage observed, "No one regarded anything besides his cruel gains. No one trembled at the remembrance of a similar event. No one did to another what he himself wished to experience."[33]

---

32 Thucydides, *History of the Peloponnesian War.*
33 Pontius of Carthage, *Life of Cyprian.* Excerpted online.

Plagues have a way of shredding communal fabrics and thus respect for consensual norms. And so too with our own plague, our own consequent sense of anomie. Without the Scouts and the Church, without the bowling league and the full-time office, without the drinks after work and the several additional rounds of drinks after work, it's not clear where that spark we need so badly as social creatures is supposed to come from.

CHAPTER 9

Of Congregationalists and Commitophobes

That's my name right there. The one you see on the book jacket. Matt Purple—that's how I've gone through life, noogies, wedgies, swirlies, and all. I'm always struck by how many people assume Purple is a pseudonym. It's as though if I could have had any last name I'd wanted I'd have jumped for the effeminate color.

I don't remember when I first became aware that my last name was different. This strikes me as strange because what is childhood memory except a catalog of embarrassments? I can clearly recall anxiety over having to wear glasses to school, self-consciousness over sucking at basketball—but little about the fact that my last name was, in fact, Purple.

The first memory I have of being teased for my name was during a stay at Boy Scout summer camp after the sixth grade. I'd signed up for the archery merit badge class, where I met a kid from a different troop with a malignantly flushed face and a crew cut. Garrett, he was called—Garretts were always bad news back then—and upon learning my name he assigned me the nickname Purple Nurple. I asked him what it meant and he proceeded to show me. He was a piece of work, Garrett, but I liked him in a jocular sort of way. The archery merit badge wasn't easy: you had to shoot a fifty with only ten arrows and a cheap wooden camp bow that was designed to be anything but accurate. I was one of only two boys who got the badge. The other was Garrett.

And how could I be mad at the other member of my little archery brotherhood? Purple Nurple? There are worse things in this vale of tears. So it was that Purple came to carry a surprisingly light stigma. Even in high school, I can only remember one particularly boring girl who used to chant "Purple" at me like an incantation, perhaps in the hopes of conjuring up for herself a life or a personality. It succeeded on neither count.

There were nicknames, to be sure, plenty of nicknames. And trust me: there isn't a single one you can try that I haven't already heard. Purple Rain. Purple People Eater. To this day, I'll still get approached by someone with a self-satisfied smile on his face like he's just invented nuclear fusion in his head, only to burst forth with: "Purple Haze!" *Bet you haven't heard that one before!* Yeah. Sure. A smile. A good-natured roll of the eyes. It's a reflex at this point.

Why didn't I get more grief over Purple? I've pondered this question and all I can think is there was a dash of Hollywood to it, a pinch of *Reservoir Dogs*. Actually there was another reason too: in any given subset of sniggering teenagers, Purple was only the second most hilarious last name on offer. There was always a Dick Cummings on hand to act as a human shield and absorb the abuse.

Still, being Purple in a classroom was one thing; being Purple as one half of a couple was another. And as the ravages of puberty descended, I began to wonder if I'd *ever* find a girl who wouldn't mind my last name. Thankfully I was dead wrong on this score: women loved it! It was almost a novelty item, an opportunity to one day vindictively tell your husband after you caught him checking out another chick at the mall that you'd dated a guy named Purple. And when I met my future wife and she told me on our second date that she would take her husband's last name no matter what it was, I thought I just might have found something here.

Yet even when I was feeling circumspect over my name, even when it put me at the mercy of the Garretts of the world (online comment sections are full of Garretts), I could never quite cast it off. A name is more than just identifying shorthand; it's a little placeholder in history, a link to your origins, where you come from. And in my case, where I'd come from was the place so many generations of Purples had come from, a town that had once bustled with factories and steamboats and river mills, yet has since crumbled into something much more grim.

* * *

The Purples of yore came to America early, during the 1670s, when they landed in East Haddam, Connecticut, a town near the mouth of the Connecticut River on Long Island Sound. A contingent of Purples remained there, but one of them, the esteemed Ezra Purple, headed north, following the river. Eventually he made his way to northwestern Massachusetts, not far from the Vermont border, where he settled in what is today the town of Greenfield. There his hue of Purples would remain for the next three centuries, farming the land and braving the frigid New England winters.

There is some dispute as to where the Purples initially came from. The most prevalent theory is they're English through and through, with whispers they might have been royalty or dye-makers—hence the last name. I have it on good authority there are several Purples buried in a churchyard in Bardfield Saling, a tiny village in eastern England with a lovely round-tower church and little else.

There is another theory about Purple, which holds it's actually French in origin and the Purples were Huguenot Protestants who fled to England after the St. Bartholomew's Day massacre in 1572. This makes some sense given that the Huguenots were persecuted Calvinists as were early American Congregationalists like the Purples. Yet it should be noted that this is a minority opinion among Purple historians (by which I mean my grandfather, my great-uncle, and a couple of researchers at Ancestry.com). It's also one I'm determined not to believe. I've spent my entire life thinking I'm descended from the ale drinkers of the British Isles and now you want to tell me I'm *French*?

Sacrebleu!

It would have been unfair to such flinty sorts as the Purples to expect them to stray too far from Greenfield. But some of them did give in to that American wanderlust. At least a few went to Boston or New York City. One of those New Yorkers, Edwin Ruthven Purple, was working as a clerk at a dry goods importing company when his boss abruptly announced he was closing his store and relocating to San Francisco. Those were the days of the 49ers, when many a restive Yankee was tempted westward by whispers of gold in them thar hills. So it was that in 1850, several months after his boss had left, Ed Purple boarded a steamship that took him through the Panama Canal and on to San Francisco.

He arrived only to find that his boss had decided opening a business in San Francisco would be too difficult (some things never change). So he'd sold what he had for a quick buck and left. Yet rather than return to New York, Purple remained in Northern California for the next decade, where he mined and kept a shop and was even elected justice of the peace. Yet by the end of the 1850s, opportunities for individual prospectors were fading. So Ed Purple turned east, first to Salt Lake City and then to Montana as it underwent its own gold rush. His journals and dispatches from Montana were later published in a 1995 collection called *Perilous Passage*, edited by the historian Kenneth N. Owens. They're a fascinating account of hard-drinking pioneers, Civil War–era tensions, and encounters with Native Americans—surely the most adventure any Purple had seen until that night I attempted to complete the Dupont Circle Pub Crawl.

It's all very exciting—until you get to Owens's assessment of Purple: "The account is valuable not because the author was a person of great charisma, remarkable abilities, or stunning insights. In professional achievement, business acumen, intuitive shrewdness, or even flair for literary expression, Ed Purple lacked any truly distinctive talents."[1]

Well! Surely genetics is an overrated discipline. Still, *Perilous Passage* was always there when I was growing up, sitting proudly on the table at my grandfather's house, its cover bordered in apropos violet and featuring a pencil sketch of old Ed holding a flintlock and looking like he was about to shoot the reader.

Yet Edwin Ruthven Purple was very much an exception. A few of my ancestors did go south and west—I still get an occasional email from a contingent of California Purples; part of having this last name is that anyone who shares it and sees your byline immediately contacts you—but most of them remained in and around Greenfield for the better part of three hundred years. Greenfield was their home. It was where they built houses, shops, families, legacies. It was where they attended the First Congregational Church of Greenfield, Massachusetts, the center of town life even after the brash upstart Second Congregational Church of Greenfield, Massachusetts, came along. It was where my great-grandfather, an electrician, started Purple Electric Company—and you already know what color he painted the

---

1   Edwin R. Purple, *Perilous Passage: A Narrative of the Montana Gold Rush, 1862–1863*, edited by Kenneth N. Owens (Helena: Montana Historical Society Press, 1995).

trucks that he ran up and down Silver Street. (Yes, purple trucks in Greenfield on Silver Street.)

All of which makes me wonder what those same Purples would think if they could see Greenfield today, if they could stroll down its streets and pop into a local establishment and marvel at how far things can fall.

***

It would be unfair to say that Greenfield today looks like a ghost town. There are still too many open shops, too many cars puttering to and fro from nearby Interstate 91. It would be fairer to say it looks like Greenfield has been ghosted, abandoned by those who were once charged with its wellbeing.

In this, it's hardly unique. The story of Greenfield is the story of a thousand other American towns. Once home to a thriving manufacturing base that produced taps and dies and metal tools, deindustrialization saw the factories move out and the capital stop flowing in. The town is ideally situated between three rivers, including the mighty Connecticut, yet with industry no longer a viable option, its geography became far less of an advantage. And with a host of competitive universities already clustered not far to the south, rebuilding via the eds-and-meds route never really stood a chance.

What was ultimately to prove Greenfield's ruin, however, was I-91. It's the main interstate in western New England, running south to New Haven, Connecticut, and north to the Canadian border, and it provides Greenfield with something many rural communities don't enjoy: an artery to both a major metropolitan area (New York) and a foreign country. In another age, this might have been an incredible asset, yet in our own time it's made Greenfield a pit stop on one of the Northeast's most harrowing drug corridors.[2] Sometimes called the Heroin Highway,[3] I-91 connects both the big-city drug scene and Canadian dealers to unsuspecting rural hamlets like Greenfield. Throw in the fact that Massachusetts has more lenient drug laws and penalties than surrounding states and you end up not just with demand but an incentive to make drugs in places like Greenfield.

The effects have been ravaging. In 2014, the late chef-turned-travel guru Anthony Bourdain brought his CNN show *Parts Unknown* to Massachusetts for an episode that focused on drugs. First it was off to Provincetown on the tip of Cape Cod, where Bourdain had worked as a chef in his younger years and where he'd become addicted to heroin. Then it was off to the other side of the state, to Greenfield, which had been ravaged by the same drug that had once ravaged him.

The most alarming moment of a very wrenching episode came when Bourdain was talking to a former druggie who had managed to kick her habit. Who was getting addicted here, he asked, who were all these small-town users? The woman chuckled. "Practically all of Greenfield," she said.

Bourdain ends his Massachusetts episode as he always does, on an optimistic note, heading to a clambake where residents have gathered flush with their region's democratic spirit to combat this plague.[4] Yet jump ahead and Greenfield has yet to heal. In 2021, Franklin County, of which Greenfield is the county seat, suffered its worst overdose rate

---

2   Patrick Johnson, "Opioid crisis: Highway to hell—how heroin infiltrates New England," Mass Live, June 16, 2015, https://www.masslive.com /news/2015/06/opioid_crisis_highway_to_hell.html.

3   "Community Remembers Those Who Succumbed To Addiction," *Hartford Courant*, November 8, 2016, https://www.courant.com/2016/11/08 /community-remembers-those-who-succumbed-to-addiction-2/.

4   "Massachusetts." *Anthony Bourdain: Parts Unknown*, starring Anthony Bourdain, directed by Toby Oppenheimer, aired on CNN, November 9, 2014.

on record.[5] Fentanyl, not heroin, is the culprit now, a drug so deadly that according to the DEA a single kilogram can wipe out half a million people. The dealers are simply innovating faster than the good guys can respond. As one county medical authority lamented to the *Greenfield Recorder*, "The numbers look so terrible, in spite of all our efforts. We've made more improvements and more changes to make it better, and it's so much worse."[6]

It sounds like a cliché, but the Greenfield I visited as a child really did feel like a postcard: rolling green pastures with lowing cows, covered bridges across burbling brooks spotted with shiny oval rocks, winding roads and Christmas tree farms and winters thick with snow. It was a place where the clock hands seemed to move a little slower, where no one ever seemed to mind sitting around for an entire afternoon and just *talking* to each other. For an impatient kid, that could be difficult to bear, as you sat and sighed and itched to visit your *other* grandparents, the ones with the Super Nintendo and the aboveground pool. For an adult with a needy toddler and a phone that won't stop buzzing, it sounds like bliss.

My dad always said it was a great place to grow up, and I'm sure many of his ancestors would have agreed. Speaking of which, the First Congregational Church of Greenfield, Massachusetts, the house of worship for so many generations of Purples, has since gone the way of so many of the town's other institutions. First opened in 1753, it survived all manner of bad winters and potential schisms, but it couldn't outlast the pandemic and closed in 2021.

---

5   Amy Sokolow, "Hampshire, Franklin counties, Athol see record-breaking opioid overdose numbers," *Boston Herald*, February 17, 2022, https://www.bostonherald.com/2022/02/17/hampshire-franklin-counties-athol-see-record-breaking-opioid-overdose-numbers/.

6   From the *Greenfield Recorder*, this article has been removed from the internet.

***

The Ballad of the Working-Class American Town is an overplayed lament, tinged with equal parts Billy Joel melancholy and John Cougar Mellencamp defiant grit. You know the lyrics: the factories closed, the fisheries shuttered, the college grads fled, and the working man was left behind with nothing but calluses on his hands and a suspiciously lovely crooning voice. It's the sort of track we yuppies listen to partly out of voyeuristic guilt and partly out of cheap solidarity—until we abruptly press pause because we're next in line at the Whole Foods register.

Likewise has there been a good deal of journalism about the spurned hard hat. The most famous book on the subject is *Hillbilly Elegy*, a memoir by J. D. Vance. Vance today is a United States senator from Ohio with a long history in finance and tech investment, but he grew up in an impoverished Appalachian town amid the demons of poverty and abuse and addiction. *Hillbilly Elegy* is his attempt to make sense of that childhood.[7] It's a good book, as books written by politicians before they know they're running for office often are (Barack Obama's *Dreams from My Father* was also compelling; 2006's *The Audacity of Hope* less so). And it turned Vance into a kind of emissary between worlds, a representative for the left-behind on *Meet the Press*. (That is, until he ran an unabashedly populist Senate campaign in 2022 and ticked off just about the entire political class.)

Against Vance, you might pit Kevin Williamson, a writer for *National Review* and native of West Texas. Williamson back in 2016 poured cold water all over those who would dare to sing lamentations to Allentown:

---

7   J. D. Vance, *Hillbilly Elegy* (New York: Harper, 2016).

> The truth about these dysfunctional, downscale commu-
> nities is that they deserve to die. Economically, they are
> negative assets. Morally, they are indefensible. Forget all
> your cheap theatrical Bruce Springsteen crap. Forget your
> sanctimony about struggling Rust Belt factory towns and
> your conspiracy theories about the wily Orientals stealing
> our jobs. . . . The white American underclass is in thrall to
> a vicious, selfish culture whose main products are misery
> and used heroin needles. Donald Trump's speeches make
> them feel good. So does OxyContin. What they need isn't
> analgesics, literal or political. They need real opportunity,
> which means that they need real change, which means that
> they need U-Haul.[8]

Trump supporters were understandably outraged by Williamson's con-
descension, and they turned that passage into an online rallying cry.
Yet credit Williamson with getting a few things right. Those in places
like Greenfield are indeed moral agents with their own responsibilities,
and to coddle them as mere victims of larger forces is to dehumanize
them almost as badly as Hillary Clinton did when she labeled them
"deplorables." And while plenty of writers love to romanticize the days
of black lung and powder factory explosions from the comfort of a New
York office building, those who live amid the industrial bones will often
echo Williamson. This place isn't what it used to be. Get out if you can.

In an exchange with the writer Michael Brendan Dougherty,
Williamson pointed out that American communities rise and fall all

---

8   Kevin D. Williamson, "Chaos in the Family, Chaos in the State: The
     White Working Class's Dysfunction," *National Review*, March 28, 2016
     edition, https://www.nationalreview.com/2016/03/donald-trump-white
     -working-class-dysfunction-real-opportunity-needed-not-trump/.

the time, often in tune with the availability of natural resources.[9] We've always been a mobile, restless people; in fact, that might be our defining quality. The pioneers headed west. The 49ers hunted for gold. Old Ed Purple bumbled around Montana.

But contra Williamson, what's different this time around is that it's not just a shuttered mine here and there. There is no precedent in American history for the widespread economic and geographic disruptions that have been wrought by deindustrialization. Those changes have been so stark as to blacken one of the great buzzwords of the twentieth century: "globalization." Once, globalization was seen as both inevitable and desirable, a made-in-China plastic toy chicken in every Fisher Price pot. But globalization in places like Greenfield has amounted to something far more ravaging. It's made some Americans feel less like opportunity seekers than toiling in the shadow of towering economic forces over which they have no control.

We usually think of individuals as being disenfranchised by oppressive government—Orwell's boot stamping on a human face forever is the most extreme example—but this can happen with private companies too, even if it's on a much smaller scale. When Xfinity refuses to credit your account despite their round-the-clock internet outages, when McDonald's charges $5 for a cold cheeseburger that was once on their dollar menu, when AT&T transfers your call back and forth within their "customer service" bureaucracy from hell, you feel helpless. Your dissatisfaction doesn't seem to matter because the corporation is so massive as to shrug you off. Your little lever of power, your threat to switch to a different company, doesn't register, because what is one customer against a huge blob? This issue of powerlessness is a consequence of the sheer bigness of globalization, and it's wrought its own consequences

---

9   Kevin D. Williamson, "More Garbuttiana," *National Review*, April 15, 2016, https://www.nationalreview.com/2016/04/white-working-class-donald/.

in turn. I doubt the market felt very "free" to the people of Greenfield who had no say over their industry picking up and leaving.

In 2023, the *Wall Street Journal* published one of the most revealing opinion polls I've ever seen. It asked simply what values people still considered important in life. What it found was that old standbys like patriotism, religion, and family had all starkly declined in perceived importance since the last time the question had been posed in 1998. There was only one value that had gone the other way: whereas in 1998, 31 percent had said making money was important, in 2023, it was 43 percent.[10]

What this suggests is that as capitalism has gotten bigger by way of globalization, as the individual has come to feel daunted by the multinational corporation, it's also encroached horizontally into people and institutions and spheres that were previously influenced by other values (almost like a cross of gold, come to think of it). Whereas the profit motive might once have existed in a balance with family life and allegiance to one's country, now those counterweights have fallen away.

Attitudes, it would seem, can trickle down too. Populists love to rail against money-grubbing CEOs who put profits before economic patriotism and basic morality. Yet even as we deplore hollowed-out flyover towns, even as we resent companies grown too big to care, our own values increasingly align with the money-grubbers. Many of us have up and left our hometowns, too, even if our motives for doing so are far more sympathetic (searching for a good job and quality of life rather than trying to reduce labor costs).

Perhaps such economic judgments are inevitable; perhaps they're even desirable in service of a robust and abundant business sector.

---

10   Aaron Zitner, "America Pulls Back From Values That Once Defined It, WSJ-NORC Poll Finds," *Wall Street Journal*, data compiled by NORC, March 27, 2023, https://www.wsj.com/articles/americans-pull-back -from-values-that-once-defined-u-s-wsj-norc-poll-finds-df8534cd.

Yet I can't help but think American capitalism has reached a kind of inflection point. Unchecked by other values, grown to enormous size, it lumbers along, elevating our GDP and unquestionably bequeathing to us a better standard of living in many respects. Yet in such untrammeled form, it also raises the question as to whether we've neglected things that matter, like the beating heart of a small town.

I have little right to talk. I left, too; went to college in the big city and stayed where the work was. My grandfather, the last Purple (to my knowledge anyway) who lived in Greenfield, was transferred to a nursing home in Connecticut years ago, and only a month before I finished this chapter, he passed away. A centuries-old historical tether was thus snapped. A place was deprived of a name, a name that had helped shape it, a name that had been shaped by it in ways I can never hope to fully comprehend.

CHAPTER 10

Dystopian Chic Comes to the Swamp

T hose who live outside Washington, D.C., love to complain about our nation's capital. They're rivaled in this only by those who live inside Washington, D.C.

We are a bunch of whiners, aren't we, my fellow Washingtonians? We complain about tourists standing on the wrong side of the Metro escalators, about the shortage of world-class restaurants compared to New York, and about the drunken interns ululating at the bar next door when we're just trying to get some sleep. We complain about living in the city, which is too expensive and noisy, and about living in the suburbs, which are too bland and bourgeois. We complain about our NFL franchise, the Washington Commanders née Football Team née Redskins, whose mediocrity is a betrayal of their deep roots in the region, and about our MLB franchise, the Nationals, whose excellence masks their lack of deep roots in the region. And we complain that we can't watch our *real* favorite sports teams, since so many of us come from somewhere else.

We complain about the crime, which has spilled out of the projects and into posher neighborhoods, as though it's anything new. Yet we complained about the crime years ago, too, when it was rarer and more contained. We complained during COVID-19 that people weren't social distancing, and we complain after COVID-19 because so many of our favorite restaurants have mysteriously shut down. We complain with particular fire about our public rail system, the Metro, which is periodically on fire. We complain about the traffic, the worst in the nation, and about the drivers, who seem like the worst in the nation. D.C. drivers have all the charm of Northern drivers and all the efficiency of Southern drivers. A Mercedes doing thirty in the passing lane with a middle finger out the window is emblematic.

I could do this all day.

We complain about the autumns, which are too short, the winters, which have too little snow except when it does snow in which case we complain about the lack of plows, and the springs, which are lovely but you can't tell because the pollen from the region's wide abundance of flora has sewn your eyes shut.

And we complain about the summers. Oh, Lord, do we complain about the summers. Live in D.C. long enough and you'll outgrow some of your complaining—I've learned to be more patient in the face of Metro delays—but bellyaching about the heat never gets old. It's the humidity that makes the difference, taking a base temperature of ninety-four degrees and kicking up the heat index to an easy 112. Step outside and it feels like the air is on fire. Head for a two-block stroll and you look like you've been hosed down by the fire department.

So we complain about our city being a literal swamp. And then we complain about those who call our city a swamp, the dreaded voters, who periodically send in their representatives to make our lives difficult. And it's here, as I finish complaining about the complaining, that the career moaners begin to separate from the mere whining wannabes. Most of those who slag off D.C. as "the Swamp" tend to be boomers who watch Fox News, but those in D.C. who trash D.C. are the young. Every year, a new class of them comes stomping off the Amtrak moaning performatively about "the corrupt establishment" and "Sodom on the Potomac" and swearing they'll move back to the Real America as soon as their fancy new jobs will allow.

You hear them and you think: those are the lifers. Those are the ones who are going to be here in thirty years, tending to their brick town houses in Shirlington and stopping by Old Ebbitt's for oyster happy hour. Because for all the flack D.C. gets, there's a lot of good to be had in this place, and like so many other places, that good isn't what it used to be.

***

Washington isn't the most culturally vibrant city in America—that would be New York. It isn't the most historically charming—Boston gets my vote there—or the most gloriously strange—New Orleans without question (pipe down already, Austin). There are areas of my city that reinforce all the worst stereotypes about it. The Farragut Square neighborhood, a commercial Duplo build of black glass and gray concrete, can feel on an overcast day like the most depressing place on earth. Capitol Hill can be a downer as well, with too many cheap-suited worker bees darting between too few good watering holes.

Yet there are some jewels in this rough. Washington isn't just a capital city; it's a *black* city, and some of its richest culture derives from its deeply rooted African American heritage. Welcome to U Street, the "black Broadway,"[1] where African Americans during the Jim Crow era ran their own "city within a city," the kind of place

---

1 "U Street: The 'Black Broadway' of D.C." *Main Street America* blog, February 26, 2020, https://www.mainstreet.org/blogs/national-main-street-center/2020/02/26/washington-dcs-u-street.

where everyone had to know each other because racism necessitated that commerce be kept local. The birthplace of jazz star Duke Ellington, U Street in its heyday was home to more than two hundred black-owned businesses. By night, it throbbed with gooey jazz notes and teemed with well-dressed men in hats and ties.[2]

While many of these venues have since shut down, replaced by more conventional bars and restaurants, there are still plenty of traces of what once was. One of the first places in D.C. that I used to haunt was a jazz club on U Street, which featured live music and allowed indoor smoking right up until the city banned it.

U Street today is a trendy nightlife district for the young—which is amusing in its own right given the way some yuppies talk about Washington's other African American bastions. When I arrived in D.C. in 2005, I didn't know much, but I knew Anacostia was Mordor. You didn't go to Anacostia. You didn't even set foot on Metro's green line, which has a stop in Anacostia. Good progressives would metamorphose into spewing Klansmen the second Anacostia was mentioned. Go to Anacostia, white people would whisper en route to bottomless mimosa brunch, and you'd be shot or stabbed or stomped to death by a giant cave troll the second you stepped off the train.

Having been to Anacostia on a few occasions—the first time out of sheer curiosity—I can attest that at least the cave troll part is untrue. The neighborhood, like many of D.C.'s largely black "east of the river" communities, struggles with poverty and crime and blight. Yet the contrast with the Farragut necropolis couldn't be starker: Anacostia is a place of life. People stop to chat on the sidewalk, play music from their cars with the windows down, and don't seem much worried about

---

2   Briana Thomas, "The Forgotten History of U Street," *Washingtonian*, February 12, 2017, https://www.washingtonian.com/2017/02/12 /forgotten-history-u-street-black-broadway/.

HOAs. Colorful murals brighten up the walls. Ornate manses from the neighborhood's better days loom behind tall fences, while so-called "abandominiums," brick buildings that have been taken over by the homeless and addicted, are reminders of complicated challenges.

Head north from Anacostia and you'll come upon Brookland, known as Little Rome for its Catholic presence, where the dome of the Basilica of the Shrine of the Immaculate Conception, the largest Catholic church in the country, towers over the Catholic University of America. At the other end of the moral spectrum, Adams Morgan to the west isn't quite Washington's "Latin Quarter," as Christopher Hitchens once put it, but its weird and debauched nightlife makes for a good time if you can steer clear of the projectile-vomiting college students (its signature establishment is a club called Madam's Organ). Nearby Dupont Circle is one of the most important historically gay locales in the country. And even Georgetown—overrated, iron-gated Georgetown—has some lovely row houses and cemeteries.

We should interrupt this episode of *Rick Steves's Swamp* to note that such diversity hardly makes Washington unique. In this way, it's just like any other city, a mix of different and jaggedly overlapping subcultures coming together to complain about the horrendous traffic. But the point is there's far more flavor here than the vanilla reputation would suggest.

There's one thing that really does set D.C. apart from everywhere else: the conversation. People from far away use the term "fast talker" as a pejorative for East Coasters, and nowhere is that truer than in D.C. The place is a natural magnet for those who have strong opinions about politics, current affairs, life—and who want to talk about them over a few Port City Monumental IPAs after work. This is a good city if you're looking to have a dialogue. The bar table is sacred here, a little democratic forum.

This is why those griping transplants always stay: their strong opinions mark them. Even boring old political Washington still has something to contribute.

* * *

If Washington is better than it's made out to be, then it's also followed the same course of late as most other American cities. Even its scrappy local industry, the federal government, hasn't been able to save it.

After decades of crime plunging in the District—a remarkable achievement given how dangerous the city had been as recently as the early 1990s—the pandemic has once again uncorked antisocial behavior. In 2023, D.C. clocked its worst homicide rate in twenty years, an increase of 36 percent over just the previous year. In addition to murders, robberies were up 67 percent over 2022 and vehicle thefts up an astonishing 82 percent.[3]

It's worth pointing out that the violent crime rate is nowhere near as high as it was at its peak in 1993.[4] Those were the days of dingy D.C., when cop cars would scream onto Fourteenth Street, now home to swanky wine bars and bistros, and send crackheads and prostitutes scattering.[5] But then an echo of the past could be heard in a viral video

3   Troy Pope and Simone De Alba, "'Grief Is a mountain' | Homicides in DC were up 36% in 2023—the most in 20 years," WUSA9, January 2, 2024, https://www.wusa9.com/article/news/local/dc/washington -dc-homicides-2023-crime/.

4   "District of Columbia Crime Rates 1960–2019," the Disaster Center, data compiled by the FBI, https://www.disastercenter.com/crime/dccrime .htm.

5   Marisa M. Kashino, "The Reinvention of 14th Street: A History," *Washingtonian*, April 4, 2018, https://www.washingtonian .com/2018/04/04/how-14th-street-came-back-reinvention-a-history/.

from 2021, which showed diners at one of those bistros scrambling as gunshots rang out (no one was hurt, thankfully).[6]

Across the city, at an Anacostia community meeting in May 2023, residents gave the mayor an earful about how juveniles seemed to serve little to no time behind bars after committing serious offenses.[7] This is a direct result of choices made by federal and local officials, starting with US attorney Matthew Graves, appointed by the Biden administration, who in 2022 declined to prosecute two-thirds of the cases that were brought to him by D.C. police.[8] (Graves blames this on a myriad of factors, including D.C.'s inept crime lab, which somehow managed to lose its accreditation between 2021 and 2023, and soft-on-crime city regulations.) Incredibly, the D.C. City Council, in early 2023, passed legislation that would have further weakened law enforcement, a measure so baffling that no less than President Biden flexed his federal authority over the capital city and blocked it.[9]

A friend tells a story: It was her first night working as a bartender at a watering hole not far from Nationals Park, where the Washington

6   Massie Graeme, "Diners flee upmarket restaurant favoured by Biden as two people shot in downtown Washington DC," *The Independent*, July 23, 2021, https://www.the-independent.com/news/world/americas/crime/diners-shooting-washington-dc-restaurant-b1889072.html.

7   Sam Ford, "Anacostia council, Mayor Bowser hear residents fears about spike in violent crime in DC," WJLA.com, May 30, 2023, https://wjla.com/news/local/gun-violence-shootings-crime-youth-anacostia-coordinating-council-mayor-muriel-bowser-lamont-mitchell-ron-moten-grapple-with-spike-in-violent-crime-in-dc-phillip-pannell.

8   Keith L. Alexander, "D.C. US attorney declined to prosecute 67% of those arrested. Here's why," *Washington Post*, March 29, 2023, https://www.washingtonpost.com/dc-md-va/2023/03/29/us-attorneys-office-charges-declined-dc-police/.

9   Claire Foran, "Biden signs measure to block controversial DC crime bill," CNN, March 20, 2023, https://www.cnn.com/2023/03/20/politics/biden-dc-crime-bill/index.html.

Nationals baseball team plays. Two men came in, ordered drinks, and began arguing. They left when the bar closed but apparently continued their disagreement just outside. My friend was stacking barstools on the tops of tables, looking forward to going home, when gunshots sounded. The two men had shot each other. One of them died.

Another story (and while I don't think much of trigger warnings, if you're a parent you may want to skip this one): A man was out for a walk with his baby girl in a stroller on a Sunday morning not far from Eastern Market, Washington's most popular farmer's market. He was accosted by a homeless man who threw a brick at the back of his head. The assailant then picked up the brick, threw it again, and hit the baby. Both father and daughter were okay, thank goodness, though a Good Samaritan who rushed in with ice and towels said there was blood everywhere. The baby had a gash on her face and was screaming inconsolably.[10]

Such stories are not unique to the post-COVID-19 era. But in a commuter city where many now have the opportunity to work from home, they only serve to turn off those who might otherwise come in. Washington's woes can be attributed not just to spiraling crime but the city's COVID-19 crackdown, which was one of the most draconian in the country. While most restaurants and other establishments in neighboring Virginia had reopened with at least limited service by late spring of 2020, and would never shutter again, Washington spasmed back and forth between limited openings and sudden closures.

The results are palpable and saddening. Washington's Seventh Street was always a bit gauche: home to the Verizon Center where the Capitals NHL team plays and a Chinatown that's little more than an

---

10 Don Parker, "'Bleeding everywhere': Man, baby in stroller attacked by brick thrower on Capitol Hill," WJLA.com, December 19, 2021, https://wjla.com/news/local/bleeding-everywhere-man-baby-in-stroller-attacked-by-brick-thrower-on-capitol-hill-mpd-anc-commissioner-denise-rucker-krepp.

Asian-themed arch, it can feel like a poor man's Times Square with flashing billboards and over-the-top sports bars. Yet head to Seventh Street today and even that's gone. Only a handful of bars remain, final redoubts against the balloon-lettered vacancy signs and real estate agent phone numbers. Windows where reflections from the Verizon Center's neon once danced with faint, alluring lights from within have gone dark.

So it's gone in drags all across the District. Entire shopfronts, blocks, neighborhoods have been euthanized by the public health regime. Walking through it, you get the sense that casualties aren't just measured in human form (though there's plenty of that as well). And when it comes to the wreckage, not all restaurants are created equal. The family-owned dive bar and the hole-in-the-wall diner naturally had less capital on hand than the franchise restaurant owned by the Dow Jones–traded company. That's another thing you notice if you stroll the D.C. streets: they feel more corporate than they used to, more steel and glass, more national chains.

***

American cities, at least relative to their European counterparts, can feel like they aren't built at a human scale. We don't go for those short store-fronts with the inviting colorful paint, those narrow streets that keep cars at bay—give us towering skyscrapers and yawning seas of asphalt.

Yet even against this, there's something about post-COVID-19 Washington that feels less natural than it did before. And what's stranger is that the people come off the same way.

The change began after the COVID-19 lockdowns as a kind of pop-ulist revolt against the Madison Avenue mandarins. The couch-bound emphasis on comfort that everyone got used to during quarantine spilled into the streets. Suddenly activewear was hot, sweatpants and other soft pants were in vogue, and skin was being shown as never before. The buzzword hanging over all this was *shameless*, as that

COVID-19-era aversion to dressing up—why should you put on a belt when no one except your goldfish was going to see you?—merged with hybrid back-to-work necessity.

Yet what we have today isn't just shameless so much as inauthentic. Crashing down on the sidewalks has come a tidal wave of piercings, ear gauges, navel stones, thick glasses, back tattoos, arm tattoos, ankle tattoos, facial tattoos, pink hair, blue hair, green hair, wigs, Botox, breast implants, BBLs, bracelets, and backturned baseball caps, all thudding and clanking by, like so much detritus after a hurricane. The obsession is with falsity, with putting on display that which is not us. It's as though what we've been given by nature isn't enough, that every wrinkle must be stapled over and every biological reality enhanced.

There's something transhumanist about it; there's also something dystopian, like we're dressing for decline. I want to make clear that, grumbling stodge though I am, I have no problem with tattoos or periwinkle hair (especially if that's your natural color). And while I'm not one for injections or piercings, if you think what your look really needs is a railroad spike shot through the skin between your nostrils, then I'm not going to ruin your fun. (I suspect much of this fashion can be blamed on Instagram. If you've decided you're an "influencer"—something you can only anoint yourself, never become—and you constantly need to look like a product for two-dimensional consumption, then a little artifice can go a long way.)

But it is curious how the look seems to fit the scenery. Our post-COVID-19, corporatized cities feel a little less human; so do the humans. Call it dystopian chic—and there are worse things than almost getting mowed down by a dude on a scooter who instead of ringing a bell just nods because his head has so many piercings that you can hear the metal ringing from miles away. But it's difficult to walk around such a place and think: *this* is where I'd pay insane rent rates to live. *This.*

***

They say that as goes California so goes America, but I'm not sure that's true. As San Francisco's Tenderloin District buckles under homelessness and addiction, Washington's public parks have been largely cleared of tents and needles. As Los Angeles struggles with smash-and-grab robberies, D.C.'s businesses aren't at the same level of risk. East Coast cities have their fentanyl problems and open-air drug markets, but generally they're better patrolled than their West Coast brethren. There is nothing out here so postapocalyptic as Portland, Oregon.

But these problems, even if they aren't applied evenly, still seem to be universal. Loosey-goosey drug policies, soft-on-crime DAs, and dispirited police departments have combined with a post–COVID-19 torpor and Drinking Alone thirst for catharsis to tarnish America's urban gems. The best one can say about Washington right now is that it's in a state of transition, struggling to discern what comes next now that its Obama-era glamor years are over. And just how do you attract bars to a downtown when only 45 percent of workers are showing up to their offices in any given week?[11] How do you lure in restaurants when the Washington power breakfast and the three-martini lunch are relics of the past? How do you bring back merchants of any kind when online shopping has had such a throttling effect on brick-and-mortar retail?

For those who tack right like myself, the temptation is to use the challenges facing our cities as political ammunition, examples of what happens when left-wing wish lists become reality. And by all means, let's scratch that itch. I'll complain about Washington again and so will you. But if America is farmhouses refracting rays

---

11   Paul Schwartzann, "Downtown D.C.'s struggles mount as many workers remain remote," *Washington Post*, data compiled by Kastle Systems, January 27, 2023, https://www.washingtonpost.com/dc-md-va/2023/01/27/downtown-dc-office-buildings-remote-workers/.

of sun across verdant pastures, then it's also the National Mall with its marble tributes to better men, the National Archives and Library of Congress preserving what was once a very written-down nation, the seat of our republican government. That D.C. is in such a state is just as much a shame as the trials that have consumed America's deindustrialized torso.

CHAPTER 11

Wokeness Is the Religion of Decline

O f all the intellectual micro-booms to come out of the twenty-first-century weirdscape, the New Atheist movement was surely among the most curious. Led by the self-styled Four Horsemen of the Apocalypse—Richard Dawkins, Christopher Hitchens, Sam Harris, and Daniel Dennett—the New Atheists emerged back in the mid-2000s with a game-changing proposition: it was okay not to believe in God. Here was a message so radical that anywhere from one to two people in any given *Daily Show* audience might not have instantly applauded it. And you could tell the Four Horsemen were an intellectual force to be reckoned with. Two of them (not one) had Oxford accents.

The New Atheists spent their time in the public eye making arguments such as: God is a spaghetti monster. And: belief in God is irrational but belief in the multiverse is not. And: Stalin's genocidal atheist regime was secretly a theocracy. And then, without warning, they disappeared. They disappeared so abruptly that revisiting them today can feel like a—forgive me, heathens—act of mercy. In Graham

Greene's masterful novel *The End of the Affair*, Sarah Miles writes in her diary about a militant atheist she's been visiting: "Could anyone be so serious, so argumentative about a legend? . . . I had gone to him to rid me of a superstition, but every time I went back his fanaticism fixed the superstition deeper."[1] This is how one feels reading the New Atheists today. The sheer effort expended in kicking a now-moribund Christianity undermines the project.

Yet I actually have a soft spot for the New Atheists. One cheer for those hellbound pencilnecks, say I. Yes, Richard Dawkins's book *The God Delusion* is a marathon exercise in running with scissors, here lacerating itself on the history of the early Church and there impaling itself on Aquinas's proofs of God until you really do leave convinced that man could only have evolved from witless apes.[2]

But then Christopher Hitchens, the brightest of the New Atheists, is on firmer ground in his book, *God Is Not Great*. Hitchens mostly ducks the thorny questions of science and philosophy in favor of cataloging the atrocities that have been committed by the religious.[3] This is the strongest argument against faith: that it can blinker man into doing terrible things he otherwise wouldn't do.

It's because of this argument that the New Atheists ended up finding their moment. The United States on September 11, 2001, was attacked by religious extremists who believed they were on a mission from God. The response to that attack was helmed by a president who seemed to think much the same. George W. Bush referred to the war on terror as

---

1   Graham Greene, *The End of the Affair* (London: Penguin Books, 1962, originally published 1951).

2   Richard Dawkins, *The God Delusion* (London: Bantam Press, 2006).

3   Christopher Hitchens, *God is Not Great: How Religion Poisons Everything* (New York: Hachette, 2007).

a "crusade,"[4] spoke about being on a mission to "rid the world of evil,"[5] and sometimes sounded like he had the Almighty Himself conferencing into the situation room.

The public initially supported Bush, even if they weren't entirely comfortable with the chain mail he kept wearing to press conferences. Yet as the war in Iraq wore on, as our "nation-building" begat sectarian strife and civil war, the rest of us began to wonder what to make of this dispensation from God gone wrong. Into this void stepped the New Atheists (ironic, given that one of them, Hitchens, had backed the war in Iraq as a means of replacing Saddam Hussein's dictatorship with a secular democracy). There was, at least in fashionable circles, a thirst for an alternative to both Bushism and Islamism, one that elevated reason over fundamentalist religion, caution over evangelical crusade. It was here that the Four Horsemen could provide.

Yet the New Atheists, for all their claims to skepticism and scientific realism, were themselves fairly utopian. They sought to argue religious belief out of existence, to ridicule it as adherence to absurd myth, a weird teething phase of our species' infancy. What they dreamed of was a new world, secular and pluralistic, where logic and science would flourish. They wanted to finish the work of the Enlightenment, which they believed would usher in more progress, more comity, more peace.

But that vision, like so many idealisms that came before it, wasn't to be. The United States today is losing its Christianity at a rapid pace, yet what's taken its place among much of the American elite has not been

---

4   Peter Waldman and Hugh Pope, "'Crusade' Reference Reinforces Fears War on Terrorism Is Against Muslims," *Wall Street Journal*, September 21, 2001, https://www.wsj.com/articles/SB1001020294332922160 #:~:text=But%20the%20president's%20reference%20to,vows%20 to%20defend%20American%20values.

5   George W. Bush, "Bush Remarks at Prayer Service," *Washington Post*, September 14, 2001, https://www.washingtonpost.com/wp-srv/nation /specials/attacked/transcripts/bushtext_091401.html.

secular rationalism but a new and strange theology, one that makes even the most barking revival-tent fundamentalism look pretty good.

***

As the New Atheists fell victim to natural selection, three important developments were greasing the rise of the new faith.

The first came in 2015 when the Supreme Court handed down its decision in *Obergefell v. Hodges*, which wiped out countless state-level laws and made same-sex marriage legal across the land. What happened next was that LGBTQ activists notably did *not* declare "mission accomplished" and go home to rake the leaves. Instead they whirled around and exclaimed, "All right, what's next?!"

What was next was trans rights, the reordering of everything around the idea that "binary" ideas of sex (i.e., men and women) were a myth and "gender"—a more elastic word—was elective. That meant bathrooms had to be desegregated, new pronouns had to be mapped out, drag queens had to be helicoptered into children's birthday parties. About three seconds after the gay marriage fight was won, the next frontier of the sexual revolution was already being blazed.

The second big development came in 2020 when a black man named George Floyd died during an arrest at the hands of Minneapolis police officers. This sparked protests in support of racial justice that quickly mushroomed into something like a panic. "Black lives matter!" cried white REI employees in Montpelier as they assembled their Molotov cocktails (carefully this time lest they accidentally set their cats on fire again). Yet even as the unrest of that dismal summer flamed out, the fixation on race never did.

There was a sense after George Floyd that everything needed to be redirected toward the struggle against racism. Even COVID-19 prevention briefly took a back seat, as public health officials discovered that bigotry was a carcinogen or something.[6] And all this was fueled by a third (and prior) development: the election of Donald Trump as president of the United States.

What Y2K was supposed to be to computers, Trump was to the human brain: millions of them just stopped working. Sprockets exploded out of ears from sea to shining sea to the tune of the "1812 Overture." And among Trump's many haters, this manifested into a feverish sense that Something Needed to be Done. That Something was ultimately for the left to double down on identity politics. Trump was saying things they didn't like about Mexican immigrants? They would defend Mexican immigrants as never before. Trump was seen as a champion of working-class whites? They would make clear that all whites had privilege, even if their fathers had died in a coal mine.

The result of all this, of channeling the left's anti-Trump absolutism through the new identity politics of sex and race, was—you've been waiting for this word, haven't you?—*wokeness*. And once upon a time that meant something very different than it does today.

"Woke" originated in the mid-twentieth century as African American slang, denoting someone who was alert to the difficulties faced by blacks in the United States.[7] It was then culturally appropriated by white liberals who, as white liberals are wont to do, found a way to make it worse. Seppuku-inducing terms entered the hipster

---

6　Georges Benjamin, "Racism is an ongoing public health crisis that needs our attention now," press release from the American Public Health Association, May 29, 2020, https://www.apha.org/news-and-media /news-releases/apha-news-releases/2020/racism-is-a-public-health-crisis.

7　Domenico Montanaro, "What does the word 'woke' really mean, and where does it come from?" NPR, July 19, 2023, https://www .npr.org/2023/07/19/1188543449/what-does-the-word-woke-really-mean -and-where-does-it-come-from.

vocabulary, such as "woke bae," which referred to a lover who was deemed sufficiently hysterical about social justice causes.

"Woke" was mainstream on the left for a few years, only to be captured by the right. Conservatives turned it into a pejorative, a way of ridiculing bougie Brooklynites who believed ordering from a socially conscious sushi joint was akin to being a Freedom Rider. The left then ditched the term, while conservatives ran with it and ultimately extended it over everything they found distasteful. I once got an email from a particularly indigestion-afflicted right-wing organization demanding I "fight the wokeness at Fox News." If Sean Hannity is woke, then not just "woke" but all words have lost their meaning.

There's no question that "woke" as a term has been devalued. But it remains the best signifier we have for a distinct school of thought, one that draws upon Karl Marx and the 1960s liberation movements, the French deconstructionists and the American critical race theorists, yet one that didn't come into its own until the blood-to-the-head rush of the Trump years. It's an ideology that's hardened into a theology, not in the sense that it believes in a god but in that it subscribes to a kind of political and cultural concept of the sacred, sacralizing as never before categories of race and sexual orientation, as well as ideas of victimhood and oppression. It would be nice if we could come up with a better word for it, given how important it is. But we haven't, and so I'll continue to use "woke" here, however reluctantly.

***

The rise of transgender ideology brought with it a zillion new genders and sexual categories. The Black Lives Matter moment catapulted skin color and ethnicity back into the public consciousness. Into the left's waiting room spilled Blacks, Latinx, Asians, Indigenous, Pacific Islanders, gays, lesbians, transgenders, agenders, pangenders, cisgenders, gender-fluids, pre-ops, post-ops, queers, questioning, BIPOCs, allies, decolonizers, and white chicks from Bed-Stuy looking lost, all motioning and clamoring while a single receptionist tried to hand out forms.

Wokeness was a kind of natural reaction to prevent the food-fight scene from *Blazing Saddles* from breaking out. These disparate identities unlocked by the trans movement and the racial reckoning needed to be cohered into some kind of political and social order. Wokeness attempted to do this via a subset concept called intersectionality. Intersectionality means simply that identities intersect, that how an individual is perceived and treated can be affected by his race, gender, and so on. Yet in practice, it came to mean common cause, that there was overlap between the struggles of Asians and trans and Latinx. Everyone was on the same team in the struggle against straight white male power (including straight white males who were willing to be "allies"). Everyone was in the same—conveniently enough—political coalition. Everyone was in the same broad church.

While wokeness is primarily political, its Trump-era absolutism has also turned it into a kind of substitute faith for a bourgeois rapidly shedding its Christianity. This is an oft-made claim but it's worth briefly examining here. Like many religions, wokeness attempts to distill competing claims—all those squawking identity groups—into a single body of dogma. And while such cohesion is important, wokeness also, like many religions, divides up its followers into a hierarchy, not of bishops and cardinals but those all-important identity groups, ranked according to how oppressed they are. "Believe all women," though not all men. Celebrate blackness, reform Latino culture into "Latinx," and dismiss whiteness as a toxin. To be a victim is the ultimate prize; to be an ally is yeoman-class; to be anything else is fascist. Intersectionality both brings together identities and dictates that under certain circumstances some must give way to the claims of others (i.e., "Latino" must be de-gendered to "Latinx" so the trans aren't offended).

Wokeness is thus an act of synthesis (some might even call it catholicity). It's collectivist, assimilating its adherents into a greater structural order, but it's also individualist. This can seem like a paradox but it's actually quite common across religions. The Catholic Church requires parishioners to submit to a single catechism, yet it also cares deeply about the individual soul. *You* have committed sins; *you* are loved by God; *you* can be saved by his grace and mercy. *Your* choices and *your* life matter, even amid a cosmos that seems indifferent to you. Catholicism thus provides the individual with structure, a set worldview, a warm place in the hierarchy, as well as personal recognition, liberation, and salvation.

This is wokeness's appeal too. It offers both a larger build for the individual based on identity politics, tells him exactly who he needs to atone to and who he needs to burn at the stake (i.e., cancel), and assures him that he counts, absolves his white guilt or validates his personal dramas by making them about larger struggles against racism or sexism. It even allows him to select his place in the hierarchy to a degree, "identifying" as different genders and even races.

For a post-Christian bourgeois that had little desire to return to the old faith but still felt disoriented amid the twenty-first century's atomizations and pressures, this sense of both positioning and attention was welcome. Even many who remained nominally Christian were drawn in, as "Black Lives Matter" banners and even trans flags were unfurled outside churches.

So it was that wokeness raced across the suburbs and metroplexes, the first ever religious awakening to catch on via social media. Corporations were opening shiny new diversity offices. Schools were shepherding teachers and students alike into seminars that informed them exactly how racist they were. Universities were offering classes with names like Queering God: Feminist and Queer Theology

(Swarthmore College)[8] and Latinx Sexual Dissidence and Guerrilla Translation (Davidson College).[9] And the military was helmed by Joint Chiefs chairman General Mark Milley, who declared that he was interested in studying "white rage."[10]

In Manhattan, a so-called "community education council" meeting descended into acrimony as the (largely white) members screamed at each other over perceived social justice shortcomings.[11] In Ontario, a trans teacher showed up to school wearing enormous prosthetic breasts and was later defended by the principal.[12] In Loudoun County, Virginia, a trans student at a high school entered a women's bathroom and raped a girl; the woke school administration then quietly covered

8　Bethany Tortenson, "College course teaches students about 'queering the Bible,'" *College Fix*, December 22, 2017, https://www.thecollegefix.com/swarthmore-course-teaches-students-queering-bible/.

9　Spencer Brown, "12 Of The Craziest College Classes In America, All Subsidized By Your Tax Dollars," *The Federalist*, February 20, 2019, https://thefederalist.com/2019/02/20/12-craziest-college-classes-america-subsidized-tax-dollars/.

10　Alex Horton, "Top US military leader: 'I want to understand White rage,'" *Washington Post*, June 23, 2021, https://www.washingtonpost.com/powerpost/republicans-joint-chiefs-chairman-critical-race-theory-congress/2021/06/23/84654c34-d451-11eb-9f29-e9e6c9e843c6_story.html.

11　Phil Shiver, "NYC education meeting turns into parody of woke politics as members spend 90 minutes scolding each other about white supremacy," *The Blaze*, July 7, 2020, https://www.theblaze.com/news/nyc-education-meeting-parody-woke-politics.

12　Joe Warmington, "Trans teacher Lemieux returning to classroom—this time in Hamilton," *Toronto Sun*, August 26, 2023, https://torontosun.com/news/local-news/warmington-trans-teacher-lemieux-returning-to-classroom-this-time-in-hamilton.

up the crime and the student was transferred to another school where he struck again.[13]

At Disney, Minnie Mouse was stripped out of her iconic red dress in favor of a girlbossing blue pantsuit (thereby finally showing up that noted stalwart of the patriarchy, Goofy).[14] At Lucasfilm, president Kathleen Kennedy became so obsessed with trying to shoehorn diversity into every production that it coined a new *South Park* catchphrase: "put a chick in it and make it lame and gay!"[15] And at Budweiser, a promo was released starring trans influencer Dylan Mulvaney that triggered such blowback that Bud Light lost its status as America's number one selling beer to the Mexican lager Modelo (the trans-versus-Latinx intersectional war the woke had long feared).[16]

The woke were infiltrating our institutions, warping our morality, suspending our common sense, and drawing our backlash. Such invincible mania can't be explained by bourgeois fashion alone. Here was an example of how overriding the religious impulse can be, and how destructive it can be when placed in the service of bad religion. It almost made you feel sorry for poor Richard Dawkins. Over the course of just a few years, a cheerily secularizing American middle class had been

---

13   "Virginia family sues school system for $30 million over student's sexual assault in bathroom," Associated Press, October 6, 2023, https://apnews .com/article/loudoun-virginia-lawsuit-transgender-bathroom-sexual -assault-a26168568cc20c2aa6cec9bef50e7c3f.

14   Jacqui Palumbo, "Minnie Mouse is trading her iconic red dress for a new look," CNN, January 27, 2022, https://www.cnn.com/style/article /minnie-mouse-stella-mccartney-pantsuit/index.html.

15   Stephanie Hamill, "'Put a Chick in It and Make It Lame & Gay!': South Park Special Nukes Woke Disney," NewsBusters, October 30, 2023, https://www.newsbusters.org/blogs/culture/stephanie-hamill/2023/10/30 /put-chick-it-and-make-it-lame-gay-south-park-special.

16   Amanda Holpuch, "Behind the Backlash Against Bud Light," *New York Times*, November 21, 2023, https://www.nytimes.com/article/bud-light -boycott.html.

abruptly conquered by a new faith. Christianity was scarcely out the door when the next creed came stomping in.

Yet if wokeness is theocratic zealotry gone mad, we should be fair and note that it's also noxiously anti-American. This is true in the most literal sense: woke theology, as we'll see, applies a simplistic litmus test of racist versus antiracist, homophobic versus allied. And since many of America's historical figures were imperfect by the standards of today, they fail that test and must be tossed out tout de suite, their names blackened and their statues torn down.

But wokeness is also anti-American in a more fundamental sense. It's the theology of a people who have lost confidence in themselves, their nation, their heritage, their blessings, their decency. It's a theology of decline. To understand why, we must turn to its bishops, those responsible for setting its doctrine.

***

Ibram X. Kendi does not strike you as a maniac. The author of *How to Be an Antiracist* and one of the most visible woke thinkers today—he was named one of 2020's most influential people by *Time*,[17] one of 1960's most influential magazines—Kendi comes off on the page as the sort who would hold the door open for you and then say sorry for being in your way.

Kendi begins *How to Be an Antiracist* by taking aim at himself over a speech he gave at an oration contest when he was in high school where he criticized black youth culture. He now says this was racist and ruefully notes the applause of the audience as evidence of systemic

---

17 Al Sharpton, "The Most 100 Influential People of 2020: Ibram X. Kendi," *Time*, September 20, 2020, https://time.com /collection/100-most-influential-people-2020/5888207/ibram-x-kendi/.

racism.[18] Later on, he tells a story of his college days when he broke up with a girl because he'd been embracing his black identity and thought she wasn't dark-skinned enough.[19] Time and again he returns to this theme: he was racist, he is racist, he struggles every day to do better.

In this, *How to Be an Antiracist* is the work of a penitent. It's the *Confessions* of the woke religion, with Kendi its soul-baring St. Augustine, the revealing chronicle of the sinner's journey into the faith. And it's for this reason that Kendi is the best spokesman wokeness has to offer. He doesn't claim to be some enlightened multiculturalist hovering over the masses on a cloud of vapor. He also doesn't deny that black people like himself can be bigoted (though he says this isn't as much of a problem because whites have far more power).

Yet it's a false modesty. If Kendi condemns himself, it's only because he's condemning an entire society wholesale in which he happens to be acculturated. The West from start to finish is awash in racism, a term defined by Kendi with extraordinary elasticity. "Racial inequity (or disparity) is when two or more racial groups are not standing on approximately equal footing," he writes. It then follows, says Kendi, that "A racist policy is any measure that produces or sustains racial inequity or injustice. An anti-racist policy is any policy that produces or sustains racial equity or justice."[20] And lest you think the vast complexities of life mean there might be other categories, Kendi brings bad news: "There is no such thing as a nonracist or race-neutral policy," he says.[21]

---

18   Ibram X. Kendi, *How to Be an Antiracist* (New York: One World, 2019), loc. 213 (note: because the Kindle edition was used, all citations will employ locations, roughly corresponding to paragraphs, rather than page numbers).

19   Kendi, *How to Be an Antiracist*, loc. 2087.

20   Kendi, *How to Be an Antiracist*, loc. 417.

21   Kendi, *How to Be an Antiracist*, loc. 422.

This is the chasm that slices through Kendi's thinking: racist versus antiracist, one or the other, take your pick. Everything we do, every action we take, must be judged on whether it combats bigotry. "The most threatening racist movement is not the alt right's unlikely drive for a White ethnostate," he writes, "but the regular American's drive for a 'race-neutral' one."[22] Even striving for equality must fall into the racist category since in the end it doesn't go far enough. What's really needed isn't equality but equity, which raises or lowers everyone to the same chalk mark on the wall regardless of circumstances or merit, a conformity of outcomes rather than opportunities.

In Kendi Land, there's no such thing as cultural responsibility and very little room for personal responsibility either. Everyone is swept along by the great algae tides of racism. Yet what of the fact that black people are far more likely to be killed by their fellow blacks than by whites or the police, while the homicide rate among blacks is far higher than among whites?[23] Isn't that a scrambling of Kendi's victimization narrative? Kendi demurs: "Internalized racist ideas are the real Black on Black crime," he sighs.[24]

This is where Kendi's sunny, buy-you-a-beer disposition sours into something crueler. The driver gunned down at random in inner-city Baltimore, the Chicago youths chewed up by gang violence—this is the fault of the ghost of the Ku Klux Klan? Or what of the fact that, back in the age of segregation, about 24 percent of black babies were born out

22 Kendi, *How to Be an Antiracist*, loc. 490.

23 "2019: Crime in the United States," "Expanded Homicide Data Table 6: Race, Sex, and Ethnicity of Victim by Race, Sex, and Ethnicity of Offender," FBI, https://ucr.fbi.gov/crime-in-the-u.s/2019/crime-in-the-u.s.-2019.

24 Kendi, *How to Be an Antiracist*, loc. 222.

of wedlock, whereas in 2008 the number was 72 percent?[25] Is the government, which reports these statistics, racist? Are numbers themselves?

It would seem so. Kendi has already smeared himself as a racist, and that only puts him in good company. Among the other things he reveals to be racist are capitalism, deregulation, denying that one is a racist, opposing Obamacare, the Bush family (all of them), distributing COVID-19 vaccines evenly to people of all races, standardized testing, the achievement gap, noticing the achievement gap, and watching reenactments of the Battle of Bull Run. Life itself is also racist because whites on average live four years longer than blacks. This presumably makes God racist, though after reading Kendi my guess is he skipped town long ago.

This is the appeal of Kendi's thinking: it doesn't require you to think. Deeply complex problems like the black crime rate are distilled down into a digestible binary of racist versus antiracist, which is then stretched to its furthest extreme.

Yet perhaps the most important thing that Kendi identifies as racist is the so-called assimilationist philosophy of the late-nineteenth-century black writer and thinker W. E. B. Du Bois. This is curious given that Du Bois is often depicted as a radical and contrasted with his contemporary, Booker T. Washington, who was willing to accept segregation until blacks were brought to educational parity with whites. Du Bois countered that blacks were ready for assimilation into American society and called for "ceaseless agitation and insistent demand for equality."[26]

---

25   Jesse Washington, "Blacks struggle with 72 percent unwed mothers rate," NBC News, November 7, 2010, https://www.nbcnews.com/id/wbna39993685#:~:text=Debate%20is%20growing%20within%20and,that%20is%20a%20complex%20issue.

26   "W. E. B. Du Bois and the NAACP," Virginia Museum of History & Culture, https://virginiahistory.org/learn/civil-rights-movement-virginia/w-e-b-du-bois-and-naacp.

For Du Bois, this was personal: he had, as he said, a double consciousness—as an American and as a black person, and only by merging the two, by properly welcoming blacks into the melting pot, could true equality and liberty be achieved. Kendi, however, asserts that because American identity is *white* identity, assimilation is nothing less than a racist policy. It forces blacks to knuckle under to a preexisting white culture, one that stamps out black identity, an effective cultural genocide.[27]

The idea that assimilation might be a matter of give-and-take—Italian Americans woven into the broader national fabric while contributing to its cuisine and traditions, for example—is alien to Kendi. The so-called American dream is nothing more than concealer for a racism that takes no prisoners and brooks no boundaries. Blacks must seek to liberate themselves from this, not conciliate with it. Remember this as we turn now from the humble penitent to the unrepentant charlatan.

***

There is no creature on this earth more pathetic than the white liberal. Those invasive lanternflies that periodically ravage Pennsylvania are preferable. No species has ever so disowned itself in favor of identifying with an out-group, *any* out-group—walleyed Latinx sex workers, bipolar peanut-allergic persons of color. The white liberal is forever on the lookout for "oppressed" demographics in need of his armchair charity.

Yet despite his allegedly good intentions, the white liberal can't ever seem to just *help* anyone. Those disadvantaged he takes under his wing always end up serving his bottom line, whether they're incorporated into a scheme that makes him a buck or turned into a token of social status à la the Black Panthers in Tom Wolfe's "Radical Chic" or just

---

27   Kendi, *How to Be an Antiracist*, loc. 741.

used to alleviate his guilt. The white liberal loves to flaunt his faith. He's the first to post a sign in his yard professing the woke Nicene Creed ("In this house, we believe . . ."). Yet serving the disadvantaged in a way that doesn't intersect with his self-interest is another thing altogether.

If this sounds like I'm stereotyping the woke the same way the woke stereotype white conservatives, that's because I am. And to be fair, I know plenty of good white liberals, just as I know some not-so-good ones. Which brings us to Robin DiAngelo. If Kendi is the Augustine of the woke faith, then DiAngelo is its evangelical retreat coordinator—and grifter.

DiAngelo is something called a diversity trainer. She speaks to corporations, universities, and nonprofits in an alleged effort to facilitate greater cohesion and antiracism among employees. Her book *White Fragility* is a journal of these seminars in which delusional whites are constantly pushing back against her accusations of racism while she emits her customary sigh and tries to get them to see the light.

To take one example: After her usual spiel, a man comes to the microphone to ask her a question. He's Italian American, he says, and as with blacks, his people were also discriminated against by the American ruling class. Why then is he being chided for bigotry on the sole basis of his skin color? Can't white people experience racism too? *Sigh.* "That he could be in that overwhelmingly white room of coworkers and exempt himself from an examination of his whiteness because Italians were once discriminated against is an all-too-common example of individualism," DiAngelo laments.[28]

First, no, that's not individualism, it's identity politics. And second, what of the man's point? "Wops," "micks," "Irish need not

---

28 Robin DiAngelo, *White Fragility: Why It's So Hard for White People to Talk About Racism* (Boston: Beacon Press, 2018) p. 12.

apply"—haven't whites in America also experienced discrimination (if not to the same brutal extent as blacks)? It's a question that deserves an answer but it also scrambles the woke's hierarchical lines, which run between skin colors with little regard for more granular matters of ethnicity. It challenges the faith, and so DiAngelo responds with disdain. Disdain and gibberish: "Poor and working-class people were not always perceived as fully white. . . . However, poor and working-class whites were eventually granted full entry into whiteness as a way to exploit labor."

May we never forget the day we finally admitted the Italians into Club White.

If you're chafing at such cartoonish thinking, please try to remember that DiAngelo is an expert: "As a sociologist, I am quite comfortable generalizing; social life is patterned in predictable and measurable ways."[29] And those "predictable and measurable ways," à la Kendi, are that racism is the sine qua non of American life. Among the things DiAngelo seems to think are racist are using terms like "underprivileged" and "good neighborhoods," attributing racial inequality to anything other than racism, buying a gun to protect your home in New Orleans, reminiscing fondly about the past, declaring "all lives matter" or "blue lives matter," and showing compassion to whites addicted to opioids.

Racism is everywhere, racism is everything—racism can never be stamped out. "Racism is deeply complex and nuanced," says DiAngelo, "and given this, we can never consider our learning to be complete or finished."[30]

This is technically true—so long as there's human nature, there will be racism—yet what it amounts to coming from DiAngelo is the

---

29 DiAngelo, *White Fragility*, p. 12.

30 DiAngelo, *White Fragility*, p. xv.

old Eric Hoffer quote about every cause eventually degenerating into a racket. If the problem of racism can never be licked, if like the cosmos it's a subject of infinite vastness and study, then DiAngelo's workshops never have to end. And isn't that just convenient.

Even more explicitly than Kendi, DiAngelo believes meaningful racism can only run in one direction: "When I say that only whites can be racist, I mean that in the United States, only whites have the collective social and institutional power and privilege over people of color."[31] Her seminars are thus directed at her fellow whites, and her trademark term, the title of her book, "white fragility," is a means of waving away any objection that might come her way. DiAngelo has shockingly encountered whites who are less than pleased with being blanketly labeled as racist. "White fragility" is her workaround. If whites argue back, however logically, it's only a reveal of their vulnerability and thus an indictment. What they're *really* up to is yelping about having had their racial power and privilege exposed.

Thus, not only does DiAngelo's work never have to end, she never has to answer any objection to her dime-store social science. It's a perfect shield drawn around a pseudointellectual hustle. In fact, so self-perpetuating is her work that at one point she pronounces that the fact that we now think racism is bad is itself a form of coded racism. Because we see bigotry as a negative, we think only bad people can be racist. And since no one wants to think they're a bad person, it enables them to claim they aren't racist. And then: *SIGH.* Just because you harbor no evil in your heart doesn't mean you aren't a bigot, people![32]

---

31   DiAngelo, *White Fragility*, p. 22.
32   DiAngelo, *White Fragility*, ch. 5.

There's no evidence DiAngelo is any kind of knowing fraud. Yet the reality is she's constructed a self-perpetuating moneymaking machine. As of 2021, DiAngelo made an average of $14,000 per speech and around $728,000 per year, putting her in the top 1 percent of income earners according to some calculations.[33] When the University of Wisconsin invited her to campus for their Diversity Week, she balked because they were only offering $10,000.[34]

Toward the end of *White Fragility*, DiAngelo relays another story from one of her seminars where a white woman is—and you'll want to sit down for this—accused of racism. The woman was in poor health and was so aggrieved by the accusation that she began to suffer a medical episode. Her colleagues worried she was having a heart attack. Yet DiAngelo was unmoved. "Of course when news of the woman's potentially fatal condition reached the rest of the participant group, all attention was immediately focused back onto her and away from engagement with the impact she had had on the people of color," DiAngelo sneers.[35]

Again, there's that cruelty. Whether it's the Loudoun County school administration covering up an inconvenient rape or Kendi waving away the devastation of inner-city crime, wokeness can be vicious.

***

33   Christopher Eberhart, "Anti-racist author DOUBLES speaking fees as America goes woke: 'White fragility' writer Robin DiAngelo charges an average of $14,000 per speech and makes '$728K a year,'" *Daily Mail*, July 2, 2021,

34   Brent Scher, "Robin DiAngelo Balked at $10k Fee From Public University, Insisted on $13k for Prerecorded Speech," *Washington Free Beacon*, March 10, 2021, https://freebeacon.com/culture/robin-diangelo-balked-at-10k-speaking-fee-from-public-university/.

35   DiAngelo, *White Fragility*, p. 111.

America is not a propositional nation. What this means is that our country is not a creed of airy notions about liberty and democracy that instantly confer citizenship upon those who believe in them. America is a place. It is a people with shared history, traditions, and touchstones. It is a culture existing within geographic boundaries and incarnate within its citizens.

Yet it's also true that one of those ideals, one of those touchstones, is a certain openness. When Ronald Reagan in 1989 quoted a letter that had been sent to him—"You can go to live in France, but you cannot become a Frenchman. You can go to live in Germany or Turkey or Japan, but you cannot become a German, a Turk, or a Japanese. But anyone, from any corner of the Earth, can come to live in America and become an American"[36]—the old man was onto something.

What sets America apart from the more antique nations of Europe is that openness, that more elastic view of citizenship. You need more than a desire to be free, for sure, but if you're willing to contribute something, to be assimilated into a common project, you're more likely to be welcomed here than in most places.

American citizenship is thus a golden mean. We have a common culture—but it allows for and even encourages subcultures. We have a language—but we tend not to mind all those Spanish radio stations down in Florida.

We are this way because we've had to be. What began as a romping ground for religious zealots and second sons expanded into a nation of estranged Northwestern Europeans and then Western Europeans and then Europeans and then beyond, as Texas harbored its rich Latino heritage and the Chinese settled in California and, of course, African

---

36 Ronald Reagan, "Remarks at the Presentation Ceremony for the Presidential Medal of Freedom," Ronald Reagan Presidential Library, January 19, 1989, https://www.reaganlibrary.gov/archives/speech /remarks-presentation-ceremony-presidential-medal-freedom-5.

Americans nurtured their own unique subculture. This diversity, *real* diversity, is a remarkable phenomenon, and put plainly, it shouldn't work. That 330 million people from so many backgrounds can be brought under the same national roof without triggering the overhead sprinklers shouldn't be possible. It runs up against so much of what we know about human history and its ugly tribal conflicts.

America somehow took the world's refuse—the poor, the huddled masses—and elevated them into the most powerful nation in human history. That's an incredible story. It's our story. As George Washington said in his Farewell Address, "Citizens by birth or choice, of a common country, that country has a right to concentrate your affections. The name of AMERICAN, which belongs to you, in your national capacity, must always exalt the just pride of Patriotism."[37]

Yet with such great unlikeliness has come great peril. Because we are so diverse—about 45 million people living here were born in other countries, about two-thirds the total population of France—the specter of dissolution is never far away. Lincoln was right when he said, "All the armies of Europe, Asia and Africa combined, with all the treasure of the earth (our own excepted) in their military chest; with a Buonaparte for a commander, could not by force, take a drink from the Ohio, or make a track on the Blue Ridge, in a trial of a thousand years."[38] There is no foreign adversary who can destroy us. Only we can do that.

There's a reason our Founders greatly feared what they called factionalism—and that was back when America was far more

---

37 George Washington, "Farewell Address," National Constitution Center, https://constitutioncenter.org/the-constitution/historic-document-library /detail/george-washington-farewell-address-1796.

38 Abraham Lincoln, "Speech to the Young Men's Lyceum of Springfield," National Constitutional Center, https://constitutioncenter.org/the -constitution/historic-document-library/detail/abraham-lincoln-speech -to-the-young-mens-lyceum-of-springfield-1838.

homogeneous. They understood that what would prove most lethal to this country was if a great factional wedge were to come cloaked in edifying ideology, if we were to forget our common culture and dissolve back into tribe not just as a matter of politics but of espoused morality. Because there are too many potential tribes here for that not to create chaos. Send us "back to blood," as Tom Wolfe worried was happening in his prescient 2012 novel of the same title,[39] and blood will be spilled.

This is what wokeness would do. By carving us up along not just racial but gender and sexual orientation lines, by acid-washing those bonds that hold us together via accusations of historical bigotry, by decrying assimilation as itself a form of tribal oppression, by reinforcing all this with the absolutism of theology, wokeness reveals itself in the main to be anti-American. It's the creed for those who have given up on the idea of a various yet singular nation united under liberty and the law. It's the way forward for those who want to exalt diversity yet who no longer care to be different.

Wokeness, of course, claims to be the opposite of a divisive creed. Its intersectionality attempts to unite its disparate identity groups under a single canvas. But who really thinks this can work? Who looks upon the dreary DEI bureaucracy of the woke and sees anything like civic unity? Who looks upon their goal of equity—absolute equivalence in all metrics across all identity groups—and doesn't see *Harrison Bergeron* crossed with circa-2024 South Africa? A political project that offers prosperity and equal rights for all—people will join hands for that. Wokeness can fracture us, but it can't put us back together again.

***

In October 2023, the terrorist gang Hamas invaded Israel and slaughtered more than 1,100 people. Israel then launched a military campaign

---

39   Tom Wolfe, *Back to Blood* (Boston: Little, Brown and Company, 2012).

against Hamas in the Gaza Strip that's drawn plenty of criticism for not doing enough to protect innocent human life. Yet wokesters on university campuses went much further. They more or less mirror-imaged their own 2020 campaign against bigotry, chanting antisemitic and even genocidal slogans, making Jewish students feel threatened. Why? Because the woke magisterium dictates that the Palestinians are a victim class, while the Israelis are colonizers and thus on par with the dreaded white man.

Somehow a theology premised on victimization offers little protection to history's ultimate victims, the Jews. It was yet another reminder of wokeness's tribalism and cruelty—and then, from out of the smoke of war, a silhouette emerged. It was Pope Francis, an emissary from the forgotten faith, Christianity, the one we'd given up on long ago. He called for Christians to pray for both Israel and Palestine. "Every war is a defeat," he said, one that leads "only to the death and suffering of so many innocent people."[40]

It wasn't a particularly useful statement so far as policy goes. Yet it was also a reminder that, in contrast to wokeness's baked-in callousness, the old faith was one of love. That's true no matter how often Christians have failed that calling, how many errors and inquisitions they've committed in its name. Not only does God love us, God is love, and the New Testament says "he who abides in love abides in God, and God in him." Because we're all loved, we all have inherent worth, regardless of our tribe, regardless of our identity categories.

This is why Christianity caught on so many centuries ago. Just as wokeness draws its identitarian lines, so too did the pagan religion of ancient Rome underpin an often brutal class system. It was the

---

40 Christopher Wells, "Pope prays for peace in Israel and Palestine: 'Every war is a defeat!'" Vatican News, October 8, 2023, https://www.vaticannews.va/en/pope/news/2023-10/pope-at-angelus-war-is-a-defeat-every-war-is-a-defeat.html.

oppressed of that system—the poor, women, slaves—who flocked to
the early Christian community. Why? Because Jesus had loved *them*.
Jesus had welcomed and forgiven *them*. They might have been from an
out-of-favor identity group, but that didn't matter: even a Samaritan
was judged by his actions, not his ethnicity.

It's difficult to express just how radical this was at the time.
Christianity gave metaphysical heft to a revolutionary concept of universal human dignity. All of our lives were precious, irrespective of
what society or ideology said, because Christ's light was in all of our
eyes. Beneath whatever temporal hierarchies Christians might establish
lurked not division or equity but true equality.

Four centuries after Christ was crucified, a Christian monk named
Telemachus descended into the arena of the Roman Colosseum. In the
midst of the usual gladiator slaughter egged on by shrieking crowds,
he jumped between the tributes and cried out, "In the name of Christ,
stop!" The spectators were so outraged that they stoned him to death,
yet when word reached the emperor Honorius, a Christian, he was so
taken aback that he banned the games entirely.[41] Such violence wasn't
entertainment; it was an affront to God, a violation of the dignity he'd
bestowed on even the lowliest captive of war. All the teachings of the
old pagan religion, all the civic constructs of Rome, couldn't conjure up
a reason to stop mass slaughter as entertainment. It took Christianity
to do that.

Something had changed, something that would outlast the crum-
bling empire around it. As the theologian David Bentley Hart writes,
"all of humanity's self-serving myths, all of its romances of power, had
been shattered at Easter, even if a great many Christians could not fully

---

41   Lawrence W. Reed, "How a Lowly Monk Ended Rome's Bloody Gladiator
     Duels," Foundation for Economic Education, January 1, 2020, https
     ://fee.org/articles/how-a-lowly-monk-ended-romes-bloody-gladiator
     -duels/.

grasp this."[42] All of us in the West are the children of this revolution, one inextricably linked to our own American Revolution, whose ideas of political equality are informed by the Christian doctrine of universal human dignity.

The United States has been shedding its Christianity for decades now. Yet by sleepwalking away from a faith we no longer care to understand in favor of a strange new theology, are we really progressing? Or are we drifting backward toward the days of tribalism and division and brutality?

One of the New Atheists' oft-heard sneers about Christianity is that it's a creed for the literal-minded, devoid of the irony we moderns pretend to treasure. Yet what could be more ironic than taking the cross, the most barbaric torture implement of the Roman Empire, and turning it into a symbol of love? What have all the late-night comedians and woke consultants ever come up with that can even approach that? The full thing is almost overwhelming in its unexpectedness. The little cruciform sitting atop the steeple of the now-empty church turns out to be the most subversive act in the history of mankind.

---

42 David Bentley Hart, *Atheist Delusions: The Christian Revolution and Its Fashionable Enemies* (New Haven: Yale University Press, 2009).

CHAPTER 12

The Battle of the Sexes Bogs Down

Remember the Battle of the Sexes? If you're under a certain age, you might not recall this particular dustup.

The Battle of the Sexes refers to many things in our popular culture: the 1973 tennis match between Bobby Riggs and Billie Jean King; a popular adult board game that pits the guys against the gals "IN THE ULTIMATE SHOWDOWN"; a 2010 album by the rapper Ludacris.

But broadly speaking it's an understanding between men and women that came into fashion during the late twentieth century. It was an arrangement born out of social reality. The sexes had achieved something like equality—not complete equality, I hasten to add, as feminists start climbing out of my TV, but as close to it as we'd ever gotten.

Women and men were coworkers and co-parents. The sexes mingled with each other in grade school and college. The 2008 Democratic presidential primary pitted a man against a woman, Barack Obama and Hillary Clinton, while the 2008 Republican presidential ticket featured both a man and a woman, John McCain and Sarah Palin (until they were crushed under the boot of the Obama/Biden patriarchy).

Yet even as equality was blooming, everyone still understood that men and women were different. This was an arcane and mist-shrouded age when one of the bestselling books was called *Men Are from Mars, Women Are from Venus*—and the author wasn't even hauled before the Hague! John Gray's self-help manual for the sexes became a smash hit precisely because men and women wanted to understand each other so they could forge successful relationships. In our time of gender fluidity, the back cover description reads like wrongspeak from a lost civilization: "Once upon a time Martians and Venusians met, fell in love, and had happy relationships together because they respected and accepted their differences. Then they came to Earth and amnesia set in: they forgot they were from different planets."[1]

None of this is to say that men and women in the Time Before were stratified into strict gender roles. I remember one girl at my elementary school who was better at basketball than all the boys on the school team. She was celebrated for her athletic skill, for putting those mouthy Martians in their place. Never was there any implication that she might really be a boy and should be prescribed puberty blockers.

The social contract between the sexes strove for equality while celebrating categorical differences. The Battle of the Sexes was thus less a battle than a fun, flirty competition between two tribes who still acknowledged they couldn't prolong the human race without each other. Think of the song "Summer Nights" from the movie *Grease*. Or the endless sex comedies from the early aughts.

This was never, we should be clear, a completely stable arrangement. For one, it assumed the goals for which the sexes were striving

---

1   John Gray, *Men Are From Mars, Women Are From Venus* (New York: HarperCollins, 1992).

were largely male-defined ones: social status, a good career, a life of partying, with historically female goals like child-rearing and home-making vanished from the picture. For another, its ideas of sex were also largely derived from men, and adolescent men at that. Women were encouraged to amass notches on their bedposts, sleep around, think nothing of their conquests in the morning. The comedic value of Alyson Hannigan's Michelle in the *American Pie* movies is that she fulfills this to an almost absurd extent: she's a girl with a filthier mouth and filthier sexual desires than most guys.

Still, there's no denying that, ironically enough, amid the Battle of the Sexes, men and women seemed to be at peace. Yet the guns of August were sounding. The real fight was about to be joined.

***

The first hint of escalation in the Battle of the Sexes came in the fateful year of 2010. That was when Democratic town criers galloped through towns across the nation to warn that it was war! Republicans had declared war on women!

The so-called war on women was an actual political trope that took hold after the GOP won the 2010 midterm elections. Stymied by an electorate that seemed to not care for White House staffers meddling in their health care, Democrats decided their best way forward was to terrify half the human race. They pointed with quivering fingers at Republican "anti-woman" measures like halting government money to Planned Parenthood and requiring women to see an ultrasound before getting an abortion. This they packaged into an endlessly repeated conceit—it literally became the name of a segment on MSNBC—called the war on women.

The real loser of the war on women, of course, was anyone with an IQ higher than a parking garage speed limit who heard such a gob-smackingly idiotic phrase and wished everyone in politics would just die. But for a while it looked like the ladies might have the upper hand. Rush Limbaugh lost advertisers after calling feminist Sandra Fluke a "slut."[2] Congressman Todd Akin lost his Senate race after making a confused and outrageous remark about "legitimate rape."[3] And that great defender of women, Barack Obama, was gloriously reelected to the presidency in 2012—and after admitting his whole opposition to lesbians getting married had been but a misunderstanding![4] Even better, on deck was a real-life woman whom it was now assumed would glide into the White House in a mere four years' time.

But then disaster struck. The men went and found themselves a generalissimo and he won the presidency.

* * *

Donald Trump's election, thanks to ample support from male voters, was the moment the Battle of the Sexes met its demise. Trump wasn't just every feminist's nightmare—loud, confident, boorish—he had won even after the infamous *Access Hollywood* tape had landed, revealing he'd once bragged about grabbing women by the you-know-where.

For feminists who had spent their careers crusading against sexual assault, this was a crushing defeat. So it was that less than a year after Trump stomped into the White House, the #MeToo movement was christened on Twitter (so you knew it was official). #MeToo was

---

2   Lyneka Little, "Rush Limbaugh's Radio Show Loses More Advertisers," *Wall Street Journal*, March 6, 2012, https://www.wsj.com/articles /BL-SEB-69219.

3   Lori Moore, "Rep. Todd Akin: The Statement and the Reaction," *New York Times*, August 20, 2012, https://www.nytimes.com/2012/08/21/us /politics/rep-todd-akin-legitimate-rape-statement-and-reaction.html.

4   Phil Gast, "Obama announces he supports same-sex marriage," CNN, May 9, 2012, https://www.cnn.com/2012/05/09/politics/obama-same -sex-marriage/index.html.

ostensibly triggered by literal and figurative pig Harvey Weinstein, who was accused of sexual abuse by dozens of women. But it was also about Trump, the sense he had inchoately given a green light to such behavior—his very existence on this planet, really.

A dumb political meme had mushroomed into a genuine culture war. And as fall turned into winter, countless celebrity men would be felled by accusations of sexual misconduct. And while some of these men (Weinstein, Matt Lauer) were clearly guilty of extraordinary crimes, others (Kevin Spacey) were later acquitted of the charges against them, while still others (Aziz Ansari) were accused of relatively minor lapses of judgment that didn't come anywhere near the venality of a Weinstein.

Then there were the outright innocent. After #MeToo took hold, the writer Moira Donegan started something she called the Shitty Media Men list, a crowdsourced spreadsheet that allowed female journalists to anonymously accuse their male colleagues of misconduct.[5] One of the names that ended up on that list was a talented sports writer whom I've edited before and whose name I'm not going to share here (though he later told his story in the *New York Post*). He was falsely accused and to this day doesn't know who listed him. Yet it was enough to get him blackballed from journalism. When he wrote the *Post* piece, he was working as a janitor at Dave and Buster's to provide for his family.[6]

Here was the problem in all its vivid cruelty: there was never any limiting principle to #MeToo, and certainly no due process. There was also something like a whiplash effect. The Battle of the Sexes had for

---

5 Moira Donegan, "I Started the Media Men List. My name is Moira Donegan," *The Cut, New York*, January 10, 2018, https://www.thecut.com/2018/01/moira-donegan-i-started-the-media-men-list.html.

6 "'Being wrongly #MeToo'd has ruined my life,'" *New York Post*, February 1, 2020, https://nypost.com/2020/02/01/being-wrongly-metood-has-ruined-my-life/.

years signaled to men that sex should be open and sybaritic, only for our entire sexual ethos to abruptly reverse itself in an authoritarian flash. For those raised on a diet of Pop-Tarts and *Wedding Crashers*, this was a momentous change indeed.

***

Where once there was the Battle of the Sexes, now there was something closer to an actual battle. Where once there had been playful competition, now there would be suspicion and even hostility.

Chaperones became a hot new trend, ostensibly to protect women from the bottomless depravity of men.[7] Several phone apps were introduced that allowed couples to sign consent forms before hopping between the sheets.[8] A Pew poll in 2020 found that a large majority of men and a plurality of women thought #MeToo had made it more difficult to know how to behave on a date.[9]

Yet despite its inquisitorial mood, #MeToo did have its positive impacts. In addition to collaring the Weinsteins of the world, it forced us to look under the sexual hood. As we retreated back into our gender tribes, men and women took stock. Men began writing more earnestly about masculinity. A new generation of feminists took a hard look at femininity. And what we found on both sides of the ledger wasn't great.

---

7   Lara Prendergast, "The sexual reformation," *The Spectator*, November 4, 2017, https://www.spectator.co.uk/article/the-sexual-reformation/.

8   Edward C. Baig, "Does 'yes' mean 'yes'? Can you give consent to have sex to an app?" *USA Today*, September 26, 2018, https://www.usatoday .com/story/tech/columnist/baig/2018/09/26/proof-yes-means-yes-sexual -consent-apps-let-users-agree-have-sex/1420208002/.

9   Anna Brown, "Nearly Half of US Adults Say Dating Has Gotten Harder for Most People in the Last 10 Years," Pew Research Center, August 20, 2020, https://www.pewresearch.org/social-trends/2020/08/20/nearly -half-of-u-s-adults-say-dating-has-gotten-harder-for-most-people-in-the -last-10-years/.

It's nearly impossible to look at the data and not conclude that boys and men are in crisis. Boys are failing out of school (or perhaps better to say schools are failing boys) at alarming rates. They receive lower grades on average than girls and consistently lag behind in reading and writing.[10] Boys are far more likely to be suspended or expelled from school than girls[11] and make up only 44 percent of young college students.[12] They're nearly twice as likely to abuse drugs and alcohol[13] and four times more likely to commit suicide.[14]

They're also far more likely to be inducted into our youth culture of mass stupefaction. According to a study at the University of Iowa, an astonishing *10 percent of children* have been diagnosed with ADHD, the vast majority of them boys.[15] Of those supposedly afflicted, 77 percent are receiving some kind of treatment with 62 percent taking

10 Richard V. Reeves, *Of Boys and Men: Why the Modern Male Is Struggling and What to Do About It* (Washington: Brookings Institution Press, 2022).

11 "Student Discipline and School Climate in US Public Schools," US Department of Education Office for Civil Rights, November 2023, https://www2.ed.gov/about/offices/list/ocr/docs/crdc-discipline-school-climate-report.pdf.

12 Richard Fry, "Fewer young men are in college, especially at 4-year schools," Pew Research Center, December 18, 2023, https://www.pewresearch.org/short-reads/2023/12/18/fewer-young-men-are-in-college-especially-at-4-year-schools/.

13 Destiny Bezrutczyk, "The Differences In Addiction Between Men And Women," The Addiction Center, December 14, 2023, https://www.addictioncenter.com/addiction/differences-men-women/.

14 "Data Brief 464: Suicide Mortality in the United States, 2001–2021," National Center for Health Statistics, https://www.cdc.gov/nchs/data/databriefs/db464-tables.pdf.

15 Felix Gussone, "10 percent of kids have ADHD now," NBC News, August 31, 2018, data courtesy of Bao, Wei, et al., University of Iowa, https://www.nbcnews.com/health/health-news/10-percent-kids-have-adhd-now-n905576.

medication.[16] An estimated 3.7 million Americans, mostly male, are thought to abuse prescription stimulants like Ritalin.[17]

After school, men are increasingly likely to struggle with employment. In 1953, 98 percent of men aged twenty-five to fifty-four had a job, yet in 2023 there were an astonishing 7.2 million men who not only weren't employed but weren't even looking for work.[18] They'd essentially dropped out of the workforce, leaving vacancies at companies that might want to employ good men. As of late 2023, there were hundreds of thousands of open manufacturing jobs in the United States, which on average paid a good wage.[19] Yet, whereas the total male employment rate at the turn of the century was 72 percent, it's since skidded down to 65.5 percent as of 2022.[20]

We know the problem isn't with the job market, but otherwise this rash of willfully unemployed men remains a mystery. One study by the Federal Reserve Bank of Richmond found a link to high rates of substance use and hours spent playing video games.[21] Further research

---

16   "Data and Statistics About ADHD," Centers for Disease Control and Prevention, October 16, 2023, https://www.cdc.gov/ncbddd/adhd/data.html.

17   "2021 NSDUH detailed tables," Substance Abuse and Mental Health Services Administration, 2021, https://www.samhsa.gov/data/report/2021-nsduh-detailed-tables.

18   Tony Dokoupil and Martin Finn, "Millions of men have dropped out of the workforce, leaving companies struggling to fill jobs: It's 'a matter of our national identity,'" CBS News, January 26, 2023, https://www.cbsnews.com/news/men-workforce-work-companies-struggle-fill-jobs-manufacturing/.

19   "Facts About Manufacturing," National Association of Manufacturers, 2023, https://nam.org/facts-about-manufacturing-expanded/.

20   "Employment rate of men in the United States from 1990 to 2022," data compiled by Statista Research Department, November 3, 2023.

21   Laura Dawson Ullrich, "Male Labor Force Participation: Patterns and Trends," Federal Reserve Bank of Richmond, First Quarter 2021,

by the Federal Reserve Bank of Boston unveiled another reason: a decline in perceived social status. Men without a college education have watched both their wages and their prestige in society erode, with a four-year degree increasingly seen as a hand stamp to the larger economy. For those who never graduated—and there are many more men in this position than women—the stress of competing with those who did graduate may have led them to give up entirely.[22]

Women, meanwhile, are stepping forward with résumés in hand. It's a good thing women are in the workforce, of course, but when 62 percent of the jobs created in November 2022 were filled by women,[23] you do start to wonder whether the arrangement has become lopsided in the other direction.

It's so lopsided, in fact, that it's tempting to call women the new dominant sex (*back! get back in the TV!*). Women are now 60 percent of college students[24] and hold more payroll jobs than men.[25] The war

https://www.richmondfed.org/publications/research/econ_focus/2021/q1/district_digest#:~:text=Over%20the%20past%2050%20years,pandemic%2C%20it%20has%20fallen%20further.

22 Pinghui Wu, "Wage Inequality and the Rise in Labor Force Exit: The Case of US Prime-Age Men," Federal Reserve Bank of Boston, Working Papers No. 22-16, 2022, https://www.bostonfed.org/publications/research-department-working-paper/2022/wage-inequality-and-the-rise-in-labor-force-exit-the-case-of-us-prime-age-men.aspx.

23 Jasmine Tucker and Brooke LePage, "Women Gain Over Six in 10 Jobs Added to Economy in November," National Women's Law Center, December 2, 2022, https://www.bostonfed.org/publications/research-department-working-paper/2022/wage-inequality-and-the-rise-in-labor-force-exit-the-case-of-us-prime-age-men.aspx.

24 Douglas Belkin, "A Generation of American Men Give Up on College: 'I Just Feel Lost,'" *Wall Street Journal*, September 6, 2021, https://www.wsj.com/articles/college-university-fall-higher-education-men-women-enrollment-admissions-back-to-school-11630948233.

25 Jack Kelly, "Women Now Hold More Jobs than Men in the US Workforce," *Forbes*, January 13, 2020, https://www.forbes.com/sites/jackkelly/2020/01/13/women-now-hold-more-jobs-than-men/?sh=179d9f748f8a.

between the sexes has become a zero-sum game: men's losses have been women's gains.

In the 1970s, women were, the data tell us, happier than men. But women's emerging economic progress and cultural dominance have coincided with a souring of their mood that is so stark as to prompt researchers to refer to it as "The Paradox of Declining Female Happiness" (the title of a famous 2009 study).[26] Start with the fact that, according to a study by Gallup and Hologic Inc., in 2022, 42 percent of women reported feeling worried, 39 percent reported feeling stressed out, and 30 percent reported feeling sad.[27] Sixty-two percent of women ages eighteen to thirty-four told the American Psychological Association they suffer from "overwhelming stress,"[28] while four in 10 women have "reached their breaking point," according to a poll by Myriad Genetics.[29]

Part of this stress gap can be attributed to those biological and psychological differences between the sexes we're no longer allowed to discuss. Research for decades has shown that women suffer more anxiety than men. But then it's also worth asking whether society is causing women to feel stressed out. What of the fact that women still do more

---

26   Betsey Stevenson and Justin Wolfers, "The Paradox of Declining Female Happiness," National Bureau of Economic Research, Working Paper 14969, May 2009, https://www.nber.org/papers/w14969.

27   Julie Ray and Jon Mehanna, "Global Study Issues Wake-Up Call for Women's Health," Hologic Global Women's Health Index/Gallup, January 16, 2024, https://news.gallup.com/poll/547712/global-study -issues-wake-call-women-health.aspx.

28   "Stress in America 2022: Concerned for the future, beset by inflation," American Psychological Association, 2022, https://www.apa.org/news /press/releases/stress/2022/concerned-future-inflation.

29   "Stressed out: 4 in 10 women have reached their 'breaking point,' survey says," Fox 13, April 29, 2022, data compiled from GeneSight Mental Health Monitor, Myriad Genetics, https://www.fox13seattle.com/news /stressed-out-women-reach-breaking-point-survey.

housework than men despite having also entered the workforce?[30] Or that more women tend to handle their family's shopping and household budgeting, exposing them more proximately to the cost of living crisis?[31] Or that single women report rising frustration with meat-market dating apps and finding a suitable guy, which only causes them to double down on their work?

Feminists long ago conceded that women can't do it all, that they can't be ideal wives and perfect mothers and hyperefficient worker bees. "Superwoman was always the enemy of the women's movement," as Gloria Steinem put it.[32] But if women can't have it all, they're increasingly doing it all, and the cultural signal being sent is that this is how it should be. The model is still the girlboss, the independent woman who wakes up at one in the morning, completes a decathlon before breakfast, showers in a pantsuit, and goes to work in a boardroom where she's forever outsassing her hopelessly moronic male colleagues.

To take just one example, in the popular Netflix biopic *Inventing Anna*, about the fabulist German heiress Anna Delvey, the actress Anna Chlumsky plays Vivian Kent, the tenacious reporter who ultimately brings down Delvey. Kent is the very epitome of what a modern women is supposed to be, a frazzled pinball of stress and competence who bounces between tasks with brilliance if not always perfect composure.

30 Megan Brenan, "Women Still Handle Main Household Tasks in US," Pew Research Center, January 29, 2020, https://news.gallup.com/poll/283979/women-handle-main-household-tasks.aspx.

31 Kathryn Tuggle, "More Than Half of Women Control Household Finances, Investment and Retirement Planning," HerMoney and Alliance for Lifetime Income, April 12, 2022, https://hermoney.com/invest/financial-planning/more-than-half-of-women-control-household-finances-investments-and-retirement-planning/.

32 "Imagining Feminism in the Marketplace: Linda Scott (University of Illinois) Interviews Gloria Steinem," Advertising & Society Review, Volume 4, Issue 4, 2003, https://muse.jhu.edu/article/50201.

Kent's husband and male coworkers are pure flying buttresses, there to support her as she yelps and spasms her way across the newsroom. At one point, Kent heads to Russia to investigate a lead *immediately after having had her baby.* It's all good though. Her husband is on hand to provide the necessary nurturing.[33]

This is the message that so often goes out to young women: you can have it all, and if you can't have it all, then just cut down on the child-rearing. Kids are just another box on the very long checklist of the Woman in Full. This as polls find women on average wish they had more children than they do.[34]

Here is the new gender arrangement, which all the time was festering beneath the gloss of the Battle of the Sexes: women are gaining ground but not happy about it, while men are falling behind with little sign of turning things around. Yet somehow the solutions are always the same. *Have you considered making abortion more accessible? Taking another swing at the patriarchy? There's this great book called* The Handmaid's Tale. *You should totally binge-watch the TV show that's it's based on.*

***

Thankfully into this morass has descended an all-powerful super-theology that can adjudicate on such matters. *This meeting of the Woke Ecumenical Council on Gender Intersectionality will come to order!* (Picture a judge wearing a pink powdered wig.)

---

33   *Inventing Anna*, created by Shonda Rhimes, produced by Shonda Rhimes, et al., aired on Netflix, 2022.

34   Lyman Stone, "How Many Kids Do Women Want?" Institute for Family Studies, June 1, 2018, https://ifstudies.org/blog/how-many-kids-do-women-want.

Wokeness is supposed to iron out the wrinkles that arise between its identity groups, yet nowhere have the woke so failed to harmonize relations as between men and women.

At issue is a schism within the woke congregation. On one side are the traditionalists, by which we mean traditional circa 2010, those feminists who see women as a class victimized by men. This sect is still at the forefront of gender thinking and is responsible for most of the slogans that filter down into popular culture ("smash the patriarchy!"). They might identify themselves as fourth or seventeenth or whatever "wave," but they trace their origins back to the women's liberation movement of the 1960s and 1970s.

On the other side are the radicals. These people care little for relations between men and women because they think men and women are just artificial constructs. The trans movement has shown the way; gender is entirely fluid now; feel free to identify as a she or a we or a xe—because it's all about me! Just don't impose any kind of gender roles onto anybody else. Even if those gender roles are signaling to women that they need to assert themselves more.

There really is no way to reconcile *women are oppressed victims* with *women aren't a set category*. Perhaps that's why the woke magisterium has largely ignored this schism. It's proceeded instead as though both claims are obviously true and need to be advanced with the usual crusading wrath of a political purge among wolverines. Already a handful of women, the so-called trans exclusionary radical feminists, or TERFs (the woke can make anything sound dull, can't they?), have committed apostasy by siding firmly with the traditionalists. And J. K. Rowling, the most popular children's author in the world, is among them.

Amid this void, the only thing left to do has been to switch on the autopilot: keep teaching women to assert themselves, keep teaching men to curb their "toxic masculinity," etc. In other words, keep going with a status quo that's proven unaccommodating to both sexes.

And perhaps the greatest irony is that it's causing us to regress: the so-called men's rights movement is just as toxic as the critics say, and it's a direct reaction to our new gender politics and the sense of disenfranchisement among men. It's enough to make you miss the days of "this one time at band camp . . ." In such a muddle, we shouldn't be surprised if the guns sound again.

CHAPTER 13

The American Dream, Now Available for
Monthly Installments of $12,999.99

S o Americans disagree about gender and race. We're divided between
the real world and the virtual one, whether we should next go to
the Moon or Mars, whether Alex Jones's inflamed tonsils are the work
of secret CIA microwave technology.

And there's still *another* culture war that's shredding our civic fabric
to ribbons: the War Between the Generations. And lately, dispatches
from the front have been looking bleak for my fellow millennials.

The War Between the Generations began on Twitter, as all wars
now do. It was the baby boomers who fired first, demanding to know
why their millennial children didn't move off of the basement futon and
buy a house already. The millennials countered that this was because a
house no longer cost $49 with coupons like it did back in 1965. And so
the generational combat was on, with the boomers attacking the millennials as spoiled and the millennials accusing the boomers of ruining
the entire country.

Thankfully we millennials had an ally in this fight: Generation Z, our juniors, those born between 1997 and 2012, who seemed to dislike the boomers just as much as we did. Yet lately this alliance has started to fray. The Zoomers have been declaring on TikTok that they're fed up with the millennials, citing everything from our affinity for skinny jeans to our being bewitched by what we call "adulting" (and everyone else calls "setting up autopay for your rent without turning it into a damn psychodrama"). This hostility came out of nowhere and it caught us by surprise. Worse, it put us in the uncomfortable position of having to moan about the state of today's youth. *You kids wouldn't have lasted ten seconds on the Aggro Crag.* That kind of thing.

Thus do we millennials find ourselves on a blasted heath as aging guys with ponytails close in on one side and teenage phone zombies shuffle toward us on the other. We'll cast our Harry Potter spells and launch our avocado mortars, but they just . . . keep . . . *coming . . .*

Even as negotiations with the Zoomers break down, the War Between the Generations is still principally one between the old and the young. And while political disagreements no doubt play a role—the millennials would like the boomers to stop voting for Donald Trump, for example—they're by no means the main grievance in play.

When Tom Wolfe noted at the turn of the millennium that traditional Marxism had all but ceased to exist, he was correct. The fact that wokeness focuses on differences of gender and race—so-called cultural Marxism—rather than any kind of economic class divide is evidence enough. Yet even if those class fissures aren't as animating as they once were, they're still there; they've just manifested as a different type of conflict.

The millennials are hacked off at the boomers not because we want to smash their way of life, as the boomers sought with their parents, but because the economy we inherited has made it more difficult for us to enjoy that way of life. The numbers tell the story: as of 2023, 51.3

percent of all the wealth in America was owned by the baby boomers, compared to just 9 percent by the millennials.[1] And while an older and more established generation is naturally going to be richer, bear in mind that the millennials as of 2023 were between twenty-seven and forty-two years old. We're middle-aged now, God help us, something we were never supposed to become, yet that bulging 401(k) still remains elusive.

By contrast, when the boomers were our age, they controlled about 20 percent of the nation's wealth, more than twice the millennials' share today.[2]

This wealth disparity is worth our attention, since, as Marxism made clear, out of great wealth disparities can come great trouble. And out of this wealth disparity has come a narrative that goes something like this: the boomers hoarded America's riches, jerry-rigging the economy to work for them while leaving their children holding nothing but a student loan bill in one hand and a CVS receipt for a Xanax prescription in the other. And the thing is, the CVS receipt is forty feet long. That's how you know a generation is decadent: by the length of its CVS receipts.

I don't wholly agree with that narrative and I certainly don't think the boomers *intentionally* rigged the economy. I also think boomer bashing has become a cop-out, a way of hiding the fact that you don't have any idea how to make things better. But then it's easy to see why

---

1   "Wealth distribution in the United States in the third quarter of 2023, by generation." Statista Research Department, December 20, 2023, https://www.statista.com/statistics/1376620/wealth-distribution-for -the-us/#:~:text=In%20the%20third%20quarter%20of,of%20the%20 baby%20boomer%20generation.

2   Christopher Ingraham, "The staggering millennial wealth deficit, in one chart," *Washington Post*, December 3, 2019, https://www .washingtonpost.com/business/2019/12/03/precariousness-modern -young-adulthood-one-chart/.

the perception exists, given just how unequal the two cohorts can appear. And it's having a dire effect on how the young perceive their country and their future.

***

Picture, if you will, the American dream: the two-story house, the green lawn, the minivan in the driveway, the dog in the front yard, the Wiffle ball crap the kids left strewn across the front yard, that one termite-infested tree you've been meaning to have removed but keep putting off because you wanted that $200 bottle of Glenfiddich instead . . .

Let's start with the house. The baby boomers first entered the housing market in the late 1960s. This drove a surge in housing prices—a large generation is going to need a lot of roofs over their heads—but the average boomer in their thirties still only paid about $82,800 for a house, or just over $300,000 in 2024 dollars.[3] The average millennial buying in late 2023? *$413,000.*[4] And it's not like millennials have higher incomes to throw around: the average millennial as of 2019 faced a 31 percent higher home-price-to-income ratio than the average boomer.[5]

---

3   Casey Bond, "How Much Did Baby Boomers Pay for Their First Homes? Millennials Would Be Shocked," *Yahoo! Finance*, December 28, 2023, https://finance.yahoo.com/news/much-did-baby-boomers -pay-120020574.html.

4   Christopher Murray, "New construction homes popular among Millennials despite high housing costs," Fox Business, December 20, 2023, https://www.foxbusiness.com/personal-finance/new-construction -homes-millennials.

5   "Baby Boomers Vs. Millennials: The Costs for Each in Buying a Home," CUToday.info, March 31, 2022, https://www.cutoday.info /Fresh-Today/Baby-Boomers-Vs.-Millennials-The-Costs-for-Each-in -Buying-a-Home#:~:text=Housing%20prices%20have%20increased%20 393,17%25%20in%20total%20since%201990.

The problem goes well beyond inflation. Inflation, first of all, has sometimes outpaced wage growth, which means even if housing prices grew at merely the inflation rate, they might still be less affordable. But home prices have spiked more than 1,600 percent since 1970 while inflation has risen by 644 percent.[6] This has served to make a house feel to the young increasingly like a pipe dream—and that's before you get to the actual pipes. Plumbers are expensive, as is all the maintenance you need to keep up any house.

The sheer price tag has seen many millennials throw up their hands at the prospect of ever owning a home. As of 2022, boomers with empty nests owned about 28 percent of American houses compared to just 14 percent of millennials with children, a gap that was nonexistent just a decade prior.[7] The boomers are fortunate, having either paid off their mortgages or locked in lower mortgage rates than what they would pay now if they moved, and so are understandably reluctant to vacate their castles. This has helped create a housing shortage that's further driven up prices. Millennials have responded by renting, but here too the generational gap yawns. In 1970, the median rent adjusted for inflation was $848,[8] compared to $2,045 in 2024.[9]

---

6 "Baby Boomers Vs. Millennials . . ." CUToday.info.

7 Dana Anderson and Sheharyar Bokhari, "Empty Nesters Own Twice as Many Large Homes as Millennials with Kids," Redfin, January 16, 2024, https://www.redfin.com/news/empty-nesters-own-large-homes/.

8 Ferran, "How US Rent Prices Have Changed Over Time," JuneHomes .com, September 9, 2022, https://junehomes.com/blog/2022/09/09 /how-rent-prices-the-have-changed-over-time/.

9 Zillow Rental Manager, "US Rental Market," March 8, 2024, https ://www.zillow.com/rental-manager/market-trends/united-states/#:~:text =How%20has%20the%20rent%20in%20US%20changed%20in%20 the%20last%20year%3F&text=The%20median%20rent%20price%20 in,%2480%20less%20than%20March%202023.

Yes, as any boomer will tell you, back in the day you had to cough up a 20 percent down payment to even think about buying a house, whereas today you can put down a Shell gas card and three Reese's Pieces and walk away with a McMansion and a lifetime of debt slavery. But then, that 20 percent amounted to a lot less than it does today. Mortgage lenders might be more irresponsible but they're also reflecting a reality: one-fifth of any contemporary house's price is difficult to cough up.

Still, some millennials have opted to buy a house, and one reason, of course, is they have kids. This is when the next cost-of-living sledgehammer swings down. Today, both parents in any given home tend to have jobs, a feedback loop of both Battle of the Sexes cultural preferences and economic necessity. This means they need childcare, yet here too they're being priced into oblivion.

The average two-parent household in 1960 spent only 2 percent of their income on childcare and education, which makes sense given that most mothers stayed at home and college was cheaper. Those costs began to rise under the boomers but they didn't truly come to a head until much more recently. In 2013, the average household spent *18 percent* of its income on childcare and education. That's about $2,600 per year, as opposed to $233 per year in 1960 (adjusted for inflation). And that only gets us to 2013.[10] Between 2010 and 2020, childcare costs jumped a further 28 percent.[11]

The biggest bite out of any childcare budget is, of course, the cost of college, a four-year-long alcohol-fueled bacchanalia that every young adult is required by law to attend. As a college education has become

10   Lam Thuy Vo, "How Much Does It Cost to Raise a Child?" *Wall Street Journal*, June 21, 2016, https://graphics.wsj.com/childcost/.

11   "How much are families spending on childcare?" USAFacts Team, April 7, 2022, https://usafacts.org/articles/how-much-are-families -spending-on-childcare/.

a necessity for most jobs, to say nothing of a cultural expectation underwritten by federal lenders, demand has surged and prices have followed. No surprise, then, that the average cost of attending college in 2020—including tuition, fees, and room and board—was 180 percent higher than it was in 1980 after adjusting for inflation.[12] Those costs can vary widely depending on whether a student attends a private or state university, whether he lives in-state, and other factors. Yet consider that at the hallowed Ivy League universities, the total cost of attendance without a scholarship is galloping toward $90,000 per year[13] (in fairness, if you're thinking of paying your way through an Ivy League college without a scholarship, you're probably not smart enough to attend an Ivy League college).

So it is that the average student will borrow more than $30,000 to pursue a four-year bachelor's degree, which he'll then take an average of twenty years to pay off.[14] This student debt is an almost universal millennial experience, and it's stunted our economic advancement. Everything begins to add up: college loans make an already pricey house even less affordable.

It's all good though. You scrimp and you save and you celebrate all your wedding anniversaries at Panera. You eventually get enough in the bank to send your son Jimmy to a good college. And then the little shit falls down at a frat party and breaks his tailbone (he was playing

12 Brianna McGurran and Alicia Hahn, "College Tuition Inflation: Compare The Cost Of College Over Time," *Forbes*, May 9, 2023, https://www.forbes.com/advisor/student-loans/college-tuition-inflation/.

13 Aimee Picchi, "Ivy League costs creep close to $90,000 per year: 'Prices just keep going up,'" CBS News, March 29, 2023, https://www.cbsnews.com/news/ivy-league-tuition-90000-per-year-prices-just-keep-going-up/?ftag=CNM-00-10aab8d&linkId=207622024.

14 Lyss Welding, "Average Student Loan Debt: 2024 Statistics," BestColleges.com, January 11, 2024, https://www.bestcolleges.com/research/average-student-loan-debt/.

Charades, he insists). Jimmy is still on your health insurance, as are most "twenty-year-old children," a dystopian term brought to you by Obamacare. And the premium for your family's health plan, provided and covered in part by your employer, runs you about $6,600 per year.[15] That's despite the fact that your deductible is $1,700, meaning you'll still have to pay for a chunk of Jimmy's medical bills out of pocket.

You think about this and flash back to the day Jimmy was born. He came out early and had to spend a couple days in the NICU. The hospital sent you a bill for $25,000.

There are plenty of other items chipping away at your checkbook. The price of gas is double what it was in 1998.[16] Post-COVID-19 inflation has sent the price of groceries soaring—a bag of Lay's potato chips is now so expensive that one of Europe's largest grocery chains literally banned them from their stores.[17] Even the damned dog is a damned liability. A thirty-pound bag of Iam's dog food costs $47 on Amazon, while his pet therapy sessions—mental health is essential for canines, your local Karen insists—run into the thousands.

---

15   Tina Reed, "Health insurance costs near $24K after big jump this year: survey," *Axios*, October 18, 2023, data compiled by KFF, https://www .axios.com/2023/10/18/health-insurance-premiums-24k-kff.

16   Carly Hallman, "Gas Prices Through History," TitleMax, 2023, https ://www.titlemax.com/discovery-center/planes-trains-and-automobiles __trashed/average-gas-prices-through-history/.

17   Sylvie Corbet and Lee-Ann Durbin, "PepsiCo products are being pulled from some Carrefour grocery stores in Europe over price hikes," Associated Press, January 5, 2024, https://www.cnbc.com/2024/01/05 /some-carrefour-stores-in-europe-pull-pepsico-products-over-price-hikes .html#:~:text=Global%20supermarket%20chain%20Carrefour%20 will,tea%20and%20its%20namesake%20soda.

Still, thinks our struggling millennial, at least there's one bright spot: he has relatively low credit card debt.[18] He's spent his money responsibly when he can (notwithstanding that brief home-brewing phase). So he goes to the store and buys a birthday card for his mother. She's been collecting Social Security and Medicare for many years, entitlements whose unfunded obligations exceed $78 trillion.[19] That's money he'll have to pay off in exchange for benefits he knows in his bones he'll never receive . . .

***

Lately millennials have been committing what in their beloved 1990s was a cardinal sin: embracing socialism. According to a YouGov poll taken in 2019, 70 percent of millennials said they were somewhat or extremely likely to vote for a socialist candidate, more than any other generation, including the Zoomers.[20] It was millennials who during the 2016 Democratic presidential primary drove support for Bernie Sanders, a self-proclaimed Democratic Socialist.

For the boomers, this has been treated as a coup de grace in the War Between the Generations. *Ha ha!* the boomers flourish, accidentally knocking off their clip-on ponytails. *These youngsters say they're socialists yet they use their Apple iPhones to deposit the birthday checks we send them at PNC Bank!* And this is kind of silly. Socialism is the

---

18 Elizabeth Gravier, "The average millennial has over $4,000 in credit card debt—other generations have more," CNBC, August 28, 2023, https ://www.cnbc.com/select/average-credit-card-debt-by-age/.

19 Romina Boccia, "The Unsustainable Burdens Posed by the So-Called Medicare and Social Security Trust Funds," Cato Institute, April 3, 2023, https://www.cato.org/blog/unsustainable-burdens-posed-so-called -medicare-social-security-trust-funds.

20 Stef W. Kight, "70% of millennials say they'd vote for a socialist," Axios, October 28, 2019, data compiled by YouGov, https://www.axios .com/2019/10/28/millennials-vote-socialism-capitalism-decline.

most discredited ideology in the history of man—the misery brought on by the Union of Soviet Socialist Republics should be evidence enough. Tweeting about how much you hate capitalism on your Google-made handheld supercomputer seems self-defeating in the extreme.

But if an "online brand development specialist" calling himself a socialist sounds dumb, then I have a theory: millennials aren't socialists. Not really. They don't support nationalizing Airbnb. They don't have strong feelings about the materialist conception of history. I grew up in a very blue state and not once did we ever storm a barricade while drunkenly belting out "L'Internationale" (well, once . . .).

Tom Wolfe is still correct: traditional Marxism is not on its way back in. Yet just as some boomers curse the word "socialism" when what they really mean is "my favorite omelet at IHOP was discontinued," so too have millennials stretched that word's definition to places it shouldn't go. Socialism to them means: *the economy isn't working for us.* It means: *too much emphasis is being placed on profit and wealth.* It means: *we need to try something new.* Laugh all you like, since socialism is hardly new, but then ask yourself: is this really a shock? Is it surprising that the generation that graduated into Wall Street's 2008 crater and then watched prices soar across the board would want to take a swing at a moneyed chimera? Socialism here, more than anything, is a cry for change.

Admittedly this theory is purely anecdotal, based on conversations with friends and coworkers. And it could be wrong. We could all wake up tomorrow and find a red flag flying over every OrangeTheory studio in America. But I doubt it. For one, millennials are long past their fist-in-the-air phase, too assimilated into the modern workforce to want to burn it down completely. For another, even the so-called socialists seem not to mind big business so long as it acts as a transmitter of their cultural priorities. In the fight between woke Disney and right-wing Florida governor Ron DeSantis, the supposed Bolsheviks sided with the money-grubbing corporation over the democratically elected commissar.

Yet if millennial socialism is confused, the response to it hasn't helped either. Those who critique the new socialists have tended to take them literally but not seriously, attacking socialism as an economic system while defending capitalism. The choice there should be obvious, but then it's also true that presenting the choice as a binary precludes any kind of needed dialogue within capitalism itself. It pretends developing a prosperous and just economy is as easy as selecting one ism over another.

The generational rift is how class consciousness—*real* class consciousness, over economic class rather than Twitter pronouns—exists in America today. And perhaps that's why the millennial embrace of socialism really is disquieting. The risk is not that we're about to all join a hippie commune; it's that, presented with serious and searing problems, we don't know how to solve them except to look back to what hasn't worked.

***

Even if millennials are checking out socialism, the way we've responded to the cost-of-living quagmire has been fundamentally capitalist. We've been innovating away, conjuring up fresh solutions in response to market forces.

To take just one example, faced with eye-watering housing prices, many young adults have decided to downsize. Enter the Tiny House Movement, which has seen millennials move into homes that are smaller than a studio apartment with bathrooms scarcely bigger than a coat closet. Millennials often build these micro-abodes themselves, spending very little on materials and nothing on labor. The disadvantages of a tiny house are obvious: less living space, less storage, less room for kids to roam. They're a solution for singles, mostly, yet the advantages are clear too: tiny housers tend to have less debt and more money in the bank than regular-sized homeowners.[21]

Even trailers and RVs are making a comeback among those in search of a more frugal life. And even if some of this is just reporters in desperate search of a trend, even if most downsizing millennials haven't quite gone *that* small, the Tiny House movement still strikes at something relatable. I grew up on a lot thoroughly colonized by the American dream: four bedrooms, three baths, two maple trees in the front yard—and there were times it simply seemed too big. I remember thinking the house could feel like an ill-fitting cloak with too many folds and pockets. And since space tends to not remain empty for very long, a bigger house can also become an excuse to hoard stuff you don't need. Then there's the sheer time demanded by all that square footage. For my hard-working and wonderful dad, weekends, his ostensible time off, meant keeping up the yard, mowing the lawn in the summer, shoveling snow in the winter.

There are even millennials who have given up on homes entirely and become outright nomads. The so-called #VanLife phenomenon took hold on social media back in 2020 as young influencers began documenting what it was like to live out of a van. As was to be expected, much of this was touched up for Instagram. One journalist who tried out the van lifestyle later wrote an op-ed for the *New York Times* reporting poor sleep, freezing temperatures, and back pain from hours of sitting in a car seat.[22] But #VanLife was still prevalent enough for

---

21 Matthew McNulty, "Tiny house trend: Why so many people are looking to live small," Fox Business, October 2, 2019, https://www.foxbusiness.com/real-estate/tiny-home-phenomena-the-pros-and-cons-of-living-in-a-micro-home.

22 Caity Weaver, "I Lived the #VanLife. It Wasn't Pretty," *New York Times*, April 20, 2022, https://www.nytimes.com/2022/04/20/magazine/van-life-dwelling.html.

my friend the writer Kara Kennedy to declare 2023 the "year of the vagabond,"[23] as people pulled up their pricey roots and cast off into the unknown.

Living in Yellowstone in a Chevy is one way to get around the pressures of having a mortgage. Yet there are also less romantic ways in which millennials have adapted to high prices. The most obvious one is that we're not having as many kids, which has helped drive America's birth rate to a record low. And while some of this is due to a decline in sex, as we discussed in chapter 2, some of it is that we view the cost of raising a child as too expensive.

Which brings up the question: what does it say about the richest country in human history that our people can't afford to repopulate the place? Or choose to live in vans to cut costs? The American dream is not a phase we went through during the twentieth century. It's linked to the fundaments of who we are, our openness, our willingness to take in others and enable them to pull themselves up, to raise their children to have a better future. If the young are being priced out of that dream, then they're going to feel less invested in the country as a whole. Their patriotism is going to wane. They're going to look abroad to more exotic solutions like socialism, or move abroad and become unbearable expats who gush about how that one time they almost got run over by a cyclist in Amsterdam was *just so liberating.*

And they're going to grumble about those for whom the American dream was a waking reality. Which in turn short-circuits another fundament of society: the need for the young to learn from and respect the wisdom of the old. The War Between the Generations has a very real casus belli—but maybe it's time for a truce. Generation X has been playing Switzerland for too long—let's all team up and attack them.

<hr>

23   Kara Kennedy, "2023 is the year of the vagabond," *Spectator World*, January 9, 2023, https://thespectator.com/life/2023-is-the-year-of-the-vagabond/.

CHAPTER 14

Capitalists Without Chests, Politicians Without Brains

Here now are six vignettes from decline-era America. The first two are about fighting words, the second two are about saving the world, and the third two are about those who dare to dream.

***

In July 2023, the world almost got what it never knew it needed: a cage match between Mark Zuckerberg and Elon Musk.

To the uninitiated, this would not seem like a fight worth airing on pay-per-view. Zuckerberg, the creator of Facebook and mortician of the metaverse, appeared unlikely to win a boxing match against his houseplant let alone a real-life human being. And while Musk might be a jack-of-all-trades—CEO of X (formerly Twitter), pioneer of space travel, owner of libs—he doesn't come off as a natural fighter either.

But then the point wasn't that either of these men could draw blood. The point was they're wealthy tech capitalists who have enough money to pretend they're MMA finalists. And *are . . . you . . . not . . . ENTERTAINED*?!

The Fight of the Century (this is a century of decline, remember) was touched off when Zuckerberg's company Meta announced it was releasing a product called Threads that was meant as a competitor to Twitter. This understandably strummed a nerve with Twitter chief Musk, who tweeted, "I'm sure Earth can't wait to be exclusively under Zuck's thumb with no other options."[1]

A fellow Twitter compulsive then informed Musk that Zuckerberg had been training in jujitsu, to which Musk replied, "I'm up for a cage match if he is lol." And so it was on. Zuckerberg texted Dana White, the president of Ultimate Fighting Championship (UFC), to see if he could make the fight happen. White agreed and began establishing the rights to the event as well as exploring venues in Vegas.[2] The Italian government then got involved and floated the Roman Colosseum as an option, raising the optimistic possibility that both men could be eaten by lions. (*ARE...YOU...NOT...*)[3] Bookies began posting odds, while newspaper headlines read like wrestling promotions: "Elon Musk vs. Zuckerberg: who would win in battle of the tech titans?"

I'm not an unbiased narrator in all this. My money was always riding on Musk (assuming you remove the asteroid from the betting

---

1   Elon Musk, "I'm sure Earth can't wait to be exclusively under Zuck's thumb with no other options," Twitter, June 20, 2023.

2   Ryan Mac and Mike Isaac, "A 'Cage Match' Between Elon Musk and Mark Zuckerberg May Be No Joke," *New York Times*, July 1, 2023, https://www.nytimes.com/2023/07/01/technology/elon-musk-mark-zuckerberg-cage-match.html.

3   "MARK ZUCKERBERG, ELON MUSK: ITALIAN GOVERNMENT OFFER . . . Fight Like True Gladiators . . . At The Colosseum!!!" The good and sober headline writers at TMZ, June 29, 2023, https://www.tmz.com/2023/06/29/elon-musk-mark-zuckerberg-mma-fight-colosseum-rome-italian-government-dana-white-ufc/.

tables, of course). Not only do I find Zuckerberg annoying, but Musk is still my best hope of seeing Twitter destroyed as he tries to "fix" that which can only be conflagrated. Yet there were early hints this may not have been the wisest of bets. For one, Zuckerberg had that jujitsu thing going for him, while Musk proudly tweeted that he almost never works out "except for picking up my kids & throwing them in the air" (my strength routine exactly!).[4] For another, Zuckerberg is thirteen years younger than Musk.

Still, there was reason to think Musk was a scrappier opponent than he was letting on, perhaps owing to some secret training regimen up in the mountains. In 2022, he challenged Vladimir Putin to a fight with nothing less than Ukraine as the prize.[5] Putin didn't reply, and thankfully Musk himself didn't then invade Ukraine, though I'm reliably informed the State Department is keeping its cage match–related options open.

Mark Zuckerberg is the inventor of Facebook, the owner of Instagram, the most successful social media entrepreneur in history, and a revolutionary who has fundamentally changed how we relate to each other and redefined words as varied as "friend" and "like." Elon Musk is the wealthiest man on earth whose company SpaceX helped pioneer private space travel and whose company Tesla forever changed the market for electric vehicles, all before he acquired Twitter, which he's proceeded to both rename and remake in his own image.

***

4   Anthony Cuthbertson, "Elon Musk confirms cage fight with Mark Zuckerberg," *The Independent*, June 22, 2023, https://www.independent .co.uk/tech/elon-musk-cage-fight-mark-zuckerberg-b2362120.html.

5   Elon Musk, "I hereby challenge ???????? ????? to single combat Stakes are ???????," Twitter, March 14, 2022.

Presidential elections are often compared to battles royale, and in decline-era America, every figurative must eventually become a literal. So it was that in 2016, then-vice president Joe Biden commented on then-presidential wannabe Donald Trump, "The press always ask me, 'Don't I wish I were debating him?' No, I wish we were in high school—I could take him behind the gym. That's what I wish."[6]

Biden, in case he hasn't personally showed up on your doorstep to tell you, grew up in Scranton, Pennsylvania, and apparently he got in a few schoolyard scraps back in his day. He was responding to the then-recently released *Access Hollywood* tapes, so he had reason to be annoyed. Still . . . you're in your seventies and you're threatening to give someone an Indian sunburn? Really?

Thankfully, Trump is really good at turning the other cheek and . . . and I'm just kidding; about three seconds later he replied, "I'd love that. I'd love that. Mr. Tough Guy. You know, he's Mr. Tough Guy. You know when he's Mr. Tough Guy? When he's standing behind a microphone by himself."[7]

This time, there was no Dana White on hand to arrange a prime-time slot. Yet click-starved newspapers still leapt into the fray: "Who would win a fist fight between Joe Biden and Donald Trump?" wondered the *South China Morning Post*.[8] The BBC, a news organization

---

6   Allie Malloy and Daniella Diaz, "Biden: I would only take Trump behind the gym 'if I were in high school,'" CNN, October 24, 2016, https://www.cnn.com/2016/10/21/politics/joe-biden-fight-donald-trump-2016-election/index.html.

7   Jeremy Diamond, "Trump: I'd 'love' to fight Biden," CNN, October 26, 2016, https://www.cnn.com/2016/10/25/politics/donald-trump-joe-biden-fight/index.html.

8   "Who would win a fist fight between Joe Biden and Donald Trump?" *South China Morning Post*, October 26, 2016, https://www.scmp.com/news/world/united-states-canada/article/2040219/who-would-win-fist-fight-between-joe-biden-and.

so buttoned-up its viewers refer to it as "Auntie," inquired, "Trump and Biden behind a barn—who has a fighting chance?" The BBC went on to describe the dustup with characteristic and frankly charitable British understatement as "one of the more unusual challenges in this most unusual of all US election campaigns."[9]

The playground rumble wasn't to happen, alas, and when Trump was sworn in as president the following year, Biden did refrain from trying to give him a noogie. Yet by 2018, the two men were at it again. Once again, it was Biden who started it, saying of Trump, "They asked me if I'd like to debate this gentleman, and I said 'no.' I said, 'If we were in high school, I'd take him behind the gym and beat the hell out of him,'" adding, "I'm a pretty damn good athlete. Any guy that talked that way was usually the fattest, ugliest S.O.B. in the room." What made this special was that Biden was speaking at a rally against assault—sexual assault, but still.

Thankfully, Trump once again took the high road and . . . and actually about fourteen milliseconds later he tweeted, "Crazy Joe Biden is trying to act like a tough guy. Actually, he is weak, both mentally and physically, and yet he threatens me, for the second time, with physical assault. He doesn't know me, but he would go down fast and hard, crying all the way."[10]

Joe Biden as president has presided over inflation, a spike in the crime rate, an increasingly sclerotic political system, and a botched troop pullout from Afghanistan. Donald Trump as president had at best

---

9   "Trump and Biden behind a barn—who has a fighting chance?" BBC, October 26, 2016, https://www.bbc.com/news/election-us-2016 -37762831.

10   Molly Nagle, "Trump assails 'Crazy Joe Biden' as 'weak' after former VP's threat to 'beat the hell out of him,'" ABC News, March 22, 2018, https ://abcnews.go.com/Politics/trump-assails-crazy-joe-biden-weak-vps -threat/story?id=53932826.

mixed results on his goals of slowing the flow of immigration, ending America's overseas wars, and managing a rising China.

***

Sam Altman is worried about climate change. That's hardly unusual—just about everyone these days is worried about climate change, an anxiety they usually assuage with joyrides on their Gulfstream jets. Yet Altman, a Silicon Valley tycoon and artificial intelligence innovator, just might have the money to pull off goodness knows what.

Altman is the CEO of OpenAI and known for his work with Y Combinator, a San Francisco-based start-up accelerator, which means it provides new tech companies with guidance and funding in exchange for a piece of the pie. YC, as it's abbreviated, is regarded by some as the best start-up accelerator in the world, and in 2018 they announced a major move: they would be investing big bucks in revolutionary new techniques to fight climate change. As Altman himself put it, these would go beyond mere investments in clean energy, which were important but also *the hour is late*. What YC would alternatively be looking at were bonkers methods of changing the very composition of the earth's atmosphere.

Said bonkers methods were at the time merely speculative, lacking the money and technology to make them a reality. But then that's where the well-heeled YC comes in, with its capacity to fund, as the company puts it, ideas that "straddle the border between very difficult to science fiction." The website Vox summarized four of these ideas: literally engineering new and better plankton that would release less carbon dioxide, capturing a natural process called mineral weathering through which rocks remove CO_2 from the atmosphere, creating synthetic enzymes that efficiently break down or dispose of CO_2, and flooding the world's deserts and turning them into algae beds that would then absorb carbon.[11]

It's here that a normal person might ask: Aren't deserts precious biomes worth preserving? And: Isn't flooding precisely what we're trying to prevent by fighting climate change? And above all: Isn't it dangerous to be tampering with the composition of the earth's atmosphere?

Such questions aren't just being asked by heteronormative climate change skeptics like ya boi. Even the United Nations has warned that "engineering-based removal activities are technologically and economically unproven, especially at scale, and pose unknown environmental and social risks."[12] (Green hysterics also tend not to like carbon removal tech because it detracts from their pet projects such as wind farms and hotel conferences.) But no matter. Among the initiatives that have received YC's seal of approval include a start-up that's building a glorified vacuum cleaner that will suck carbon out of the earth's atmosphere.[13] (The start-up's name, Legion of Doom LLC, probably should have raised a few red flags.)

Altman is at the crest of a wave of interest in green investment that's been sweeping Silicon Valley, shifting climate change research out of the university and into the boardroom. So when YC invests in,

---

11   Kelsey Piper, "Silicon Valley wants to fight climate change with these 'moonshot' ideas," Vox, October 26, 2018, https://www.vox.com/future-perfect/2018/10/26/18018454/silicon-valley-sam-altman-yc-climate-change-carbon-moonshot.

12   Hiar Corbin, "U.N. slams carbon removal as unproven and risky," E&E News by *Politico*, May 24, 2023, https://www.eenews.net/articles/u-n-slams-carbon-removal-as-unproven-and-risky/.

13   Tasmin Lockwood, "How Y Combinator–backed Seabound is using carbon-capture tech to tackle the shipping industry's problematic emissions," *Business Insider*, August 29, 2023, https://www.businessinsider.com/y-combinator-backed-startup-seabound-carbon-capture-wave-shipping-2023-8#:~:text=Seabound%2C%20backed%20by%20the%20famed,sold%20as%20a%20building%20material.

for example, a biosciences company that seeks to alter the digestion of cows so they emit less methane when they burp—I am not making that up—you have no choice but to take them both literally and seriously.[14] YC brags that as of December 2022 they'd already funded over one hundred climate tech start-ups, which together are worth more than $10 billion.[15]

Sam Altman is the CEO of OpenAI and is regarded as the god-father of ChatGPT, the artificial intelligence bot whose research and communication capabilities will likely one day make it to AI what the Model T was to automobiles. Before that, he cofounded the company Loopt, a smartphone location sharing service, and was briefly the CEO of Reddit. A prolific tech investor, he's funded companies from Airbnb to Asana to Pinterest. In 2018, he considered a run for governor of California as a Democrat.

***

Alexandria Ocasio-Cortez had only been in Congress for a month when she introduced the most unimportant bill you've forever heard of. The Green New Deal was unveiled by both AOC and Senator Ed Markey in 2019, and as with FDR's signature legislative blitz, it promised nothing less than a national transformation. Yet whereas the New Deal sought to haul America out of the Great Depression, its green doppelgänger had in its sights our rapidly sautéing planet.

What would change under the Green New Deal? Everything, give or take. The legislation's stated goals seem innocuous enough: more good-paying union jobs in marginalized communities to reduce

---

14 Haje Jan Kamps, "Alga Biosciences wants to help climate change, one bovine burp at a time," *Techcrunch*, April 6, 2023, https://techcrunch .com/2023/04/06/alga-biosciences-series-seed/.

15 "Request for Startups: Climate Tech." Y Combinator, December 15, 2022, https://www.ycombinator.com/blog/rfs-climatetech.

misogynist greenhouse gases, etc., etc., etc. Yet dig a little deeper and the sheer radicalism of the thing comes to surface. Among the Green New Deal's proposals was to gut a modest 100 percent of the country's buildings and retrofit them with new energy-efficient insulation, electricity, plumbing, stoves, windows, and doors.[16]

The bill would also invest massive amounts of money in green energy and effectively end fossil fuel extraction in America as we know it, displacing millions of workers and forcing them into other jobs—assuming those jobs existed at all. AOC herself seemed to acknowledge the sheer scale of what she was proposing, given that a previous version of the Green New Deal had guaranteed economic assistance to those "unable or unwilling to work" (because their jobs had been crushed by bureaucrats, presumably). The bill was "massive," AOC admitted,[17] but then those were just the eggs that needed to be cracked if we were to get our net-zero emissions omelet.

Also included in the Green New Deal were less environmentally relevant measures like universal health insurance and affordable housing. This wasn't a serious legislative package so much as a list of bullet points to make Democrat Capitol Hill staffers feel tingly in their feet. There was also no blueprint as to how any of it was supposed to work. AOC merely set the vision while unelected regulatory agencies like the

16 David Harsanyi, "The New and Improved Green New Deal Is Still Insane," *National Review*, April 20, 2021, https://www.nationalreview.com/corner/the-new-and-improved-green-new-deal-is-still-insane/.

17 Anders Hagstrom, "AOC admits 'massive' scale of Green New Deal, says climate change will be even worse," Fox News, April 23, 2023, https://www.foxnews.com/politics/aoc-admits-massive-scale-green-new-deal-says-climate-change-even-worse#:~:text=Rep.,with%20MSNBC%20host%20Jen%20Psaki.

EPA were expected to sort out the details. Exasperated economists who tried to price the thing ended up with numbers like $93 trillion.[18]

The Green New Deal was dead on arrival in Congress, with every Senate Republican and four Senate Democrats blocking it from even receiving a vote. Alexandria Ocasio-Cortez is known chiefly for her Twitter clapbacks, TikTok videos, and being in something called the Squad. In 2021, she was rated by the Center for Effective Lawmaking as one of the least effective members of Congress.[19]

***

Aubrey de Grey is a British-born California millionaire, and while he's long had a Mines of Moria–style beard down to his sternum, his old age may now be manifesting in other ways. De Grey is perhaps the most vocal living advocate of human immortality, harnessing scientific innovation to enable man to live forever.

In fairness to de Grey, he isn't seeking to abolish the human condition solely out of self-interest. He readily concedes that a man his age has only a 40 to 50 percent chance of escaping death's sting. Yet for the on-average younger general population, he kicks up the odds to 80 to 90 percent.[20] That means there's a good chance I could be writing

18   Chris Mills Rodrigo, "Center-right group: Ocasio-Cortez's Green New Deal could cost $93 trillion," *The Hill*, February 25, 2019, https://thehill .com/policy/energy-environment/431460-center-right-group-says-ocasio -cortezs-green-new-deal-could-cost-93/.

19   Jon Levine, "Study declares AOC one of the least effective members of Congress," *New York Post*, April 3, 2021, https://nypost .com/2021/04/03/aoc-was-one-of-least-effective-members-of -congress-study/#:~:text=When%20looking%20at%20the%20 legislative,state%2C%20she%20ranked%20dead%20last.

20   Brian Wang, "Scientific Progress to Radical Antiaging, Aubrey Sees 50+% of Longevity Escape Velocity by 2035," NextBigFuture.com, March 24, 2021, https://www.nextbigfuture.com/2021/03/scientific-progress-to -radical-antiaging-aubrey-sees-50-of-longevity-escape-velocity-by-2035 .html.

snarky books about decline until our planet superheats (a mark against scientific progress, if you think about it).

These odds are part of what's called the "longevity escape velocity," or LEV, a term de Grey throws around a lot. It refers to the moment when our capacity to extend life will outpace our aging. So, while in 2024 you might age one year (five years if you're writing a book), if research and development is able to prolong the average human life in 2024 by two years, and the innovation only accelerates from there, then you've effectively cheated death. You'll live forever. Naturally such R&D takes money, and that's where the Methuselah Foundation comes in. Cofounded by de Grey in 2003 as a medical charity, it funds antiaging initiatives with the stated goal of making "90 the new 50 by 2030."[21]

There are all kinds of methods that might be used to reach the LEV, from 3D bioprinting healthy human tissue to replacing atrophied cells with stem cells.[22] And while de Grey himself might look like the (notably dead) Rasputin, there are other signs he isn't necessarily the guru he's made himself out to be. De Grey has long inspired consternation among scientists, who point out that outwitting biology to such an extent—stopping aging goes far beyond curing cancer or osteoporosis—will take a lot more than media-friendly enthusiasm. Yet it's also true that as time has worn on, more researchers have come around to his ambitious point of view.

21 "Return on Mission," Methuselah Foundation, 2023, https://www
    .mfoundation.org/what-we-do#:~:text=Our%20mission%20is%20
    to%20make,%2C%20investors%2C%20and%20donors%20focused.

22 Brian Wang, "Aubrey de Grey Thinks Robust Human Longevity Might
    Be Here by 2037," NextBigFuture.com, February 28, 2019, https
    ://www.nextbigfuture.com/2019/02/aubrey-de-grey-thinks-robust
    -human-longevity-might-be-here-by-2037.html.

Perhaps no one since Gilgamesh, the ancient Sumerian king who sought eternal life, has quested so hard for immortality. And de Grey's crusade has proven contagious among his fellow Silicon Valley elites. In 2022, Jeff Bezos made a major investment in a start-up called Alto Labs that's researching cellular rejuvenation,[23] while in 2013 Google launched a company with the goal of curing death.[24] And just in case this is starting to sound like a Michael Crichton novel where scientific hubris goes catastrophically wrong but it's still just fiction, consider it may just be scientific hubris gone catastrophically wrong. The Silicon Valley elites have revolutionized our world before; if anyone is going to do it again, it's the likes of de Grey.

Aubrey de Grey is a biomedical engineer, software programmer, AI researcher, and amateur mathematician who teaches at the Moscow Institute of Physics and Technology and has been interviewed widely across the media. He's the author of the book *Ending Aging* and has an estimated net worth in the millions.

***

Back in the Mesozoic mists of 2012, a curious moment came to pass during one of the Republican presidential primary debates. Newt Gingrich, the former speaker of the House, was asked about his support for building a colony on the Moon. He defended the idea by saying that America never returning to the lunar surface would amount to "a path of national decline."

23   Caroline Delbert, "Jeff Bezos is Paying for a Way to Make Humans Immortal," *Popular Mechanics*, January 26, 2022, https://www.popularmechanics.com/technology/startups/a38867242/jeff-bezos-altos-labs/.

24   Jay Yarow, "Google Is Launching A Company That Hopes To Cure Death," *Business Insider*, September 18, 2013, https://www.businessinsider.com/google-is-launching-a-company-that-hopes-to-cure-death-2013-9.

Music to my ears, darling! Except then along came the buzzkill dad from *Stranger Things* to ruin everyone's fun. "I spent twenty-five years in business," droned Mitt Romney as the audience fell out of their chairs into a state of paralysis and the moderator died. "If I had a business executive come to me and say they wanted to spend a few hundred billion dollars to put a colony on the Moon, I'd say you're fired."[25]

There's so much happening in that quote: the cross-eyed notion that boasting about your corporate experience is going to win over GOP voters, the ridiculing of a Moon base when Romney's presidential campaign would turn out to be a far worse investment, the unwitting utterance of the tagline of the man who four years later would go where no Romney had ever gone before. And, of course, the sympathy it created for Gingrich. You knew you wanted that space mall, didn't you?

Gingrich, once upon a time, was the sharpest ideas man in the Republican Party and perhaps its last dreamer. Many of his ideas were focused on outer space and inspired by his love of the science fiction writer Isaac Asimov. Some of them, the colonization of the Moon by 2020, were good ideas, even if all we got that year were anti-colonization riots. Others, such as his plan to install giant mirrors in space so we wouldn't need streetlights, make you think Romney had a point.[26]

But then that's just living out loud for Newton Leroy Gingrich. The man entered the limelight as the face of the Republican Revolution, the 1994 GOP wave elections that ended half a century of Democratic

25 "Romney mocks Gingrich's 'moon colony' idea." YouTube. Uploaded by CBS News, January 26, 2012.

26 Linda Feldmann, "Newt Gingrich: 8 of the GOP idea man's more unusual ideas," *Christian Science Monitor*, December 15, 2011, https://www.csmonitor.com/USA/Elections/President/2011/1215/Newt-Gingrich-8-of-the-GOP-idea-man-s-more-unusual-ideas/Establishing-a-moon-colony-to-extract-minerals.

congressional control, and even back then he was brimming with ideas. Elected Speaker of the House, Gingrich became part politician and part professor, educating his caucus (and anyone else who would listen) on conservative principles while pushing through one of the most creative blitzes of legislation in American history. And while the remark of one Republican that "Newt has 10 ideas a day. Two of them are good, six are weird, and two very weird" is probably lowballing the very weird,[27] who really cares in the end?

This is the man who said in 1996 that beach volleyball was a blessing of a free society.[28] It's the man who in 2007 created a digital version of himself via the computer game Second Life and had it give a speech on the steps of the Capitol.[29] And while he did not then jump aboard a giant purple pterodactyl and fly through the skies of D.C. gunning down enemy airships, such is Newt Gingrich that you could have seen it. You could have.

Newt Gingrich is a former Speaker of the House who successfully cut taxes, reformed welfare, and helped balance the federal budget, all over the objections of a Democratic president, while rewriting the rules of Republican politics. He's more recently known for pushing ads that claimed the 2020 election had been stolen from Donald Trump.[30]

* * *

27   Jonathan Weisman and Brody Mullins, "House Divided on Ex-Leader," *Wall Street Journal*, December 6, 2011, https://www.wsj.com/articles /SB10001424052970204083204577080732531879426.

28   "Beach Volleyball, Child Labor, and Other Craziest Newt Gingrich Comments," *The Daily Beast*, July 13, 2017, https://www.thedailybeast.com /beach-volleyball-child-labor-and-other-craziest-newt-gingrich-comments.

29   Paul Rice, "Newt Gingrich Loves Second Life," *The Escapist*, September 19, 2007.

30   Aila Slisco, "Newt Gingrich Pushed Election Fraud Ads to 'Arouse Anger': Jan. 6 Committee," *Newsweek*, September 1, 2022, https://www .newsweek.com/newt-gingrich-pushed-election-fraud-ads-arouse-anger -jan-6-committee-1739185.

What unites all these vignettes is that uniquely decline-era combo of privilege and wackiness. It's akin to what Ross Douthat in one of his books defines as a "decadent society," one both successful and stagnant, vain and campy.[31]

What divides these scenes is their economic geography and their seriousness. Zuckerberg, Musk, Altman, and de Grey are all in the private sector, and whatever you think of them, they've racked up some impressive and truly revolutionary successes. When they say they want to remake the world again, or just playact modern-day gladiators, you believe them. The same can't be said about politicians like Biden and AOC. They've got all of the show with none of the seriousness.

While our capitalists are innovating away, our legislators lack that problem-solving spirit that's so necessary in a self-governed liberal democracy. Once upon a time, America had a reputation for getting itself into big messes that it then hauled itself out of with big solutions. Sometimes those big solutions—Prohibition comes to mind—were grave mistakes, but others were successful if compromised attempts to respond to the problems of their times. (This is what makes Gingrich so interesting: he bridges the two eras, having passed the aforementioned welfare reform only to now spend most of his time on cable news.)

In the private sector, the decadence is largely a sideshow and sometimes even has a deeper purpose: the Zuckerberg/Musk fight was probably a PR ploy by both men to call attention to their respective brands. Yet in the government, the decadence is increasingly the point.

Our political system has become sclerotic. Our government is both too big and too ineffective, too unaccountable and too pandering. At least Mark Zuckerberg has some idea how to run a big institution. It's to this political dysfunction that we now turn.

---

31 Ross Douthat, *The Decadent Society: How We Became Victims of Our Own Success* (New York: Simon & Schuster, 2020).

CHAPTER 15

Our Godzilla Versus Mothra Politics

We were partisans once, and young.

The first election I followed with any real consciousness was the 2000 contest between George W. Bush and Al Gore. There were hundreds of other campaigns that year—state legislators, governors, congressmen, senators—but all of them have since been lost to the campaign button enthusiasts and the annals of Ballotpedia. There was one race that mattered back in 2000. It was George W. Bush and Al Gore.

I remember hearing over and over again that year that said race between George W. Bush and Al Gore was "the most important election of our lives." And in fairness, it did seem like the stakes were higher than four years earlier in 1996, which I faintly recalled as a sleepy affair with an often asleep Republican candidate. But I was only thirteen in 2000, and that year's election was also said to be the most important to voters in their nineties who had been around when FDR was leading the country during World War II. And that did seem like a stretch.

Yet it was also difficult to tell because four years later the pundits were pronouncing the 2004 election to be the most important of our lives. That was the year the Bush war agenda was on the line via a half-hearted challenge from international sex symbol John Kerry. The 2008 election was the most important of our lives because Obama was going to usher in world peace or something. The 2012 election was the most important of our lives because . . . actually, I'm not sure why on that one, but several people did say that, including Fox News leading man Bill O'Reilly.[1] The 2016 and 2020 elections had real claims to be the most important of our lives, but by then everyone was just numb. The entire electorate was sitting in the bathtub with the water up to their chins plugging their ears and screaming.

I'm always tempted to throw a curveball and declare, say, the 2009 election to be the most important of our lives. *This country has never recovered from Bill Owens winning the special election for New York's 23rd congressional district and it never will.* But then you could probably find a paid-in-full consultant who would argue that doomed Plattsburgh independent Doug Hoffman really was the most consequential figure of the twenty-first century. It's a strange business, politics, and I'm worse off for having ever made contact with it.

Why do we do this to ourselves? Why is it that every four years we come together to pretend the very fate of the universe has been balled up into a burping contest between two geriatrics?

There are many reasons the stakes of American presidential elections seem so high. One is that our elections tend to be close when compared

---

1   Conor Friedersdorf, "It's Time to Retire the Phrase, 'This Is the Most Important Election . . .'" *The Atlantic,* May 2, 2012, https://www
.theatlantic.com/politics/archive/2012/05/its-time-to-retire-the-phrase
-this-is-the-most-important-election/256623/.

to those of other countries, which underscores the need to drive out every vote. Another is that we're the ones who revolutionized the idea of politics as entertainment, with even early American campaigns featuring band-stands and slogans. You could even argue some of this urgency makes sense as a reflection of our time, a response to the decline we perceive around us and a need to elect politicians who will reverse it before it's too late.

But this doesn't explain why presidential elections in particular have taken on such an apocalyptic tone. As a voter, I'm far more affected by local issues like road construction and residential zoning than national ones like defense funding or even federal tax rates. Yet I have no idea who my city council representative is, let alone my state senator. But I'll be damned if I don't know that Joe Biden is the president of the United States and at this very moment he's plunging his arthritic fist into the very chest cavity of Traditional America. (The irony is that my city council is far more functional than the federal government, which means I'd probably be happier if I paid more attention to it!)

What's happened is that as business and government and media have grown bigger, politics has grown bigger too, flush with money from big business, power from big government, and visibility from big media. Our attentions have drifted upward toward the presidency, the biggest office in our system, whose candidates have become stand-ins for literally everything in existence. Think of two monsters duking it out over a densely packed cityscape. And then cut to the title card: *Godzilla 46: The Most Important Election of Our Lives.*

Yet if every four years we pit Godzilla against Mothra, then the rest of us increasingly feel like that general from every monster movie. You know the one: grizzled face, chomps a cigar, wears his fatigues even if he's just going to Starbucks. The general always advises nuclear weapons as the solution to the monster problem, and we feel the same way. Can't we just tune out both of them and be done with it already? We're trying to take a bath here.

***

The question of when American politics became too big is ultimately a question of presidential power and perception. There have been big presidents before: George Washington cut quite the figure; Abraham Lincoln consolidated authority to fight the Civil War; Teddy Roosevelt wielded Washington like a mallet to squash the trusts; FDR tried to pack the Supreme Court and then refused to pack his own belongings after his second term.

But for the purposes of this book, it makes sense to examine the more recent bloating of presidential power. The new millennium began with one George W. Bush who, having barely squeaked out a win against former vice president Al Gore, at first didn't seem like a particularly big president. He was inarticulate, new to Washington, and, as Democrats never failed to remind everyone, in the White House on only the thinnest of mandates. He was also hardly a celebrity president in the mold of JFK (despite having done a stint in rehab). But the attacks of 9/11 would elevate his presidency to a height no one had ever anticipated. And its real influencer potential would lie not with Bush himself but with those lurking in the background.

Bush's vice president, Dick Cheney, took that usually irrelevant office and made it an administration command post. Donald Rumsfeld became one of the most important defense secretaries in history, overseeing the invasions of Afghanistan and Iraq. Both Cheney and Rumsfeld were bureaucratic streetfighters who had cut their teeth as operatives in the Ford administration. They knew how to manipulate the federal government better than Bush, a former governor of Texas, ever could.

And they used that knowledge in the wake of 9/11 to amass enormous power in the executive branch in the name of keeping America safe. The CIA was given the authority to torture (excuse me, *interrogate*) suspected terrorists in foreign dungeons. The National Security Agency (NSA) was permitted broad access to Americans' phone data.

The observation by Randolph Bourne that "war is the health of the state" had rarely felt so time-tested.

And that state would be defended at all costs. When the Bush Justice Department's second-in-command, a fella by the name of James Comey, refused to sign a reauthorization of the NSA's expansive surveillance program over concerns it violated the Fourth Amendment's privacy protections, Cheney's lackeys literally ambushed a half-dead attorney general John Ashcroft in the hospital and tried to make him sign. Ashcroft heroically sat up and told them where to stick it, but a message had been sent. Unconstitutional war powers would be preserved at all costs. The surveillance program was eventually reauthorized with only minor tweaks.[2]

So far as presidential monsters go, George W. Bush was himself a minor ogre. Yet his administration was nonetheless a turning point because it was when the twenty-first-century administrative state came into its own. The security bureaucracy was given unprecedented autonomy. A new agency was created, the Department of Homeland Security. And it wasn't just the security side: Bush expanded the federal government's role in education through the No Child Left Behind reforms and created a new health entitlement called Medicare Part D. Bush himself summed up his administration's ethos this way: "When somebody hurts, government has got to move."[3] And government did indeed move—into your text messages, your browser history, your health care.

The Church Committee in the 1970s had used Congress's power to rein in the security state. The Clinton administration had worked

---

2 Bart Gellman, *Angler: The Cheney Vice Presidency* (New York: Penguin, 2009), ch. 12.

3 Bruce Bartlett, "How Bush Bankrupted America," Cato Institute, January/February 2006, https://www.cato.org/policy-report/january /february-2006/how-bush-bankrupted-america.

with Republicans in Congress to balance the federal budget and trim the defense bureaucracy. The Bush administration marked the moment when the executive branch again began to eclipse the legislative. And while these things ebb and flow, Congress has never since gotten serious about clawing back its powers.

One reason for this was that no one really cared. In post-9/11 America, it was assumed that a godlike executive branch would at least keep us safe. The 2000s weren't as politically apathetic as the 1990s, but there was still a sense that government could be left on autopilot, that the war on terror was just a couple dry coughs amid the clean air of history's end. Yet this indifference was about to meet its own challenge. A political savior was to descend from the heaven that is inner-city Chicago. And while his campaign slogan, "hope and change," didn't really mean anything, you could still *feel* it, couldn't you?

Barack Obama burst onto the scene determined to Make America Trite Again. He'd first garnered attention at the 2004 Democratic convention when he'd uttered this line: "There is not a liberal America and a conservative America; there is the United States of America!" And what a profound insight into the human condition that was. The country under Obama became like one of those corporate seminars where executives utter focus-grouped lines about "synergy" while everyone else doodles TIE Fighters in the margins of their notebooks. Obama: "We are the ones we have been waiting for!" *Next we'll be having a catered lunch. . . .*

After the failed war in Iraq and the 2008 economic crash, Americans were in the mood for national renewal. Just make it national renewal we could print on the inside of a birthday card. Obama was the celebrity president Bush never was, and he took on a curious mix of roles in the national psyche. He was our therapist, the calm presence who promised it was all going to be okay in fifty words or less. He was also a kind of national dad, with his cornball sense of humor and glamorously functional family strolling around Martha's Vineyard.

What he was not was what many conservatives said he was: a third-world Marxist, a foreign interloper. Many on the right became convinced there was something exotic about Obama, a whiff of anti-Americanism that threatened our very way of life. To be fair, Obama didn't exactly help himself by saying he wanted to "fundamentally trans-form" the country. But in practice, he turned out to be kind of a dork. He was obsessed with policy. He thought weatherizing homes was cool. The truth was far more boring: he was just another doctrinaire liberal.

The opposition to him was likewise fairly predictable. Conservatives had watched George W. Bush shore up power in government and Barack Obama meddle in their health care, none of which seemed to have worked. Out of this sprang the Tea Party, which countered "yes, we can" with "don't tread on me" and "do you have these colonial pan-taloons in a trim-fit?" The Tea Party was a libertarian reaction against the statism of both political parties, and at first, contrary to how it was portrayed, it was relatively civil and idea-driven. Yet as the conspiracy theories grew out from the edges, the opposition to Obama grew more feverish and on occasion self-discrediting.

This was another important trend of big politics: As presidents grew big, so did the accusations against them. This had begun under Bill Clinton, one of the most corrupt presidents in American history, whom a handful of Republicans somehow managed to smear as a murderer and an Arkansas drug kingpin. It continued under George W. Bush, who was called a fascist, a racist, and a warmonger (the trifecta!). Presidents were now not just to be criticized but otherized as criminals and interlopers. Such demonization has a long history in our politics, but during the twenty-first century it's reached a china-rattling pitch. Mothra would throw at Godzilla whatever I-beams he could find.

Yet even if Obama wasn't a socialist shaman, beneath the glowing exterior was a dark side. Obama had been elected as a former constitutional law professor who'd promised to end the executive oversteps of the Bush years. Instead he fell head over heels for the administrative state.

Not only did Obama create several new government programs to fight the Great Recession, he brought a paranoia and ruthlessness to the security bureaucracy that sometimes exceeded that of Dick Cheney. He expanded warrantless surveillance of Americans' internet searches.[4] He pioneered drone warfare and assembled "kill lists" of foreigners targeted for assassination.[5] He waged an unprecedented war on whistleblowers.[6] His Justice Department spied on the phone records of Associated Press journalists[7] and baselessly investigated a Fox News reporter as a "criminal co-conspirator" under the Espionage Act.[8] His IRS targeted conservative nonprofit groups for audits.[9]

4   Tessa Berenson, "New Snowden Documents Reveal Obama Administration Expanded NSA Spying," *Time*, June 4, 2015, https ://time.com/3909293/edward-snowden-obama-nsa-spying/.

5   Jo Becker and Scott Shane, "Secret 'Kill List' Proves a Test of Obama's Principles and Will," *New York Times*, May 29, 2012, https://www .nytimes.com/2012/05/29/world/obamas-leadership-in-war-on-al-qaeda .html.

6   Tim Shorrock, "Obama's Crackdown on Whistleblowers," *The Nation*, March 26, 2013, https://www.thenation.com/article/archive /obamas-crackdown-whistleblowers/.

7   Kim Zetter, "Obama Administration Secretly Obtains Phone Records of AP Journalists," *Wired*, May 13, 2013, https://www.wired.com/2013/05 /doj-got-reporter-phone-records/.

8   Jan Crawford, "Fox News reporter secretly monitored by Obama administration: court documents," CBS News, May 23, 2013, https ://www.cbsnews.com/news/fox-news-reporter-secretly-monitored-by -obama-administration-court-documents/.

9   Peter Overby, "IRS Apologizes For Aggressive Scrutiny Of Conservative Groups," NPR, October 17, 2017, https://www.npr .org/2017/10/27/560308997/irs-apologizes-for-aggressive-scrutiny-of -conservative-groups.

He behaved in some respects more like a war president than Bush had, and eventually voters began to ask: "for what?" Obama's administration was supposed to be all balmy breezes and skywritten platitudes, but the economy hadn't fully recovered from the 2008 crash, the troops were still bogged down in the Middle East, and partisanship was at its most vicious tenor yet. America had gone all in for optimism and watched it sour. So perhaps it wasn't a surprise that so many voters, and even so many Obama voters, decided it was time to try the opposite approach. Perhaps the funniest thing about Donald Trump's election is that it was an act of pragmatic calculation.

***

Given what a shock to the system Trump was, it's curious how similar he can seem to his predecessor. Both Obama and Trump were celebrity presidents. Both thrived on the campaign trail. Both extensively utilized television and social media. Both had their earworm slogans, with Trump pledging to "make America great again."

The difference is that, whereas Obama was depicted as a messianic hero, Trump was an antihero. He was the metalhead warrior from *Mad Max* strumming his flamethrower electric guitar while his MAGA convoy gleefully crunched over the norms of government.

This was exactly how his voters would have had it. Obama had glamorized a bland technocratic liberalism—whereas the nineties had gotten comfortable with big business, he'd tried to make the 2010s cool with big government as a corrective. Trump's approach was to use big politics to assail big government, big business, and especially big media. No more screwing about: the electorate had tried that and gotten something called Cash for Clunkers. The Trumpists were in a mood to smash.

In theory, this made Trump the most daunting threat the administrative state had ever faced. Not only had he pledged to roll back government and deregulate the economy, he had a personal beef with the security state (or, as he called it, the deep state). The FBI had improperly surveilled his campaign,[10] while records revealed agents chattering about how they would step in if necessary and stop him from getting elected.[11] The time seemed ripe for a serious rollback of bureaucratic power.

The Trump presidency had its successes on this front, starting with economic deregulation. Yet if deregulation was a success, it was in part because Trump wasn't paying much attention to it. The limitations of an antihero presidency became clear: that guitar thrashed and throbbed as much against Trump's own allies as his enemies. New cabinet secretaries motored up to the White House in a town car and clattered away in a tumbril a few days later. Trump's first and most reliable ally in Congress, Senator Jeff Sessions, a true believer in his agenda, lasted a year and a half as attorney general before resigning at Trump's insistence.[12]

The attack on the deep state turned out to be primarily rhetorical. In practice, Trump defended torture,[13] reauthorized the NSA's expansive

---

10   Samantha Raphaelson, "FBI Apologizes to Court for Mishandling Surveillance of Trump Campaign Adviser," NPR, January 11, 2020, https://www.npr.org/2020/01/11/795566486/fbi-apologizes-to-court-for -mishandling-surveillance-of-trump-campaign-adviser.

11   Michael S. Schmidt, "Top Agent Said F.B.I. Would Stop Trump from Becoming President," *New York Times*, June 14, 2018, https://www .nytimes.com/2018/06/14/us/politics/fbi-texts-trump.html.

12   Peter Baker, et al., "Jeff Sessions is Forced Out as Attorney General as Trump Installs Loyalist," *New York Times*, November 7, 2018, https://www.nytimes.com/2018/11/07/us/politics/sessions-resigns .html#:~:text=Trump%20berated%20Mr.,and%20stop%20him%20 from%20leaving.

13   Jenna Johnson, "Trump says 'torture works,' backs waterboarding and 'much worse,'" *Washington Post*, February 17, 2016, https ://www.washingtonpost.com/politics/trump-says-torture-works-backs

eavesdropping,[14] and showed few qualms about using drones. A law-and-order president understandably had a difficult time reining in his law-and-order agencies—he might rail against them, but when riots broke out in Portland, he itched to deploy them. Not only did this prevent needed reform, it didn't even stop Trump's opponents from claiming he was a threat to national security. Whereas Obama was otherized by the right as a Kenyan interloper, Trump was tarred by virtually the entire media and political establishment as a plant of the Russians.

Mostly what Trump did was to put on good TV. *The Donald Trump Show* was must-see viewing from 2016 into early 2021. It was one of those serialized programs like *24* that never quite let you rest easy. You *thought* order had been restored to the government—and then there goes Nancy Pelosi launching another impeachment inquiry. Certain episodes of *The Donald Trump Show* rank up there with some of the best television America has ever produced ("The One with the Shithole Countries" is a personal favorite). So how disappointing to find that, after a narrative arc that ended with rioters literally storming the Capitol, we got a new president who was pure ratings arsenic.

How to best sum up Joe Biden? He was once strong-armed away from journalists by his own White House Easter Bunny.[15] The writers did attempt to pulp some drama out of Biden's dysfunctional son Hunter, but then Twitter refused to even air those episodes. Generally,

---

-waterboarding-and-much-worse/2016/02/17/4c9277be-d59c-11e5-b195
-2e29a4e13425_story.html.

14 Dustin Volz, "Trump signs bill renewing NSA's internet surveillance program," *Reuters*, January 19, 2018, https://www.reuters.com/article/idUSKBN1F82MI/.

15 Steven Nelson, "Staffer dressed as Easter Bunny stops Biden from answering reporter's question," *New York Post*, April 18, 2022, https://nypost.com/2022/04/18/easter-bunny-stops-biden-from-answering-reporters-question/.

it was agreed that *The Donald Trump Show* without Donald Trump had jumped the shark.

Biden is *not* a celebrity president—he's too old, too mumbly, too susceptible to brain freeze when he eats vanilla ice cream. What he is—and this is important—is the most pro–deep state Democratic president in at least a generation. As a senator, Biden wrote the 1994 crime bill that Bill Clinton signed into law, which dramatically increased federal law enforcement powers. He also wrote the Patriot Act all the way back in the 1990s when he wanted to use it against right-wing terrorists (natch).[16] Libertarians would have to spend another four years vaping therapeutically. There was zero chance Biden would ever rein in the administrative state.

***

From this deeply comprehensive history of the American presidency, we can see a few trends taking shape. The first is a tendency toward celebrity presidents in the age of twenty-four-hour news and social media (even if Biden represents a momentary departure from this tradition). The second is that the administrative state only ever grows larger. The third is that the accusations leveled by the opposition have likewise grown larger and more vitriolic. And the fourth is that the public clearly hates this arrangement and tries with each new president to in some way repudiate his predecessor. (Obama was the idealistic civil libertarian to the wartime Bush, Trump was the antihero to Obama's hero, Biden was the senile old man to Trump's old man.)

The writer Gene Healy has dubbed this latter pattern the cult of the presidency, whereby voters project all their hopes and dreams and fears onto a single leader only to inevitably be disappointed. The president is

---

16   "User Clip: Joe Biden says he wrote the PATRIOT Act," "Counterterrorism Efforts, Part 1—Senate Judiciary Committee," C-SPAN, June 7, 2002.

a sun god who ends up a scapegoat. This cult, as Healy notes, has been building for decades, fed by early progressives' appetite for executive power, the transition of the State of the Union from a written address to a speech, the Cold War, and other factors.[17]

Yet in our own time it's fed into something else: America has become an empire. I don't mean that just in the sense that the United States has military bases overseas (though Lord knows we have military bases overseas). I mean that our system of government itself has become arranged in an imperial fashion.

In ancient Rome, the emperor was a celebrity in his own right: his face was on the coinage and he was sometimes regarded (or at least self-regarded) as a god. He was also very powerful: he could govern beneficently, as did Augustus and Hadrian, or sadistically, as did Caligula and Nero, with little to stop him except through the check and balance of assassination.

Yet what the Roman emperor could not do was to govern on his own. Rome was simply too big to be the province of one man and his advisors. During the Roman Republic, administrative tasks were assigned to elected magistrates with strange names like quaestor and aedile. But as the Romans began to conquer more territory, a bureaucracy became necessary to manage the expanding empire. This bureaucracy was small at first—the early empire vested more power in local authorities than centralized administration—but over time it grew into a force in its own right.

Eventually, even the emperor position itself was bureaucratized, with Diocletian dividing imperial power between two emperors and two successors. Yet from this we can see something emerge like a model of empire: a visible and possibly omnipotent emperor lording

---

17   Gene Healy, *The Cult of the Presidency: America's Dangerous Devotion to Executive Power* (Washington: Cato Institute, 2008).

over an administrative state that chugs through the immense details of governing. Throw in a cabinet of advisors drawn from the nation's elite and a powerful military to keep order, and you've got yourself a mockery of self-government. The legislative bodies that had made decisions during the Roman Republic, the Senate and various elected councils, were either abolished or tamed. Democratic representation gave way to entrenched and centralized power.

Sound familiar?

The biggest difference between America's current system of government and the Roman Empire is, of course, the opposition. Every four years, we have an opportunity to replace our emperor with a different emperor of equivalent size and ambition. Hence the monster battle. Why has politics become so big? Because the stakes really are that high. Those monsters are fighting to be the very face of modern-day Rome—to say nothing of being able to kill anyone with the push of a button and then destroy the planet with the push of another button.

For those of us who support small-r republican government, consensus-based democratic decision-making, and limited federal powers, this is a dire state of affairs. And as the monsters begin to snarl and snap again, it's worth asking: where in the world have the people who are supposed to be governing us gotten off to?

CHAPTER 16

Advise and Descent

O n an autumn day in 2023, in the esteemed Congress of the United States, in what's often referred to as the "world's greatest deliberative body," a sitting senator challenged a union boss to a slap fight.

It began months earlier when Teamsters president Sean O'Brien—who is every ounce the Boston-accented cueball his name and profession would suggest—took to Twitter to call Senator Markwayne Mullin, Republican of Oklahoma, a "greedy CEO," a "clown," and a "fraud." O'Brien added, "You know where to find me. Anyplace, Anytime cowboy." Mullin then tweeted back: "Okay, I accept your challenge. MMA fight for charity of our choice. Sept 30th in Tulsa, Oklahoma."[1]

---

[1] Alex Griffing, "Republican Senator Challenges Union Boss to a Cage Fight Following Testy Hearing Exchange," Mediaite, June 26, 2023, https://www.mediaite.com/politics/republican-senator-challenges-union -boss-to-a-cage-fight-following-testy-hearing-exchange/.

It's become a feature of decline-era America that grown men challenge each other to spectacles of violence they have no intention of following through on. Mullin's flourish should have been the end of it—except come November, O'Brien was summoned as a witness to a hearing of a Senate committee on which Mullin sits. Mullin proceeded to read the Twitter exchange to O'Brien in person and made him an offer: "We can finish it here," he said.

"Okay, that's fine. Perfect," O'Brien replied.

"You want to do it now?" Mullin asked.

"I'd love to do it right now," O'Brien said.

"Well, stand your butt up, then," Mullin said.

"You stand your butt up," O'Brien said.

You're a penis-head. No, you're . . .

Things eventually got so heated that Senator Bernie Sanders had to step in and restore order.[2] And in fairness to Mullin, as he later pointed out, the Senate had once been a more rough-and-tumble place. "You used to be able to cane," Mullin declared,[3] referring to when Congressman Preston Brooks nearly beat Senator Charles Sumner to death with a cane on the Senate floor. That this is widely considered a prelude to the Civil War, which broke out five years later and killed 620,000 people, seems like a relevant bit of context.

---

2   Alex Griffing, "Bernie Sanders Stops Fist-Fight Between Republican and Union Boss During Hearing: 'Sit Down! You're a United States Senator!'" *Mediaite*, November 14, 2023, https://www.mediaite.com /politics/bernie-sanders-stops-fist-fight-between-republican-and-union -boss-during-hearing-sit-down-youre-a-united-states-senator/.

3   Jennifer Bowers Bahney, "'You Used To Be Able to Cane': Republican Senator Who Nearly Threw Down with Union Chief Discusses the Good Old Days," *Mediaite*, November 14, 2023, https://www.mediaite.com /politics/you-used-to-be-able-to-cane-republican-senator-who-nearly -threw-down-with-union-chief-discusses-the-good-old-days/.

Still, we shouldn't dwell too much on the Mullin confrontation. Because elsewhere under the Capitol dome, Congressman Tim Burchett was accusing Congressman Kevin McCarthy of elbowing him in the kidneys.[4] Congresswoman Marjorie Taylor Greene was calling Congressman Darrell Issa a "pussy."[5] Congressman James Comer was observing that Congressman Jared Moskowitz looked like a Smurf.[6]

And the thing is, this all happened on the same day.

In the era of big politics, power has largely ascended to the federal level. Localism is a thing of the past; subsidiarity is a hazily remembered term from Catholic school; the pro–states' rights Tenth Amendment is a dead letter. This has made Congress all the more important. With so much power centralized, Congress is now the organ closest to the people on a good number of policy matters, the means through which they can affect change. They might not be able to vote out the transportation secretary or the chief justice of the Supreme Court, but every two years they can pass judgment on their congressman. In a republic, where power is supposed to flow upward rather down, few things could be more important.

There's a reason the Founders made Congress Article I of the Constitution—legislative primacy was supposed to be a cornerstone of our system. The legislature acted first, proposing and voting on laws, while the president approved and enforced them, and the courts

---

4   Caitlin Yilek, "GOP Rep. Tim Burchett says Kevin McCarthy elbowed him in the back after meeting," CBS News, November 14, 2023, https://www.cbsnews.com/news/tim-burchett-kevin-mccarthy-elbow-in-kidneys/.

5   Taegan Goddard, "Marjorie Taylor Greene Calls GOP Colleague a 'Pussy,'" Political Wire, November 14, 2023, https://politicalwire.com/2023/11/14/marjorie-taylor-greene-calls-gop-colleague-a-pussy/.

6   "'You look like a Smurf': Comer gets into heated exchange with Moskowitz during hearing," *USA Today*, November 14, 2023, https://www.usatoday.com/story/news/politics/2023/11/14/you-look-like-a-smurf-comer-moskowitz/71584650007/.

reviewed them. Yet today, the executive branch has subsumed the legislative both in terms of lawmaking power and public perception. Joe Biden on a good day can get 40 percent of the country to like him; Congress's approval rating as of February 2024 was stuck at 12 percent.[7]

The perception is of Congress as a circus that politics—meaning presidents—must rise above in order to get anything done. And then members of Congress go and behave like clowns. Given the legislative giants like Henry Clay and Joseph Cannon who once trod the Capitol halls, it's starting to feel a bit unseemly.

***

Our Congress was once the envy of the world.

I'll pause here so you can stop laughing.

What made our Congress great was, first of all, the expertise of its members.

I'll pause again so you can peel yourself off the floor with a snow shovel.

After the Revolutionary War, the United States was determined to be different from Great Britain. Not for us was all that driving on the left side of the street, and also not for us was that seething House of Commons where drunken members mooed and ululated at each other while a slightly less drunken speaker tried to restore order. (My favorite story from British Parliament is of the minister who in 2010 was reprimanded for calling another member a "stupid, sanctimonious dwarf." He later apologized—to dwarves.[8]) America's Founding Fathers were

---

7   "Congress and the Public," Gallup, https://news.gallup.com/poll/1600
     /congress-public.aspx.

8   "Minister apologises for branding Speaker John Bercow 'a stupid dwarf,'"
     The Independent, June 30, 2010, https://www.independent.co.uk/news
     /uk/politics/minister-apologises-for-branding-speaker-john-bercow-a
     -stupid-dwarf-2014731.html.

inspired by older ideas of government, rooted in grand Greco-Roman conceptions of republicanism.

If Britain's parliament was characterized by constant heckling, Congress would, in due course, come to vest its power in committees, which would place a premium on expertise, allowing members to bring specialized knowledge to bear on legislation before it ever came up for a vote. If Britain's House of Lords was a glorified hospice care unit for aging politicians, America's upper house, the Senate, would be a vibrant and coequal wing of government that would need to approve all bills before they reached the president's desk. If Britain's House of Commons was run by party bosses and whips, Congress, and especially the Senate, would afford greater power to individual members and place an almost fetishistic emphasis on bipartisanship.

Many of these differences evolved over time, and some of them can be overstated. (The House of Representatives functions more like a parliament than the Senate, for example.) Yet at their root was a sense on the part of the Founders that good legislators ought to make decisions based on reason and evidence rather than passions and party loyalty. A system that enabled the latter, they worried, would lead to factionalism and mob rule. The Founders hated mob rule. They wanted to see the will of the people prevail within reason, but they also wanted it slowed, tempered, subjected to input from all sides. They understood the majority didn't have a monopoly on wisdom—often quite the opposite—and that political minorities should have their say too.

In retrospect, this can seem a bit doe-eyed. The Founders were so determined to keep factionalism at bay that they gave short thought to any role of political parties within their system, even as such parties quickly became an essential part of American politics. But then, you can do a lot worse than a government that aspired to set aside intrigue in the name of freedom and the general welfare. And the problem we have today is that Congress has been infiltrated by powerful factions that pressure legislators to do the opposite, that block their reason and good sense in favor of spectacle and ulterior agendas.

The first bad faction influencing our Congress should be obvious enough: lobbyists. There are an estimated thirteen thousand lobbyists squatting in our national legislature, up from fewer than one hundred in the 1960s and outnumbering elected representatives by a factor of about twenty-four.[9] Spending on federal lobbying reached $4.1 billion in 2022, which is more than the GDP of the nation of Liberia.[10] (And that seems like a call to action. Can a rich nation like ours not afford a single lobbyist for the Liberians?)

These lobbyists are how powerful interests infiltrate elected government, factionalism multiplying into more factionalism. Why can't Congress pare back our bloated defense budget? One reason is that weapons contractors like Lockheed Martin and Boeing spend tens of millions of dollars every year on lobbyists to guarantee votes in favor of their favorite defense appropriations. Why can't Congress ever seem to figure out what it wants to do about powerful social media companies like TikTok? Perhaps because big tech has flooded D.C. with lobbyists who these days are the city's de facto ruling class, buying up Washington's nicest historic town houses and footing the bill at its swankiest restaurants.[11]

---

9 Bruce Love, "Money Talks: Lobbyists Pulling the Strings on Capitol Hill," *National Law Journal*, January 27, 2022, https://www.law.com/nationallawjournal/2022/01/27/money-talks-lobbyists-pulling-the-strings-on-capitol-hill/.

10 Taylor Giorno, "Federal lobbying spending reaches $4.1 billion in 2022—the highest since 2010," Open Secrets, January 26, 2023, https://www.opensecrets.org/news/2023/01/federal-lobbying-spending-reaches-4-1-billion-in-2022-the-highest-since-2010/.

11 Hailey Fuchs and Emily Birnbaum, "These days, Capitol Hill townhomes aren't for living in. They're for lobbying," *Politico*, November 23,

This leads to another problem: brain drain. The median salary for a staffer in the House of Representatives is just $59,000,[12] and while that might sound like a decent amount if you live in the Sun Belt, in Washington it's barely enough to scrape by. Around D.C., Hill People, as they're known, are the city's Jos. A. Bank–besuited working poor who grab a couple $3 Miller Lites till eight o'clock and then retreat back to the mildewing closets they share with seven roommates.

Denied enough money to support himself, the average congressional staffer remains on the Hill for just three years. And since lobbying organizations are able to pay far better than congressional offices, and since lobbying organizations value employees who have connections in Congress, enter the revolving door, which sees former congressional staffers sell out to lobbyists so they can make a decent wage and then return to the Capitol with agendas in hand.[13] Thus do you end up with hungover twenty-three-year-olds shuttling billions of dollars around the government. Only the diehards stay past puberty.

Giving anyone on Capitol Hill a raise these days might sound like a terrible idea, given the quality of the output. But there's plenty of money in politics; it's just not being distributed to the right places. And that brings us to the next big, bad faction: donors. Yes, there are candidates who gloriously defy the big donor model, starting with Donald J. Trump, whose 2016 campaign was funded largely by small

2021, https://www.politico.com/news/2021/11/23/lobbyists-capitol -hill-real-estate-523246.

12   Chris Cioffi, "This was supposed to be a big year for Hill pay. Staffers aren't holding their breath," *Roll Call*, November 18, 2021, https ://rollcall.com/2021/11/18/this-was-supposed-to-be-a-big-year-for-hill -pay-staffers-arent-holding-their-breath/.

13   Alexander C. Furnas and Timothy M. LaPira, "Congressional Brain Drain: Legislative Capacity in the 21st Century," New America, September 8, 2020, https://www.newamerica.org/political-reform/reports /congressional-brain-drain/.

contributions.[14] But generally they're the exception—you need bundles of cash if you're going to run for office. The cheapest congressional campaign in 2022 still cost more than $143,000, while Senator Raphael Warnock, locked in a tight race in Georgia, raised north of $100 million.[15]

The intricacies of modern campaign finance law are so boring as to risk putting anyone who reads about them into a persistent vegetative state, so we won't delve into them here. But suffice it to say that whereas committee assignments and prestige used to be the currencies of Congress, today it's much more about money. That's especially true after the Supreme Court's 2010 *Citizens United* decision, which opened the floodgates to money in politics. Elections get more expensive every year. Parties are glorified fundraising apparatuses. Members of Congress end up spending as much time telemarketing as they do legislating.

This intrusion of money into politics reached an apex in 2023 when Kevin McCarthy was elected speaker of the House of Representatives. McCarthy is the opposite of a policy mind, an uninspiring orator, a sack of ambition wrapped in a suit. Yet he's also a prolific moneyman. McCarthy is so good at raising money that he broke GOP fundraising records in the first six months of 2023.[16] His time at the top wasn't to last: he was deposed as speaker after a rebellion in the Republican

---

14   Shane Goldmacher, "Trump shatters GOP records with small donors," *Politico*, September 19, 2016, https://www.politico.com/story/2016/09/trump-shatters-gop-records-with-small-donors-228338.

15   Andrew Stanton, "The Cheapest Congressional Victory Cost Less than $150K," *Time*, November 9, 2022, https://www.newsweek.com/cheapest-congressional-victory-cost-less-150k-1757497.

16   Paul Steinhauser, "House GOP leader Kevin McCarthy breaks another fundraising record," Fox News, July 11, 2022, https://www.foxnews.com/politics/house-gop-leader-kevin-mccarthy-breaks-fundraising-record.

caucus. But his ascent said something important. Kevin McCarthy was the first truly post–*Citizens United* Speaker.

Then there's the final, and in some ways most important, bad faction on Capitol Hill: cable news. Fox News and MSNBC both have studios a stone's throw from Capitol Hill, and that proximity is telling. Cable news was once a kind of relay system, a way of radioing back to your most engaged supporters that you were still taking the fight to the bad guys. Today, members from both parties all but hibernate in greenrooms, lying in wait for their *big close-up* (that is, a fourteen-second hit on CNN). This desperation to get on TV has skewed the legislating process. The thing to do today is to give a thundering speech on the floor of the Senate denouncing a fellow member and then post it to YouTube. If you're lucky, it'll go viral and you'll do a hit on *Fox & Friends* discussing it the very next morning. (And then your staff will send out a fundraising email and cash in!)

Which is fine. If members of Congress want to pretend they're celebrities by courting both of Lawrence O'Donnell's viewers, then the nation has bigger fish to fry. The problem is that the Fox News and MSNBC audiences are respectively to the right and left of most of the country (to say nothing of the other, less-watched, even more ideological cable and YouTube offerings). This leads both parties to act in ways that are unrepresentative. It also encourages theatrics. You're not going to get booked on CNN if you don't call *someone* a fascist (preferably with a giant easel behind you showing a black-and-white picture of Mussolini motoring into Rome in case the point wasn't clear).

There are many, many other reasons political scientists might argue Congress is broken—too many earmarks, too few earmarks, election primaries, the direct election of senators, first-past-the-post electioneering—but from the new factionalism we can see the outgrowth of the disease. Big lobbyists encourage members to represent big interest groups rather than their constituents and the general welfare.

They also suck away talented staffers, robbing Congress of its expertise and perpetuating the revolving door. Big donors force members to spend time courting big money rather than solving the nation's problems. They also reward glorified salesmen at the expense of real leaders and policy minds. Big media incentivizes individual showmanship and ideological catharsis rather than the consensus that's necessary for any democratic body to function.

To see how this works, consider one of Congress's worst failings: the national debt. Everyone knows the national debt is a problem. Get four beers into a Keynesian economist and even he'll admit the national debt is a problem. All the way back in 2010, Admiral Michael Mullen, the chairman of the Joint Chiefs of Staff, warned that the debt was "the most significant threat to our national security."[17] And that was when it amounted to just $13.5 trillion. As of January 2024, it's a cool $34 trillion and counting, or about 124 percent the size of the American economy.

Incredibly, after World War II and the immense military spending it necessitated, the United States actually had a smaller ratio of debt to gross domestic product than we do today.[18] The Truman administration brought down that ratio even during the Korean War, while Dwight Eisenhower, one of our most underrated presidents, accelerated the budget balancing. As a result, the ratio of debt to GDP plummeted all the way down to 54 percent in 1960.

Today, there's no evidence of a similar correction in store. The 2008 bank bailout, the 2009 Obama stimulus plan, the COVID-19 spending extravaganza, the American Rescue Plan Act of 2021, ballooning

---

17   "Mullen: Debt is top national security threat," CNN, August 27, 2010, http://www.cnn.com/2010/US/08/27/debt.security.mullen/index.html.

18   Julien Acalin and Laurence Ball, "Reassessing the fall in US public debt after World War II," VoxEU, October 20, 2023, https://cepr.org/voxeu/columns/reassessing-fall-us-public-debt-after-world-war-ii/.

entitlement programs, and a wasteful Pentagon desperately in need of reform have all unleashed the red ink. Congress might be gridlocked, but when it comes to spending money, it operates with feline efficiency. All the Tea Party rallies, the government shutdowns, the debt ceiling fights have failed to trim the state. (The one exception, the so-called Budget Control Act of 2011, was a decent law but nowhere near strong enough and much of it was rolled back two years later.)

Big lobbyists want to keep taxpayer money flowing to their clients, whether it's defense firms that don't want anyone touching the military budget or senior citizen groups like the AARP that demand hands off Social Security and Medicare. Big donors have other things on their minds these days, and the wealthy are unlikely to be affected much by a debt crisis anyway. And big media is more concerned with visceral issues like immigration and prizes fleeting partisan gotchas over any kind of fiscal consensus. Boring budgeting might have been somewhat in vogue during the Tea Party era but those days are long gone.

Part of the problem too is basic democratic representation. Politicians need to get reelected somehow and bringing home the bacon is one way to keep your constituents happy. There's no guarantee, however, that the laws of economics have been suspended in our favor, that unlimited borrowing will continue forever, or even that the dollar will remain the world's reserve currency as China rises and our debt continues to balloon. Basic rationality suggests the national debt is a problem but legislative irrationality points a very different way.

***

There's an old trope that says the best government is divided government. If you elect Republicans to Congress and a Democrat to the White House, they'll spend the next two years fighting like rats in a sack and won't be able to fix what ain't broke. The private sector will then flourish, sprouting smokestacks and farms and new Amazon distribution centers across the fruited plain while the townsfolk empty into the streets and sing carols about their bulging stock portfolios.

From this point of view, it might be tempting to think the new factionalism is a good thing. If members of Congress are too busy making foghorn sounds on CNN or placing donor calls, then at least they can't strangle everyone else in red tape.

If only this was how it worked.

There are some responsibilities that only the federal government can carry out and some national issues that only the feds are poised to tackle. And if Congress becomes useless, it creates a void of power that will only be filled by another part of the government. In this case, that part of the government has been and will continue to be the administrative state, the endless bureaucracies that are technically part of the executive branch but seem increasingly to operate autonomously.

The permanent federal bureaucracy is well-positioned against the new factionalism: it's less vulnerable to pressure from lobbyists; it doesn't need to worry about funding campaigns or electoral pressures; and it has no use for media visibility.

This is how the executive branch has colonized the legislative branch—and often with the legislative branch's express consent. To take just one particularly egregious example, consider the Clean Air Act. Initially passed in 1963 and bolstered as recently as 1990, the Clean Air Act is the most important environmental legislation in American history. Its purpose is to make sure our skies aren't choked with smog by enabling the government to regulate air quality.

Yet to do this, the Clean Air Act handed the Environmental Protection Agency (EPA), the executive department charged with regulating air quality, nearly unlimited power over greenhouse gas emissions. It transferred from Congress to unelected bureaucrats the authority to regulate pollution standards, and whereas Congress might have been forced to consider all sides before cracking down on a pollutant, weighing economic costs against environmental benefits, facing pressure from constituents who might be adversely affected, the EPA has no such motivation. The public is allowed to file comments on proposed regulations before they take effect and can sue after the fact. But those are about the only checks and balances in place.

For green hysterics, this is good news, as it allows their wish list to be implemented without any of that democratic messiness. Yet it's also a circumventing of how representative government is supposed to work. The Supreme Court in 2022 neutered some of the EPA's authority to curb carbon emissions from power plants, but the bulk of the Clean Air Act remains in effect. One reason is that name.[19] You don't oppose clean air, *do you?*

Which brings us to another standout case of emotional blackmail: the Patriot Act. Oppose that and you might as well be a card-carrying member of Hezbollah. The Patriot Act is actually the USA PATRIOT Act, which stands for Uniting and Strengthening America by Providing Appropriate Tools Required to Intercept and Obstruct Terrorism. (I sometimes think there's a special office in Congress that does nothing but come up with these acronyms. Annual operating budget: $160 billion.)

The Patriot Act was introduced in the House of Representatives a month and a half after 9/11. It was passed the next day and was signed into law by President Bush two days after that, so you know they put some serious thought into it.[20] The law did nothing less than overhaul

19 Andrew Chung, "US Supreme Court rulings darken forecast for EPA powers," Reuters, May 31, 2023, https://www.reuters.com/world/us/us-supreme-court-rulings-darken-forecast-epa-powers-2023-05-31/.

20 "H.R.3162—Uniting and Strengthening America by Providing Appropriate Tools Required to Intercept and Obstruct Terrorism (USA PATRIOT ACT) Act of 2001," Congress.gov, https://www.congress.gov/bill/107th-congress/house-bill/3162/text.

America's traditional civil liberties, with enormous new powers ceded to the security state. Onto the statute books came exciting new tools like the sneak-and-peek warrant, which allowed federal officers to break into your house and search it without notifying you,[21] and the national security letter, which allowed the FBI to demand revealing information while prohibiting you from telling anyone except a lawyer.[22]

The Patriot Act has since expired as law, though most of its provisions remain in effect. But it stands as an archetype of how Congress works today, writing vague paper-towers of legislation that cede massive authorities to the bureaucracy which then fills in the blanks. The same holds true for No Child Left Behind, Obamacare, and the Dodd-Frank financial legislation. It also holds true for Congress's budgeting process, where party leaders increasingly negotiate enormous spending packages with the White House over the heads of the congressional appropriations committees, and then submit the bill to members at the last minute, with any proposed cuts to the bureaucracy screamed about like they're high treason.

Forbes magazine reports that in 2020 Congress passed 178 laws, while 3,353 new regulations were imposed unilaterally by the federal bureaucracy.[23] That is, the unelected federal bureaucracy issued about *nineteen times* more regulations than the number of laws passed by the

---

21 Charles Doyle, "The USA Patriot Act at 20: Sneak and Peek Searches," Congressional Research Service, October 27, 2021, https://crsreports .congress.gov/product/pdf/LSB/LSB10652.

22 "National Security Letter." Legal Information Institute, Cornell Law School, July 2023, https://www.law.cornell.edu/wex/national _security_letter.

23 Clyde Wayne Crews, "The 2021 'Unconstitutionality Index': 19 Federal Rules and Regulations for Every Law Congress Passes," *Forbes*, February 2, 2021, https://www.forbes.com/sites/waynecrews/2021/02/02/the-2021 -unconstitutionality-index-19-federal-rules-and-regulations-for-every -law-congress-passes/?sh=2cbcb9625522.

democratically elected members of Congress. And remember, this was still under Donald Trump, whose administration did its best to slash red tape. In 2016, under the far more regulation-happy Barack Obama, the bureaucracy issued 3,853 regulations, exactly 500 more.[24] When it comes to Congress, the rule seems to be: legislate in haste, and then let the bureaucracy regulate at leisure.

***

You may have noticed something about the Clean Air Act and the Patriot Act: both were underpinned by a sense of emergency. Whether greenhouse gases are melting the planet or Islamists are flying planes into buildings, the common denominator is that something must be done—*and it must be done now.*

And if it must be done *now*, does Congress really have time for "civil liberties"? Or "reading legislation"? Or "retaining its power to declare war"?

That last one in particular. Because national emergencies beget expediency, it's no surprise that nowhere has Congress been so derelict as with its warmaking powers. The last time Congress bothered to declare a war was after Pearl Harbor was bombed and the last time it bothered to pass any kind of legislation initiating military force was before the Iraq war.

Every time war powers comes up, suddenly every member of Congress has an orthodontist appointment. It's so much easier to let the executive branch decide. Thus has war become just another bureaucratic process of the administrative state, detached from democratic

---

24   Clyde Wayne Crews, "How Many Rules And Regulations Do Federal Agencies Issue?" *Forbes*, August 15, 2017, https://www.forbes.com/sites/waynecrews/2017/08/15/how-many-rules-and-regulations-do-federal-agencies-issue/?sh=5a1d523f1e64.

accountability and public scrutiny. Since many airstrikes are now carried out by drones rather than human pilots, and since those airstrikes are funded more by debt than taxes, the public rarely even feels the effects of these conflicts in terms of casualties or tax hikes. Occasionally, Congress has to be troubled to approve another pricey grab bag for the Pentagon, but then dissenters are easily shut down as denying our military men and women a raise.

And that brings us back to the problem of empire. You don't necessarily need a war to cement an imperial system of government, but it sure does help. Or better yet, dozens of so-called police actions that most Americans aren't aware of and thus will never be troubled to ask questions about.

CHAPTER 17

From the Halls of Okinawa to the Shores of Benghazi

Back in middle school, there came a day when my social studies teacher decided she was going to do something about Americans' notorious ignorance of geography. Every one of us was assigned a continent and told to memorize the locations of its countries for a quiz. Just as I was about to try to flip a Capri-Sun straw into my friend's eyeball, I was told my continent was Africa.

This was bad luck. Africa isn't just on the other side of the planet, it has more nations than any other continent on earth (whoever got Antarctica was a fortunate bastard). And in Western Africa, those nations start to look like a sub-Saharan New England: tiny rectangles with names like Ghana and Guinea and Guinea-Bissau. I somehow studied my way to a passing grade on that quiz, but man. Learning to keep Zambia and Zimbabwe straight was no easy A.

So it should say something that when it was reported in 2013 that our government was deploying troops to the African nation of Mali,[1] I had no idea where that was. At first I thought it was the blocky one on the west coast with the northern border shaped like a staircase, but that was Mauritania. I was pretty sure it was in Northern Africa . . . or was it? Was it that little enclave that's completely surrounded by South Africa? Lesotho or whatever it's called? That is something we would do, isn't it? A nation is literally surrounded by South Africa and we're the ones who send in the troops.

The rest of America seemed to share my befuddlement. From garages to barbershops to Walmarts, the nation was at once united in not knowing anything about the Mali situation. Apparently Mali is in Northern Africa, to the east of Mauritania, and Islamic extremists there had been consolidating power in the north and were pushing toward the capital. The French had done what they do, which is to flex muscle they didn't have in a former colony they no longer controlled, deploying thousands of troops to help the government stop the extremist advance. And we had done what we do, which is to bail out the French, flying in matériel and providing logistics and refueling.

As of 2024, American troops were still involved in military operations in Mali—in 2017, four of them were killed just over the border in Niger during a firefight in the town of Tongo Tongo (which I thought was a racist cocktail).[2] In 2023, the American government did what it

1   Craig Whitlock, "Pentagon deploys small number of troops to war-torn Mali," *Washington Post*, April 30, 2013, https://www.washingtonpost.com/world/national-security/pentagon-deploys-small-number-of-troops-to-war-torn-mali/2013/04/30/2b02c928-b1a0-11e2-bc39-65b0a67147df_story.html.

2   Rukmini Callimachi, et al., "'An Endless War': Why 4 US Soldiers Died in a Remote African Desert," *New York Times*, February 20, 2018, https://www.nytimes.com/interactive/2018/02/17/world/africa/niger-ambush-american-soldiers.html.

does by accidentally sending hundreds of sensitive documents to Mali after using the web suffix .ml on an email instead of .mil.[3] This, arguably, was too much aid.

But it's all in a day's work for a government whose definition of "terrorism" has been stretched into Silly Putty. After the 9/11 attacks, Congress passed an authorization for use of military force (AUMF), which green-lighted President Bush to take the fight to al-Qaeda. Yet the government's counterterrorism powers didn't stop there: according to Section 127e of Title 10 of the US Code, the Defense Department is permitted without consulting Congress to "provide support to foreign forces, irregular forces, groups or individuals engaged in supporting or facilitating authorized ongoing military operations by United States special operations forces to combat terrorism."[4]

This vague permission slip has been used to justify American troops not just in the vital theater of Mali but other African nations like Somalia, Kenya, Egypt, Libya, Niger, Nigeria, Tunisia, and (thank goodness) Mauritania. It's been used to maintain troop presences in Iraq, Yemen, Syria, and Lebanon. It's been used to keep a light footprint in Afghanistan despite our supposed pullout in 2021. And those are just the deployments we're aware of: the military has a, shall we say, spotty record of keeping both Congress and the public informed about where it spends taxpayer money.

In addition to the known 127e operations, the Quincy Center for Responsible Statecraft points to another devilish provision, Section 333

---

3   Jonathan Lehrfield and Colin Demarest, "Sensitive US military info exposed in accidental emails to Mali," *Military Times*, July 17, 2023, https://www.militarytimes.com/news/your-military/2023/07/17/sensitive-us-military-info-exposed-in-accidental-emails-to-mali/.

4   Katherine Yon Ebright, "What Can a Secretive Funding Authority Tell Us About the Pentagon's Use of Force Interpretations?" Lawfare, October 11, 2022, https://www.lawfaremedia.org/article/what-can-secretive-funding-authority-tell-us-about-pentagons-use-force-interpretations.

of Title 10 of the US Code, which gives the government broad authority "to conduct or support programs providing training and equipment to national security forces of foreign countries" for the purposes of everything from counterterrorism to combating narcotics trafficking to border security. (American troops are permitted to secure the borders of other countries, just not their own.) The Defense Department runs an estimated fifty programs under Section 333 in countries ranging from Indonesia to Peru.[5]

Then there's the World War II LARPing. Oh, there's the World War II LARPing. The United States still operates military bases in Germany in the event the Nazis rise to power again. US troops are still stationed in Italy to keep Mussolini at bay. Dozens of American military bases are still in Japan, which has the third-largest economy on earth. And those are just some of the 750 bases the Pentagon maintains across eighty countries or about four in ten of the total nations on earth.[6]

Here we see empire in its most popular-definition sense. Zoom out the lens and you'll find the United States attempting to snuff out Islamic jihadism across the Middle East, working with South Korea to keep North Korea contained, protecting Ukraine from the invading Russians, and countering a rising China. America's navy is almost solely responsible for guarding global waterways and trade routes. We've

---

5   Jim Lobe, "The US military is operating in more countries than we think," Quincy Center for Responsible Statecraft, November 8, 2022, https://responsiblestatecraft.org/2022/11/08/the-us-military-is -operating-in-more-countries-than-we-think/.

6   David Vine, et al., "Drawdown: Improving US and Global Security Through Military Base Closures Abroad," Quincy Institute for Responsible Statecraft, September 20, 2021, https://quincyinst.org/research/drawdown -improving-u-s-and-global-security-through-military-base-closures -abroad/.

contributed $3.75 trillion in foreign aid since the end of World War II[7] and cover close to a quarter of the budget of the United Nations.[8] We regularly host and lead peace talks in all corners of the globe. We provide collective defense for virtually every other NATO member, footing the bill as militaries stagnate across Western Europe.

We've been doing this for decades. And perhaps, as the national debt sails through the treetops, it's time to ask: does this still make sense? Should a nation saddled with massive domestic problems still be the world's policeman? To say nothing of its fireman, paramedic, construction foreman, marriage counselor, and Salvation Army Santa?

* * *

When those missiles of steel and flesh hit the Twin Towers on a clear fall morning, when the buildings collapsed into a demonic rosebush of ash and soot, when the Pentagon got hit too and heroes sacrificed their lives over a field in Pennsylvania, like so many others, I was changed. This was not because of any heartfelt attachment to New York—"why would we go *there*?" my Massachusetts parents used to wonder—nor because I knew anyone who had been harmed in the attacks.

It was because 9/11 was a moment of profound emotional nationalization. It was silly to say, as some did, that on that day we were all New Yorkers; I would have sooner choked on my New England clam chowder, and the attacks hadn't been limited to New York at any rate. More accurate to say we were all Americans, and not just us but people

---

7   "Which countries receive the most foreign aid from the US?" USA Facts, July 15, 2023, https://usafacts.org/articles/which-countries-receive-the-most-aid-from-the-us/.

8   "Meeting the Moment: the US and the UN in 2023," Better World Campaign, https://betterworldcampaign.org/the-un-budget#:~:text=Over%20time%2C%20the%20U.S.%20has,the%20U.S.%20was%20assessed%2025%25.

all over the world who stood in solidarity. It was a rare moment of intense clarity, when the infinite hues of life coalesced into black and white. "You're either with us or you're with the terrorists," President George W. Bush said, and his rhetoric might have been grander. "Us" was civilization, tolerance, vibrancy, freedom; "them" was barbarism, tribalism, thuggishness, totalitarianism.

The problem was we took this moment of clarity and stretched it to places it could not go. We acted like this was a clash between Platonic forms rather than a real war rooted in place and time with costs and casualties and limits on what could be achieved. "Our responsibility to history is already clear," said George W. Bush three days after the attacks, "to answer these attacks and rid the world of evil." That's some war.

It's worth pointing out that as recently as September 10, 2001, America's foreign policy had been something of a paradox. It was a unipolar moment, as Charles Krauthammer had put it, with America cast as the world's lone superpower, but we were also ornery with our singular status. Under the Clinton administration, the United States had cut its military budget, withdrawn troops from Somalia, whistled nervously during the Rwandan Genocide, and only intervened to stop the killing in Kosovo after much lobbying from the British. Clinton's predecessor, Bush the First, had launched Gulf War the First, but crucially had refrained from removing Saddam Hussein from power. His son, Bush the Second, had run for president opposing "nation building."[9]

What the 9/11 attacks had done was to empower certain radicals both inside and outside the Bush administration who had long been dissatisfied with this state of affairs. These radicals were high on the

---

9   "Bush a convert to nation building." *Washington Times*, April 7, 2008, https://www.washingtontimes.com/news/2008/apr/7 /bush-a-convert-to-nation-building/.

exhaust of American Humvees and wanted to put them to good use. They had a particular itch for going after Saddam Hussein, whom they viewed as an international crime kingpin who should have been deposed under the first Bush. They also believed, as the philosopher Allan Bloom put it, that "there is no intellectual ground remaining for any regime other than democracy," and as Krauthammer said, that "supporting democracy is a vital American endeavor. It is nothing to be ashamed of and nothing to be stingy about."[10]

Some of these thinkers, like Robert Kagan, Bill Kristol, David Frum, and Richard Perle, wanted nothing less than a global campaign to destroy totalitarianism and spread democracy. These people are sometimes called neoconservatives, though there's nothing conservative about them. I like the term coined by my former professor Dr. Claes Ryn: neo-Jacobins.[11] Just as the Jacobins had viewed the French Revolution as a call to export their ideology across not just France but the entire world, so too did the neo-Jacobins see the war on terror as an opportunity to plant American values in soil where they had never before been cultivated.

The exemplary text of the neo-Jacobins was a deranged little war-on-terror manual by Richard Perle and David Frum called *An End to Evil*, published in 2004. The sheer lunacy of the title is your first clue as to what lies ahead. And that title was no clickbait dreamed up by the publisher: Perle and Frum say on page eight that America is on a mission "to end this evil before it kills again and on a genocidal scale." And are you feeling just a bit ambivalent about rolling the tanks into Hell itself? Too bad: "There is no middle way for Americans," Perle and

---

10   Bloom and Krauthammer quotes from: Claes Ryn, *America the Virtuous* (New Brunswick: Transaction Publishers, 2003).

11   Ryn, *America the Virtuous*.

Frum pronounce. "It is victory or holocaust."[12] Anyone who questions the mission is an appeaser and thus on Team Holocaust.

So determined are Perle and Frum to root out appeasement that at one point they declare the nation of South Korea to be an appeaser because it prefers to avoid nuclear war with the North.[13] With American troops already fighting in Iraq and Afghanistan, Perle and Frum say "we must move boldly against [Iran and North Korea] and against all the other sponsors of terrorism as well: Syria, Libya, and Saudi Arabia."[14] And while the Libyans no doubt posed an existential threat to humanity as we knew it, some third-world mud huts were asking for it more than others. "Really there is only one question to ask about Syria: Why have we put up with it as long as we have?"[15] The entire nation, apparently.

It was a whole new world that Perle and Frum could envision from atop their American Enterprise Institute-issued magic carpet. "A world at peace," they sang, "a world governed by law; a world in which all peoples are free to find their own destinies: That dream has not yet come true, it will not come true soon, but if it ever does come true, it will be brought into being by American armed might and defended by American might, too."[16]

That sounds clinically insane (it's also extraordinarily bad writing), but there was a time when many Americans thought this way—not the average voter, whose patience ran out after Baghdad descended into anarchy, but powerful political elites. Iraq was just the beginning, "a

---

12 Richard Perle and David Frum, *An End to Evil: How to Win the War on Terror* (New York: Ballantine Books, 2004) p. 8.

13 Perle and Frum, *An End to Evil*, p. 85.

14 Perle and Frum, *An End to Evil*, p. 85.

15 Perle and Frum, *An End to Evil*, p. 98.

16 Perle and Frum, *An End to Evil*, p. 237.

test," as Perle and Frum called it.[17] Iran was on deck—"real men go to Tehran," as the saying went—and Syria was in the White House's crosshairs as well.

The failure of the Iraq war to usher in a new era of democratic peace and comity, combined with the subsequent sputtering of the Arab Spring revolutions in 2011, would dash the neo-Jacobin dream of a democratized Middle East. Yet such thinking still became institutionalized in organs of government and elite thinking. To take just one example, David Frum is now an esteemed "centrist" pundit with a lofty perch at the *Atlantic* magazine and a million Twitter followers. He's never once had to answer for the counsel he gave in *An End to Evil*.

***

In 2001, the United States invaded Afghanistan and crushed the Taliban government, which had aided and sheltered al-Qaeda. What followed was a twenty-year-long occupation that might have seen Afghani women start going to school but that also saw their country become one of the most corrupt and dysfunctional on earth. Unable to control an ancient land we'd never bothered to understand, Afghanistan's new so-called democracy became more like a kleptocracy, with factions and warlords looting the public purse.[18]

It also became something else: a narco-state. Deeply impoverished despite the United States waving its modernizing magic wand, the locals turned to poppy crops in order to make ends meet. The result was that Afghanistan soon accounted for 90 percent of the world's illegal poppy,

---

17   Perle and Frum, *An End to Evil*, p. 31.

18   Craig Whitlock, "Consumed by Corruption," *Washington Post*, December 9, 2019, https://www.washingtonpost.com/graphics/2019/investigations /afghanistan-papers/afghanistan-war-corruption-government/.

much of which would end up in opioid drugs like heroin.[19] Here was an irony too macabre to contemplate: the United States blew through about $2.3 trillion in Afghanistan to finance an addiction crisis on its own shores.[20] Another irony: the Taliban back in 1997 had banned opium and tried to control the poppy crop (though they weren't especially successful).[21]

That same Taliban was all the while taking advantage of local misery and slowly retaking the Afghani heartland. So it was that in 2021, when Joe Biden pulled out most of the American forces, anyone who had been paying attention knew what was coming next. The Taliban regained control of the country two weeks before the troop withdrawal was even scheduled to be complete,[22] while the Afghan security forces, which the United States had spent $90 billion training, melted away in the face of their assault.[23] The head of security at the

---

19   "What does Taliban control mean for Afghanistan's opium economy?" *The Economist*, September 1, 2021, https://www.economist.com/the-economist-explains/2021/09/01/what-does-taliban-control-mean-for-afghanistans-opium-economy.

20   "Human and Budgetary Costs to Date of the US War in Afghanistan, 2001–2022," Costs of War, Watson Institute for International and Public Affairs, Brown University, August 2021, https://watson.brown.edu/costsofwar/figures/2021/human-and-budgetary-costs-date-us-war-afghanistan-2001-2022/.

21   "Fact Sheet: The Taliban And The Afghan Drug Trade," Bureau of South Asian Affairs, US Department of State, 2001, https://1997-2001.state.gov/www/regions/sa/facts_taliban_drugs.html.

22   Joseph Krauss, "Taliban take over Afghanistan: What we know and what's next," Associated Press, August 17, 2021, https://apnews.com/article/taliban-takeover-afghanistan-what-to-know-1a74c9cd866866f196c478aba21b60b6.

23   Paulina Smolinski, "How US, Afghan governments failed to adequately train Afghan security forces after spending $90 billion over 20 years," Associated Press, February 28, 2023, https://www.cbsnews.com/news/afghanistan-security-forces-us-failures-special-inspector-general-report/.

presidential palace shook hands with the Taliban commander as he handed the place over.[24] Today, women have once again been marginalized from public life while opium has once again been banned.[25] Untold billions and an estimated 176,000 lives purchased a return to the status quo ante.

In 2003, the United States invaded Iraq and within three weeks Baghdad had fallen to coalition forces. It was a lightning military victory that culminated with the pulling down of a bronze statue of Saddam Hussein in Firdos Square by an American military vehicle while Iraqi onlookers cheered. And it was all downhill from there. American officials "de-Baathified" the Iraqi state, expelling all members of Saddam Hussein's formerly ruling Baath Party, driving thousands of ruthless and knowledgeable men into the hands of extremist groups overnight. Such extremist groups, largely divided between Sunnis and Shias, soon became the real power players in Iraq. And they proved far more interested in war against both us and each other than in democracy.

The first election to Iraq's newly created parliament was boycotted by the Sunnis, who noted the sectarian violence being waged against them by the Shias and questioned whether a fair vote was possible.[26] The first prime minister of Iraq, Nouri al-Maliki, a mentee of President

---

24 "Taliban Takeover of Afghanistan Updates: Fear Spreads in Kabul as Taliban Take Charge," *New York Times*, August 16, 2021, https://www.nytimes.com/live/2021/08/16/world/taliban-afghanistan-news.

25 "Taliban's Poppy Ban in Afghanistan: Can It Work?" United Nations, August 17, 2023, https://www.un.org/en/video/talibans-poppy-ban-afghanistan-can-it-work.

26 Michael Howard, "Main Sunni party pulls out of Iraqi election," *The Guardian*, December 28, 2004, https://www.theguardian.com/world/2004/dec/28/iraq.michaelhoward.

Bush, allowed Baghdad to be ethnically cleansed of Sunnis.[27] Bombings against both coalition forces and civilians (even mosques weren't spared) were constant, courtesy of both Shia militias like the Mahdi Army and a new al-Qaeda chapter in Iraq, which quickly gained a reputation as the most vicious on earth. In 2013, al-Qaeda in Iraq changed its name to the Islamic State (or ISIS) and rapidly captured a vast swath of Iraq and Syria, subjecting Shias and other religious minorities to horrific atrocities and genocide. American and Iraqi forces were eventually able to drive out ISIS but the group maintains a network of underground infrastructure.

Today, Iraq, like Afghanistan, is essentially a kleptocracy, with rampant corruption divvying up the government among thieves who also happen to control their own militias.[28] The underlying factors that drove young men into the arms of ISIS—poverty, lack of jobs—have not been addressed. In a kind of bitter coda to the war, one of the Iraqis who helped the Americans tear down that statue back in 2003, Kadhim al-Jabbouri, much of whose family was wiped out by Saddam, told the BBC in 2016 that he would put the statue back up if he could. "Saddam killed people, but it was nothing like this current government," he said. "Saddam has gone, but in his place there are 1,000 Saddams."[29]

In 2011, the United States intervened in Libya's civil war, where an Arab Spring–inspired rebellion was fighting the regime of dictator Moammar Gaddafi. Gaddafi had cooperated with the West in the past—not eight years earlier, he'd willingly divested Libya of its

27 Juan Cole, "Iraq Needs an Inclusive Leader," *New York Times*, June 15, 2014, https://www.nytimes.com/roomfordebate/2014/06/15/how-to-stabilize-iraq-and-stop-the-march-of-isis/iraq-needs-an-inclusive-leader.

28 Robert F. Worth, "Inside the Iraqi Kleptocracy," *New York Times*, July 29, 2020, https://www.nytimes.com/2020/07/29/magazine/iraq-corruption.html.

29 "'I toppled Saddam's statue, now I want him back,'" BBC Radio, July 5, 2016, https://www.bbc.com/news/av/world-36712233.

weapons of mass destruction[30]—but we helped topple him all the same. Libya then descended into chaos, fracturing between east, west, and a million militias in between. It got so bad that Libyans began to pine for the days of Gaddafi when at least there was electric power and the ATMs had cash.[31] As of publication, Libya's democratic government still doesn't have control of the entire country, the next presidential election has been delayed indefinitely,[32] and the parliament building in 2022 had been stormed and torched by protesters irate over their crumbing quality of life.[33]

In 2013, the United States intervened in Syria's civil war, which had begun as another Arab Spring protest only to become an armed rebellion against Bashar al-Assad's dictatorship. The Obama administration decided to send American arms and aid to the Syrian rebels, with the only problem being that the rebels were by then dominated by Islamic extremists. Our weapons ended up in the hands of the local al-Qaeda chapter[34] and later ISIS.[35] The Defense Department

30   Flynt L. Leverett, "Why Libya Gave Up on the Bomb," Brookings Institution, January 23, 2004, https://www.brookings.edu/articles /why-libya-gave-up-on-the-bomb/.

31   "Libyans Regret, Miss Life Under Gaddafi," *Sunday Mail*, September 18, 2016, https://www.sundaymail.co.zw/libyans-regret -miss-life-under-gaddafi.

32   Omar Hammady, "Why Libya's Elections Didn't Take Place," *Foreign Policy*, February 18, 2022, https://foreignpolicy.com/2022/02/18/libya-elections -2021-postponed/.

33   Robert Plummer, "Libya protesters storm parliament building in Tobruk," BBC, July 2, 2022, https://www.bbc.com/news/world-africa-62018882.

34   "US-trained Syrian rebels gave equipment to Nusra: US military," Reuters, September 26, 2015, https://www.reuters.com/article /idUSKCN0RP2HO/.

35   Mallory Shelbourne, "Study shows US weapons given to Syrian rebels ended up in ISIS hands," *The Hill*, December 14, 2017, https://thehill .com/policy/defense/364917-study-shows-us-weapons-given-to-syrian -rebels-ended-up-in-isiss-hands/.

subsequently admitted that a $500 million initiative to train so-called moderate rebels had produced about sixty fighters.[36] Donald Trump officially ended Washington's failed attempt to prop up the Syrian rebellion, and Assad ultimately won the civil war with a leg up from the Russians and Iranians.

In 2015, the United States intervened in Yemen's civil war, which saw a coalition of Arab nations led by Saudi Arabia attack a local Shia rebellion called the Houthis. America took the Saudis' side and provided them with intelligence, weapons, and other services like midair refueling for their bombers. The Saudis' campaign was vicious and shards from US weapons were soon found sprayed amid civilian corpses everywhere from a farm to a wedding.[37] Into the void—surprise!—came al-Qaeda, whose Yemeni franchise soon had free rein in the country's largest province and was later determined to be plotting to attack the United States.[38] America and the Saudis were never able to dislodge the Houthis and as of early 2024 we'd started bombing them ourselves after they attacked dozens of commercial ships in the Red Sea in response to Israel's war in the Gaza Strip.

***

---

36 Richard Sisk, "$500M US Program Has Only Trained 60 Syrians to Fight ISIS," Military.com, July 7, 2015, https://www.military.com/daily -news/2015/07/07/500m-us-program-has-only-trained-60-syrians-to -fight-isis.html.

37 Nima Elbagir, et al., "Made in America: Shrapnel found in Yemen ties US bombs to string of civilian deaths over course of bloody civil war," CNN, 2018, https://edition.cnn.com/interactive/2018/09/world /yemen-airstrikes-intl/.

38 Bruce Riedel, "Al-Qaida's Hadramawt emirate," Brookings Institution, July 12, 2015, https://www.brookings.edu/articles /al-qaidas-hadramawt-emirate/.

If you read carefully, a pattern does start to emerge. Yet amid all the failure and farce, the opium fields and the burning mosques, the unintended consequences and the knowledge problems, it's the damned gas station that always gets me.

In 2011, the United States at last figured what was needed to win the war in Afghanistan: more clean energy. The country has large reserves of natural gas, which burns cleaner than gasoline, and so the Pentagon decided to build Afghanistan its own natural gas station. There was reason from the start to think this was not the wisest allocation of resources. Converting a car from gasoline to natural gas was estimated by the Pentagon to cost $700, while the average Afghani income was just $690.

Still, the project went forward, and it soon snowballed into the most expensive gas station in history. When all was said and done, an audit by the Special Inspector General for Afghanistan Reconstruction (SIGAR) placed the total cost at an astonishing $43 million.[39] Subsequent audits have revised this down to as low as $5 million,[40] but it's still an eye-watering amount of money for a project that proved almost entirely useless.

We had set out to export democracy to the Middle East. In the end, we hadn't been able to export a Sheetz.

Nowhere is American decline so palpably realized as in this climb-down from late-2001 idealism to mid-2020s brute reality. The limitations of imperialism and central planning have rarely been so

39   Tom Vanden Brook, "Watchdog: Military blew $43M on useless gas station," *USA Today*, November 2, 2015, https://www.usatoday.com/story/news/nation/2015/11/02/pentagon-afghanistan-gas-station-boondoggle/75037032/.

40   Jeff Goodson, "No, the US did not spend $43 million on a gas station in Afghanistan," *The Hill*, January 17, 2018, https://thehill.com/opinion/international/369340-no-the-us-did-not-spend-43-million-on-a-gas-station-in-afghanistan/.

blatant. It's difficult now to think about 9/11 and not just feel sad. Sad for the victims, but sad also that the war in its aftermath went bust, that a genuine moment of unity was hijacked by fanatics, that perhaps we didn't even manage to win. Al-Qaeda had set out not so much to conquer Washington and New York as inspire fear and futility in the American psyche. Given where we are today, can it be argued they failed?

Yet on we go. In 2022, Russia invaded Ukraine in a move that came as a shock to everyone save for those who had been paying attention. This is a European war through and through—it's the first ground invasion on European soil since World War II—yet the Biden administration is leading the way, footing most of the bill as Germany and France tag behind. And while Ukraine is not in the Middle East or North Africa, as have been most of America's larger military interventions since 9/11, the familiar pattern is taking shape. Combat has bogged down; the war appears frozen. As of early 2024, Ukraine hasn't taken any new territory since November 2022 while deaths on both sides number in the hundreds of thousands.[41]

The longer the Ukraine war goes on, the more it feels like we're pumping fuel into a charnel house. Yet on the bureaucracy whirs, churning out more weapons and provocations and death. War is the health of the state. And all the better if the war isn't just limited to far-flung corners of the globe but is being waged right here at home too.

---

41 Daniel DePetris, "Year Three: Limiting US Ambitions in Ukraine," Defense Priorities, February 23, 2024, https://www.defensepriorities .org/explainers/year-three-limiting-us-ambitions-in-ukraine.

CHAPTER 18

American Gladiators

CNN's *Crossfire* was always a silly show, but it was especially silly round about the years 2002 to 2005.

That was when The Most Trusted Name in News—remember when CNN could almost credibly call itself that?—decided that what its signature political debate program really needed was more Thunderdome. *Crossfire* was moved to a colosseum-style studio at the George Washington University in downtown D.C. with a live audience. Blazing graphics and pulsing music were introduced; possibly Michael Bay was brought in to direct. The show's intro began this way: "*CROSSFIRE!* On the left: James Carville and Paul Begala! On the right: Robert Novak and Tucker Carlson!"[1] The camera then soared

---

1   "VHS 36 IRAQ WAR MARCH 19 2003 CNN WNT Countdown to War Crossfire Tucker Carlson," YouTube, posted by Gregory Golda, November 7, 2022.

over a whooping audience as that day's two prizefighters sized each other up. At the end of every episode, a Mack truck was blown up just because they could.

The idea of political debate as popcorn entertainment today seems not novel at all. Yet, back then the new *Crossfire* format didn't work especially well. Robert Novak was a brilliant and hard-nosed conservative journalist, but he was also seventy years old by the time *Crossfire* was repurposed. And while Tucker Carlson in those days could play the GOP partisan when he wanted to, he always seemed too smart for the format, amused by the manufactured drama and winking at the fourth wall. Contrast that to Carville and (especially) Begala, generals of the Clinton administration's political wars, who landed their blows with ease and were reliably applauded by the Washington audience.

The dynamic really struggled during the run-up to the Iraq war. Republicans were supposed to be onboard with the Bush administration's foreign policy, yet Novak flatly opposed the invasion and Carlson would soon turn against it. So when one Jon Stewart stopped by for an on-air segment in 2004 and *courageously* accused the show of being in the pockets of big corporations, he was punching at that which was already on life support.[2] *Crossfire* was canceled less than a year later. CNN CEO Jonathan Klein later said he agreed with some of Stewart's criticisms.[3]

Crossfire was silly, yes, but it was also wonderfully, gloriously silly. Watching old episodes today—that forced mix of "Democrats risk exacerbating the deficit if they expand the earned income tax credit"

---

2   "Jon Stewart on Crossfire," YouTube, posted by Alex Felker, January 16, 2006.

3   Bill Carter, "CNN Will Cancel 'Crossfire' and Cut Ties to Commentator," *New York Times*, January 6, 2005, https://www.nytimes.com/2005/01/06/business/media/cnn-will-cancel-crossfire-and-cut-ties-to-commentator.html.

and "yippee-ki-yay motherf***er"—can make you nostalgic for an era when things were merely silly.

Since then, CNN has gone from a nominally objective news channel that at least seemed interested in debate to a finely tuned left-wing propaganda network that would probably find Carville and Begala too wet. There are no John Williams scores now, just the gray faces of state TV reminding you what you're supposed to think. And the irony is, in going this way, CNN has become far more warlike than when Begala and Carlson were scrapping.

***

The question of Where American News Went Wrong is an oft-debated one, though given that those having the debate are usually journalists, the answers tend to be self-interested and self-flattering ("no one seems interested in *the truth* anymore . . .").

Still, when journos lament that the news business has changed, if anything it's an understatement. Come the mid-twentieth century, American journalism was close to the opposite of how it is now: stodgy, buttoned-up, just-the-facts-ma'am. That's not to say bias and color didn't seep in, but there was little of that Fleet Street flavor, that sense that the journalist ought to be a character in his own story (or even in general). The reporter was the voice of God, the Oz-like authority who was indivisible from the truth and whose craft was so indispensable as to be enshrined in the First Amendment.

This model was far from perfect. When Walter Cronkite became more critical of the Vietnam War after the Tet Offensive, it had a serious impact on American public opinion, which raised questions of just how much influence journalists should have. Yet, I also challenge you to watch a news broadcast from the sixties and not come away better informed than you would be after watching hours and hours of MSNBC today.

So what happened? A progressive would argue that an Australian billionaire named Rupert Murdoch touched down on American soil and brought with him his right-leaning political views and a flair for tabloid journalism. This begat Fox News, one of the most evil forces this world has ever known, last seen . . . actually it was last seen calling Arizona for Joe Biden before anyone else, but *still*. A conservative would counter that Fox was necessary because the media had by then grown overwhelmingly liberal: one poll from the mid-1990s found that 89 percent of Washington journalists had voted for Bill Clinton in 1992 compared to just 7 percent for George H. W. Bush.[4]

Less partisan observers might point to William F. Buckley's debates with Gore Vidal on ABC during the 1968 political conventions, which culminated in Buckley growling at Vidal, "Now listen, you queer, stop calling me a crypto-Nazi or I'll sock you in the goddamn face you'll stay plastered."[5] (Couldn't he have said all that in two words?) That exchange is often seen as the advent of scream-o pundit debate.

Yet as a scream-o pundit myself, I can't help but think this only gets us so far. It explains how we got to *Crossfire* but it doesn't explain how debate itself was phased out, how the cable news channels became partisan organs. Less than forty years after Buckley and Vidal sparred, *Crossfire* was canceled. Fox News's right-versus-left hour *Hannity & Colmes* was amputated to *Hannity*. MSNBC went from an eclectic all-over-the-map lineup (they gave Carlson a show after CNN axed him) to lip-synching Obama speeches.

---

4   Howard Kurtz, "Poll Takes Liberal View of the Press," *Washington Post*, May 26, 1996, https://www.washingtonpost.com/archive /lifestyle/1996/05/27/poll-takes-liberal-view-of-the-press/2df59569-e9af -47f1-9af7-6186b5f6a1f5/.

5   "Gore Vidal vs William Buckley Democratic Convention Debate 3," YouTube, posted by Thomas G, December 4, 2012.

The problem today isn't that cable news is too combative but that it's too smug. Its anchors assume the old voice-of-God approach but apply it to partisan talking points. Whereas journalists once behaved almost like a priesthood because they were convinced they alone could be objective, now they behave like a priesthood because they're subjective, because they believe they take the only correct view. It's the result of a years-long campaign against the very idea of objectivity.

The war on objective journalism began overtly on the left during the Bush administration. Stung by the failures of the Iraq war, a chorus of left-wing voices began to decry balanced reporting. Shouldn't the goal be to report the truth rather than trying to give equal time to all sides? A bad odor came to surround a new term, "bothsidesism," the idea that you had to get both sides of a story in order to be fair.

As Donald Trump came into his own, as Twitter epistemically closed off journalists in their little ideological cocoons, as the stakes came to feel even higher, the attack on "bothsidesism" blossomed into an attack on objectivity itself. Why should a reporter strive to be unbiased given that he inevitably has biases that will affect his coverage? Here was an extraordinarily cynical view—can we not expect well-paid journalists to at least *try* to expand their horizons?—and it called to mind not any idea of a free press but the antidemocratic philosophy of a thinker named Carl Schmitt.

Schmitt believed there was no such thing as an apolitical or value-neutral state. Moral biases were insurmountable and therefore those in power would always end up acting on them. Any kind of detachment from questions of values—think Lady Justice wearing the blindfold—was a fantasy. Supposed political neutrality, the sort that sunny classical liberals attempt to practice ("I might believe X and you might believe Y, but we're all after the truth, aren't we?"), was just a shell concealing the biases of whoever happened to be in power. Schmitt probably would have agreed that objective news was impossible too, influencèd inevitably by the views and values of journalists. And so why even try to be fair?[6]

Schmitt was one of the twentieth century's leading critics of liberal democracy. He was also, it seems worth pointing out, a member of the Nazi Party who defended the Night of the Long Knives in which dozens if not hundreds of Hitler's political opponents were murdered.[7] And no wonder. If value-neutrality was impossible, then disinterested laws and norms were likewise impossible. We were all at the subjective whim of whoever happened to hold power. And so may as well drop the act and brandish the gun.

It's curious, isn't it, how journalists who style themselves anti-fascist are now validating Schmitt's ideas? "As a member of a marginalized community (I am transgender), I've never had the opportunity to pretend I can be 'neutral,'" pronounced journalist Lewis Wallace in 2017, adding, "Obviously, I can't be neutral or centrist in a debate over my own humanity."[8] The standard of objectivity, wrote former *Washington Post* executive editor Leonard Downie Jr., "was dictated over decades by male editors in predominantly White newsrooms and reinforced their own view of the world."[9]

6   Carl Schmitt, *Political Theology: Four Chapters on the Concept of Sovereignty*, translated by George Schwab (Chicago: University of Chicago Press, 2006).

7   Detlev Vagts, "Carl Schmitt's Ultimate Emergency: The Night of the Long Knives," *The Germanic Review*, 87: 203–9, 2012, https://www.tandfonline.com/doi/abs/10.1080/00168890.2012.675795.

8   Lewis Wallace, "Objectivity is Dead and I'm Okay With It," Medium, January 27, 2017, https://medium.com/@lewispants/objectivity-is-dead-and-im-okay-with-it-7fd2b4b5c58f.

9   Leonard Downie, "Newsrooms That Move Beyond 'Objectivity' Can Build Trust," *Washington Post*, January 30, 2023, https://www.washingtonpost.com/opinions/2023/01/30/newsrooms-news-reporting-objectivity-diversity/.

The right has its own version of this, though it's a bit more compli-cated and disparate. It's less ideologically involved—conservatives right now are in a state of ideological flux—and more centered on certain truths about Donald Trump. There are some Trump voters who refuse to ever hear that he lost the 2020 election or that January 6 was a dire moment for the country. These voters are ironically open to historically liberal ideas like protecting entitlements and throttling corporate power. The tropes they defend tend to be more personal and circumstantial.

Yet those tropes are still powerful motivators. Fox News's early call on Election Night 2020 that Joe Biden had won Arizona drove thousands of its viewers into the arms of more pro-Trump channels like Newsmax and One America, which were willing to cater to those tropes. And reporters there would probably agree with their CNN counterparts. Objectivity is dead. Why even bother? The left is ruining the country and we have to fight back.

***

One peril of ditching objectivity is that, like so much else in decline-era America, the news descends into farce. When ideology comes into col-lision with reality, it's the former that wins out. Thus did CNN air a report from Kenosha, Wisconsin, during an Antifa riot with the chyron "FIERY BUT MOSTLY PEACEFUL PROTESTS" while an entire street burned in the background.[10]

Another problem is it makes everyone else distrust the media more than they otherwise would. According to Gallup polling, 39 percent of Americans said in 2023 they had no trust in the press, a record high and

---

10 Joseph Wulfson, "CNN panned for on-air graphic reading 'fiery but mostly peaceful protest' in front of Kenosha fire," Fox News, August 27, 2020, https://www.foxnews.com/media/cnn-panned-for-on-air-graphic -reading-fiery-but-mostly-peaceful-protest-in-front-of-kenosha-fire.

up from 4 percent in 1976.[11] This is not, by the way, to say Americans have no trust in any journalists—they tend to believe those who are on their side. But because most opinionated journalists posture as voices in the wilderness, claiming to be telling truths you won't get anywhere else, the media writ large ends up as a discredited foil.

This is a particular problem given the nature of the work. You're not supposed to trust a lawyer, for example, given that lawyers are charged with serving the interests of their clients above all else. The same goes for politicians, even if politics in theory isn't supposed to be *that* transactional. But journalists' entire job is to tell the truth. That's why you get into the industry in the first place. It's why you accept the low pay and long hours and creeping alcoholism: because it's the one profession where you get to be totally honest. Yet as objectivity has died in supposed pursuit of the truth, what's really happened is that truth has given way to ideology. And that all-important trust has vanished.

Still another peril is that opinionated journalism is exhausting. One study from 2017 found that reading articles that were biased in favor of your identity or opinion, and specifically those that made said identity or opinion feel threatened, triggered anger. And that anger only led readers to click on even more incendiary news.[12] Another study published in *Nature* tried to quantify the presence of positive and negative words in the headlines of articles shared online. What it found was that every negative word in a headline increased the chance the article would

---

11   Megan Brenan, "Media Confidence in US Matches 2016 Record Low," Gallup, October 19, 2023, https://news.gallup.com/poll/512861/media-confidence-matches-2016-record-low.aspx.

12   Yi-Hsing Han and Laura Arpan, "The Effects of News Bias-Induced Anger, Anxiety, and Issue Novelty on Subsequent News Preferences," *Advances in Journalism and Communication*, Vol. 5, No. 4, December 2017, https://www.scirp.org/journal/paperinformation?paperid=81300#:~:text=Bias%2Dinduced%20anger%2C%20but%20not,on%20identity%2Dthreatening%20information%20preferences.

be clicked on by 2.3 percent.[13] No wonder the American Psychological Association warns that the overconsumption of news is "hurting our mental health."[14]

I was one of those opinionated journalists on and off for about fifteen years, until I got laid off for the first time in my life in 2023. And while losing your job is always harrowing, there was a silver lining in it too. The reason was I had run out of things to say.

After the massacre at Sandy Hook Elementary School in my home state of Connecticut—that one hit hard: those blue license plates, those trees just so—I wrote an essay in which I said everything I had to say about mass shootings. Yet those mass shootings kept coming, one grisly slaughter after another, and on most of these occasions I was expected to comment, to provide some novel insight even though I'd long ago run dry. The same was true of the endless debt showdowns on Capitol Hill. Did anyone really think *this* was the time Republicans were finally going to trim the budget? Yet we were all required to pretend it might be, to participate in the hype.

Because Congress and our other problem-solving mechanisms are broken, our civic liturgy is stuck on Groundhog Day, with the same spectacles repeating themselves on loop. This enables newsrooms to keep serving up the same opinions and the same outrage over and over again. *Can you believe there was a gun massacre . . . again?! Can you believe the GOP is threatening to shut down the government . . . AGAIN?! Can you believe Donald Trump was just indicted . . . AGAIN?!?!* The same lines get said, the same hopes that This Time

13   Claire E. Robertson, et al., "Negativity drives online news consumption," *Nature Human Behaviour* 7, 812–22, 2023, https://www.nature.com/articles/s41562-023-01538-4.

14   Charlotte Huff, "Media overload is hurting our mental health. Here are ways to manage headline stress," *Monitor on Psychology* 53, no. 8, p. 20, 2022, https://www.apa.org/monitor/2022/11/strain-media-overload.

Could Be Different get teased, and the same hopes get dashed as it turns out This Time Won't Be Different. All you're left with is fear and anger.

Which brings us back to Carl Schmitt. There's a reason dictatorships, or just imperial systems of government, love to keep their subjects afraid. There's also a reason why those same imperial systems love to keep people afraid not just of a foreign foe but of each other. Loosen the bonds between citizens, allow fear to dissolve those local associations that balance and check state power, and the government can rule unopposed.

This is why state TV in a dictatorship is concerned with neither the truth nor robust debate but with parroting the party line. That party line keeps people in line, parading before them an endless procession of traitors and crises. The thing to do is to create the ethos of a civil war without a civil war actually breaking out. And that means never allowing on a dissenting voice that could question whether any of this makes sense.

The United States is not there yet—we still have a free press and plenty of journalists across plenty of platforms who are interested in getting at the truth. (I'll even swallow my revulsion here and admit that Twitter can sometimes be a tool for disseminating that truth.) But then ask yourself: does the CNN of today more closely resemble *Crossfire* circa 2004 or *Pravda*? Does the treatment by the mainstream press of dissident journalists like Matt Taibbi smack more of a free society or an imperial crackdown?

And since that mainstream press is largely left-leaning, and since that enemy of all leftists Donald Trump feuded constantly with the security state, the media has effectively taken sides with the security state. They love to lionize the FBI now, to say nothing of the endless probes into Trump's conduct. You might even say the press has been institutionalized into the imperial system to a degree, defanged as the powerful bureaucracy chugs away in peace.

***

So it was that in September 2022, American empire came into full bloom. In a twisted parody of republican government, President Joe Biden shambled out to a podium in Philadelphia to declare war on half the country.

His administration wasn't even pretending anymore. The backdrop to the speech was the brick façade of Independence Hall, which had been bathed in red light, casting two Marines standing on either side in silhouette. Between them, a giant American flag had been draped between two marble pillars.

His imperium duly projected, Biden declared that at that very moment there was an ongoing "battle for the soul of the nation" between decent people and "MAGA Republicans." "Donald Trump and the MAGA Republicans represent an extremism that threatens the very foundations of our republic," Biden said. And who were these scoundrels? "MAGA forces are determined to take this country backwards—backwards to an America where there is no right to choose, no right to privacy, no right to contraception, no right to marry who you love."

Amid this "assault on American democracy," the country had reached an "inflection point." "MAGA Republicans have made their choice," Biden said. "They embrace anger. They thrive on chaos. They live not in the light of truth but in the shadow of lies." He continued, "MAGA Republicans look at America and see carnage and darkness and despair."[15]

Here was a jarring spectacle, almost as jarring as January 6, which Biden (rightly) professed to be outraged about. And while the real

---

15   Joe Biden, "Remarks by President Biden on the Continued Battle for the Soul of the Nation," transcript from the White House, September 1, 2022, https://www.whitehouse.gov/briefing-room/speeches -remarks/2022/09/01/remarks-by-president-bidenon-the-continued -battle-for-the-soul-of-the-nation/.

purpose of the speech was almost certainly political—the midterm elections were a mere two months away and the Democrats were lagging in the polls—it felt more like a confluence of all the strands of American empire. The president appeared bathed in power. His speech implicitly reinforced the power of the security agencies and attacked their critics. His team showed no deference to Congress, where several of those MAGA Republicans had been elected to serve by the people. His effect was to make you afraid and/or angry. His words were almost universally hailed by the mainstream press.

And, of course, he made no mention of America's failed wars abroad, which he had so often supported as a senator. It was a stunning reveal of what had been building for decades, yet it came and went like so much smoke on the wind, just another comic-book happening in decline-era America. Not long after the speech, Biden's imperial image was turned into a meme. It was called Dark Brandon, and like all online ephemera, it flashed on by.

Afterword: It Begins with Us

This book is a snapshot. It's a look at a very narrow span of American history, and by the time you read it, some of the trends it documents may have been eclipsed by events.

So it is that many are now predicting the death of not just Twitter (hallelujah!) but the age of social media altogether. The conspiracy culture of the Trump era has abated slightly. Inflation has slowed, bringing some relief in the cost of living crisis.

In Boston, the Center for Antiracist Research, run by Ibram X. Kendi, announced mass layoffs in 2023,[1] suggesting wokeness is

1   Sara Weissman, "Ibram X. Kendi Defends Boston University Center After Layoffs," *Inside Higher Ed*, September 25, 2023, https://www.insidehighered.com/news/quick-takes/2023/09/25/ibram-x-kendi-defends-antiracism-center-after-layoffs.

hitting unforeseen headwinds. Layoffs are also hitting CNN[2] and MSNBC,[3] as more viewers cut their TV cords, heralding a reckoning for cable news's outsize role in our politics. And in Franklin County, Massachusetts, home to Greenfield, the latest numbers on record have seen a merciful and hard-earned decrease in the overdose rate.[4]

This book is a snapshot, and the fortunate thing about snapshots is the scenes they capture always change. Yet they can also change for the worse, and so it's gone for other subjects we've discussed. Our next trip to the Moon has been delayed yet again. Congress has discovered new and exciting ways of beclowning itself, as the narrowly Republican-controlled House of Representatives comes to look even more like the Lebanese Civil War.

Yet it's in this fluidity that perhaps there is hope. Because, again, determinism is still bunk. Our decisions matter. The United States has gotten itself into plenty of trouble in its history, from that whole Civil War thing to the tumult of the 1960s when many predicted the country would come apart. But within a quarter century of each ordeal, we were back on our feet and charging forward. In 1890, the United States claimed its place as the largest economy on earth, while in 1989, the Berlin Wall fell, leaving American power uncontested.

So may it be in 2050. Perhaps that will be the year when my son, who by then will be in his late twenties, will read this book for the first

---

2   Ted Johnson, "NBC News Undergoes Layoffs Impacting 'Double Digit' Number Of Employees," *Deadline*, January 11, 2024, https://deadline.com/2024/01/nbc-news-layoffs-1235716799/.

3   Alex Sherman, "CNN Lays Off Hundreds of Staffers," CNBC, December 2, 2022, https://www.cnbc.com/2022/12/01/cnn-lays-off-hundreds-of-staffers-read-the-memo.html.

4   Kristin Burnell, "New report details rates of opioid-related deaths in western Massachusetts," Western Mass News, August 3, 2023, https://www.westernmassnews.com/2023/08/03/new-report-details-rates-opioid-related-deaths-western-massachusetts/.

time, roll his eyes, and say, "Sure, Pops." He'll then hop aboard the new warp-speed rail that crisscrosses the country, blink into gleamingly safe Washington, D.C., for a light snack at the new Brazilian/Martian fusion joint, and mull which of that year's thirtysomething-year-old multiracial JFK lookalikes he should vote for.

Could it happen? Stranger things have.

This book is a snapshot, and at least one thing has come into greater focus since I finished writing it: America might be in decline but its global position is still secure. Doomsayers love to herald the end of American global power, but who could ever fill the void we leave behind? Russia? That paper grizzly bear can't even conquer Ukraine. The European Union? I can't even type that without a laugh track sounding.

Since last we checked in on the Western Europeans critics, they've gone from sneering at the United States to sticking out their hands to the United States demanding protection from Russia and access to natural gas exports—while also sneering at the United States. The Euros insist they still have a better quality of life, and if by "quality of life" they mean "lax attitudes on cigarettes and paid vacations to Saint-Tropez," then they may have a point. (That's no putdown: I really do mean that by "quality of life.") Yet America's economy is still far more dynamic and growth-oriented than anything in the European Union. And with low birth rates and less ability to attract economic migrants, Europe's populations are rapidly graying. This has turned many of their vaunted welfare states, which rely on the young to pay in so the old can cash out, into time bombs that are ticking faster than our own Social Security and Medicare.

Even China, which is unquestionably an American adversary, isn't all it's cracked up to be. China has been the subject of what my friends in the international relations community call "threat inflation" and what everyone else calls "our government scaring the sneeze out of us." For all its size and saber-rattling, China has massive problems. Its economy sits atop a mortgage bubble. Its authoritarian system of government encourages passé central planning and hamstrings its ability to adapt. Its vaunted navy isn't engineered to operate far from its shores. Its leader looks like a Sino Grimace.

In the short and medium term, China will no doubt rise. In the long term? My money is still on the United States. And that money is still denominated in dollars.

So it is that we return to the civilizational hubris we examined at the beginning of this book. America is no longer a "unipolar power" and few would call us the "indispensable nation," but the weird thing is that, for all the inanity and chaos of recent years, we're still on top. Our economy is still the best in the G7; our military is still the most powerful on earth. If you think the cost of living here is bad, try buying a house in Canada or Australia. Or check the economic growth numbers for Germany or the UK. No one else has our advantages, from our enviable geography to our abundance of natural resources to our willingness to pair bacon with steak and call it a meal. And as the future becomes the present, our dominance only looks more secure.

The twentieth century was an American age. What few of us were expecting was that the twenty-first century is looking like an American age too. The question then is what kind of American age it's going to be.

***

The most famous case of national decline in human history is, of course, the Roman Empire. And my favorite quote about the Roman Empire comes from the poet W. H. Auden: "What fascinates and terrifies us about the Roman Empire is not that it finally went smash, but that it managed to last for four centuries without creativity, warmth, or hope."

It's a quote a historian might quibble with. The gleaming marble we've come to associate with ancient Roman majesty only came to exist in those last four centuries; before that Rome was constructed largely of brick and dingy in comparison to more cosmopolitan centers like Athens and Alexandria. Yet you can also see where Auden was coming from. The late Roman Republic and Roman Empire was a place of hideous violence and political strife. From Sulla's wicked purges to the roving mobs of Clodius and Milo, from the brutality of Caligula to the astonishing thirty-seven emperors who were assassinated, Rome became saturated in the same mad carnage it had once pointed outward at enemies like Carthage.

Yet Rome still hung on, if only because there wasn't anyone else who could do what they did. So may it be for this American century. Forget being displaced by China; forget power supposedly shifting to the Global South; forget all the talk from the EU. The question for our time is whether America will revert to form, fix our problems at home, and burnish our reputation abroad. Or whether we'll lumber along like a blindfolded giant, widely disliked yet reluctantly followed, if only because we're the baddest creature around and it's a bad idea to get in our way.

Will America be good, true, and beautiful? Or will it merely exist, unloved and uninspired, lurching toward goodness-knows-where?

The Rubicon in ancient Rome wasn't so much a river as a stream, and when Caesar famously crossed it he didn't say "the die is cast" as is often claimed but rather "let the dice be thrown." Caesar understood he was making a choice and that choice was laden with risk. Yet there's another salient fact about his stomping across that glorified trickle: he wasn't the first Roman to do so. The general Sulla had marched on Rome four decades earlier, and about this the historian Mary Beard makes an observation. "Forty years had made a big difference," she writes. "When Sulla turned his army on the city, all but one of his senior officers had refused to follow him. When Caesar did the same, all but one stayed with him."[5]

Norms can give way quickly. This is why Edmund Burke said that "manners are of more importance than laws." What stayed Sulla's men wasn't any threat of legal penalty but rather the long-standing civic norm that armed Roman soldiers should never enter the city. Yet once the precedent was chipped away, once Rome had suffered through decades of political violence, the unthinkable became plausible. The legions stormed in.

Likewise are Americans going to have to reclaim some of the norms that we've damaged: that debates should be conducted respectfully and sympathetically rather than with all the viciousness of a Twitter flame war; that an argument is not a Molotov cocktail and vice versa; that individuals should be judged on their merits rather than their identity categories; that politics should be about protecting rights and bettering community rather than some abstract monster battle. None of these axioms has ever held completely true in the United States but once upon a time we were better at them than we are today.

Thankfully what gives us such an advantage over the likes of China is that we can change course, that our individual choices matter in the aggregate, that our national destiny is determined more organically than in a command-and-control top-down state. This is why liberal democracy, freedom of speech, and, yes, capitalism are worth fighting for: because they allow us the creative liberty and space to both get ourselves into messes and escape from them. They allow us to reform, to progress, to avoid the kind of entropy that can stagnate a society, even if a conservative like myself thinks that progress needs to happen slowly and in constraint to tradition.

---

5   Mary Beard, *SPQR* (New York: Liveright, 2016), p. 219.

But if such bottom-up change is going to happen, then it has to begin with us. We need to take it upon ourselves to make things better. We need to indulge in the ultimate act of creative destruction: getting off the couch and going outside. We need to be doers and builders, not just complainers.

Speaking of which, it's about time I wrapped up my own three-hundred-page act of complaining. I'd like to go be with my family, whom I haven't seen in two years and whom I'm informed are pretty nice people. As a conservative, it's my God-given right to end this book with a quote from Ronald Reagan, and that's exactly what I'm going to do: "The crisis we are facing today does not require of us the kind of sacrifice that . . . so many thousands of others were called upon to make. It does require, however, our best effort and our willingness to believe in ourselves and to believe in our capacity to perform great deeds, to believe that together with God's help we can and will resolve the problems which now confront us. And after all, why shouldn't we believe that? We are Americans."[6]

6 Ronald Reagan, "Inaugural Address 1981," Ronald Reagan Presidential Library and Museum, https://www.reaganlibrary.gov/archives/speech/inaugural-address-1981.

Index

A
absolutism, 72
Adams, John, 65
ADHD, 179–180
adolescents, 44, 118
Afghanistan, 4, 205, 255–257, 261
Akin, Todd, 176
alcohol, 90–91, 115–117
alerts, from phones, 53–55
al-Maliki, Nouri, 257–258
Altman, Sam, 206–208
Anacostia (Washington, D.C.),
    138–139
Andersen, Kurt, 14
Anderson, Gilliam, 67
Andrews, Lewis M., 76
anonymity, 26–28
Ansari, Aziz, 177
Apollo program, 78–81

Arendt, Hannah, 84
Asimov, Isaac, 213
atheism, 147–149
Auden, W. H., 84, 278

B
Ballmer, Steve, 57
Beard, Mary, 279–280
Bell, Art, 66–68, 72
Bezos, Jeff, 212
Biden, Hunter, 227–228, 269, 274
Biden, Joe, 204–206, 227–228,
    262, 273
Black Lives Matter, 154. *See also*
    Floyd, George
blogging, 23
boomers, 3, 187–189, 191–192,
    195–196
Bourdain, Anthony, 127

Bowling Alone (Putnam), 103–105
boys, 179–181
Boy Scouts, 105–108
Brooks, Preston, 232
Buckley, William F., 266
Burchett, Tim, 233
Burroughs, William, 95
Bush, George H. W., 11, 14, 266
Bush, George W., 148–149,
   217–218, 220–222, 252–253
Byrd, Robert C., 79

C
cancer, 93
Cannon, Joseph, 234
car crashes, 93–94
carjacking, 117–118
Carter, Chris, 67
Catholic Church, 59–61, 108–110,
   154
Cathy, Don, 47–48
Challenger (space shuttle), 80
charitable giving, 113–114
chat rooms, 22–23
Cheney, Dick, 220, 224
Chesterton, G. K., 72–73
Chick-fil-A, 47–49
childcare, 192–193
China, 277–278
Christianity, 59–61, 108–110,
   149–150, 153, 169–171
Church Committee, 221
Citizens United, 238
class consciousness, 197
Clay, Henry, 234
Clean Air Act, 242–243
climate change, 80–81, 206–209
Clinton, Bill, 6, 14, 66, 103,
   221–222, 266

Clinton, Hillary, 130, 173
Cold War, 83
college education, 192–194
Comer, James, 233
Comey, James, 221
communitarianism, 104–105
conspiracy theory, 63–74
Constellation program, 80
Corey, James S. A., 85–86
COVID-19 pandemic, 4, 90–91,
   96–98, 105, 115–116, 142–144,
   150–151
crime, 4, 117–118, 140–141, 205
Crossfire (television), 263–265
cyberbullying, 38–39

D
Dark Side of the Nineties, The
   (documentary), 7–9
Dawkins, Richard, 148
deaths, 92–95, 211–212
debt, 195, 240–241, 251
de Grey, Aubrey, 210–212
deindustrialization, 131
Delvey, Anna, 183–184
DeSantis, Ron, 196–197
DiAngelo, Robin, 162–165
Disney World, 20–22
Donegan, Moira, 177
Dougherty, Michael Brendan,
   130–131
Douthat, Ross, 215
Downie, Leonard, Jr., 268
Dreams from My Father (Obama),
   129
drug overdoses, 94–95
Du Bois, W. E. B., 160–161
Duchovny, David, 67
Dworkin, Andrea, 34

E

education, 192–194
election of 1924, 10
election of 1996, 10
election of 2000, 217–218, 220
End of the Affair, The (Greene), 147–148
epistemic closure, 71
erectile dysfunction, 33–34
Esolen, Anthony, 15
Estonia, 89–91
Expanse, The (television), 77, 85–86

F

Facebook, 42–45
factionalism, 235–236
"Fairy Tales" (Chesterton), 72
fakeness, 36
Fauci, Anthony, 96
firefighters, 111
Floyd, George, 4, 150
Fluke, Sandra, 176
Franklin, Benjamin, 110
friendship, 100–102
Frum, David, 253–255

G

Gaddafi, Moammar, 258–259
Gaisford, Mark, 99–100
gay rights, 150
Gaza, 168–169
gender, 150. *See also* transgender; women
generations, 187. *See also specific generations*
Generation X, 199
Generation Z, 188, 195
Gingrich, Newt, 212–214
globalization, 131–132
God, 148, 169

God Delusion, The (Dawkins), 148
Gore, Al, 217–218, 220
Graves, Matthew, 141
Great Recession, 4, 224
Greene, Graham, 147–148
Green New Deal, 208–210
groceries, 194
gun violence, 94–95

H

Hamas, 168–169
Hannity, Sean, 68
Hart, David Bentley, 170–171
Haskins, Dwayne, 38–39
health insurance, 194, 209
Healy, Gene, 228–229
heart disease, 92–93
Heaven's Gate (cult), 67
heroin, 126–128
Hillbilly Elegy (Vance), 129
Himes, Jim, 24
Hitchens, Christopher, 139, 147–149
Hoffman, Doug, 218
housing, 190–192, 197–198
How to Be an Antiracist, 157–158
Hussein, Saddam, 257

I

inflation, 4, 191–192, 194
Infowars, 69
Instagram, 39–40, 42–44, 198–199
internet, 22–23, 105. *See also* social media
intersectionality, 153
Interstate 91, 126–128
Inventing Anna (miniseries), 183–184
iPhone, 52–54, 57–58
Iran, 255

Iraq War, 4, 254–255, 257–258
Islamic State, 257
isolation, 104–105, 110. *See also*
loneliness
Israel, 168–169
Issa, Darrell, 233

J
January 6, 4, 64–65, 273
Jefferson, Thomas, 65
Jews, 169
Jobs, Steve, 57
Johnson, Andrew, 65–66
Jones, Alex, 68–70, 72–73

K
Kagan, Robert, 253
Kavanaugh, Brett, 19
Keith, Toby, 114
Kendi, Ibram X., 157–161, 165, 275
Kennedy, John F., 65, 220
Kennedy, Kathleen, 156
Kent, Vivian, 183–184
Kerry, John, 218
Kim Jong-un, 73
King, Billie Jean, 173
Klein, Ezra, 23
Klein, Jonathan, 264
Klosterman, Chuck, 9–10
Krauthammer, Charles, 252
Kristol, Bill, 253

L
Latvia, 90
Lauer, Matt, 177
Legends of the Hidden Temple
(television program), 12–13
legislative primacy, 233–234
LEV. *See* longevity escape velocity
(LEV)

Lewis, C. S., 85
libertarianism, 45–46, 67
Libya, 258–259
life expectancy, 91–92
Limbaugh, Rush, 66, 176
Lithuania, 91
lobbying, 236–237
loneliness, 98–101, 104–105
longevity escape velocity (LEV), 211

M
Mali, 248–249
Marin, Sanna, 40
Marxism, 188, 196
masculinity, 69–70
Massachusetts, 127–128
McCain, John, 174
McCarthy, Kevin, 233, 238–239
McLuhan, Marshall, 30
McVeigh, Timothy, 66–68
Melian Dialogue, 29
men, 179–181, 185–186
*Men Are from Mars, Women Are
from Venus* (Gray), 174
MeToo, 176–179
Meyer, Urban, 38
Mikulski, Barbara, 24
military, 112–113, 191, 249–250
millennials, 1–6, 15, 111, 187–189,
195–199
Moon, 80, 82, 84–85, 212–213
Moskowitz, Jared, 233
Mueller, Robert, 65
Mullin, Markwayne, 231–232
Mulvaney, Dylan, 156
Murdoch, Rupert, 266
Murthy, Vivek, 98–99
Musk, Elon, 30, 76, 201–203, 215
MyPillow, 65

N

NASA, 75–76, 78–82

National Security Agency (NSA), 45–46, 220–221, 226–227

neo-Jacobins, 253–253

neoliberalism, 3, 20, 56

New Atheists, 147–149

New World Order, 68–69

Nineteen Eighty Four (Orwell), 30, 47

Nineties, The (Klosterman), 9–10

Nisbet, Robert, 109

No Child Left Behind, 221

nomadism, 198–199

NSA. *See* National Security Agency (NSA)

O

Obama, Barack, 24, 80, 129, 173, 176, 218, 222–223, 225, 227–228, 259

Obamacare, 4

Obergefell v. Hodges, 150

obesity, 92–93

O'Brien, Sean, 231–232

Ocasio-Cortez, Alexandria, 40, 208–210

"okay" hand symbol, 17–20

Oklahoma City bombing, 66, 68

opioid crisis, 94–95

O'Reilly, Bill, 218

Orwell, George, 30, 47

Owens, Bill, 218

Owens, Kenneth N., 125

P

Palin, Sarah, 174

PalmPilot, 57

Patriot Act, 228, 243–244

Perelandra (Lewis), 85

Perle, Richard, 253–255

pornography, 31–34, 36

Powell, Sidney, 65

powerlessness, 131–132

Prohibition, 215

Putin, Vladimir, 203

Putnam, Robert, 103–105

Q

QAnon, 70, 73

R

racism, 17–19

rape, 176

Reagan, Ronald, 80, 166, 281

Reality Bites (film), 10

Reddit, 65, 71

regulations, 244–245

religion, 59–61, 108–111, 148–150, 153, 169–171

Riggs, Bobby, 173

Ring door cameras, 46–47

Roman Empire, 278–280

Romney, Mitt, 213

Rousseau, Jean-Jacques, 2–3

Ruby Ridge, 66

Rumsfeld, Donald, 220

Russia, 262

Ryan, Paul, 24

Ryn, Claes, 253

S

Sanders, Bernie, 232

Sarah, Robert Cardinal, 59–61

Schmitt, Carl, 267–268, 272

screen time, 52

September 11 attacks, 4, 68–69, 148–149, 220–221, 249, 252–253

Sessions, Jeff, 226

sex, 33–35
sex abuse, 107–109
Silent Generation, 6
Simon Personal Communicator, 57
smartphones, 52–58
Smith, Adam, 27
social capital, 104–105
socialism, 195–197
social media, 23–27, 36, 38–40,
　42–45, 52–53, 118, 198–199
space program, 80, 82, 84–85. *See
　also* NASA
Spaceship Earth (Disney ride),
　20–22
SpaceX, 203
Spacey, Kevin, 177
Stewart, Jon, 264
Stone, Roger, 70
stress gap, 182–183
suicidality, 44
Sumner, Charles, 232
surveillance, 42–43, 46–47
Syria, 254, 259–260

T
Taliban, 255–257
Taylor Greene, Marjorie, 233
teenagers, 44, 118
television, 12–13
Tesla, 203
Theory of Moral Sentiments, The
　(Smith), 27
Thompson, Hunter S., 94
Thucydides, 118
TikTok, 118, 188, 236
Tiny House Movement, 197–198
Tocqueville, Alexis de, 110
transgender, 150, 152–153,
　155–156

transparency, 109–110
Trump, Donald, 4, 64–65, 70, 82,
　130, 151, 176–177, 204–206,
　214, 225–228, 237–238, 245,
　268–269
Truther movement, 69
Twitter, 23–29, 188, 201–202, 232

U
Ukraine, 203, 262

V
Van Buren, Peter, 82–83
Vance, J. D., 129
VanLife, 198–199
Vidal, Gore, 266
video games, 13–14
Viper Room, 8–9
volunteering, 110–113

W
Waco, 66, 68
Wallace, Lewis, 268
Warnock, Raphael, 238
Washington, Booker T., 160
Washington, D.C., 135–146
Washington, George, 167
Weinstein, Harvey, 177
White, Dana, 202, 204
White Fragility (DiAngelo),
　162–163, 165
Williamson, Kevin, 129–131
Wilson, Rick, 28
Wilson, Woodrow, 61–62
wokeness, 106–107, 151–171,
　183–186, 275
Wolfe, Tom, 161, 168, 188, 196
women, 173–179, 181–185, 257
World War I, 61–62

X

X-Files, The (television), 66–67

Y

Y Combinator, 206–208
Yemen, 260

Yglesias, Matt, 23
YouTube, 52–53

Z

Zoomers, 188, 195
Zuckerberg, Mark, 201–203, 215